THE PLURALIST STATE

The Pluralist State

The Political Ideas of J. N. Figgis and his Contemporaries

Second Edition

David Nicholls

St. Martin's Press

in association with
ST ANTONY'S COLLEGE, OXFORD

First edition 1975
Second edition 1994

Published in Great Britain by
THE MACMILLAN PRESS LTD
Houndmills, Basingstoke, Hampshire RG21 2XS
and London
Companies and representatives
throughout the world

This book is published in the *St Antony's/Macmillan Series*
General Editor: Alex Pravda

A catalogue record for this book is available
from the British Library.

ISBN 0–333–61762–2 hardcover
ISBN 0–333–61763–0 paperback

Printed in Great Britain by
Antony Rowe Ltd, Chippenham, Wiltshire

First published in the United States of America 1994 by
Scholarly and Reference Division,
ST. MARTIN'S PRESS, INC.,
175 Fifth Avenue,
New York, N.Y. 10010

ISBN 0–312–12163–6

Library of Congress Cataloging-in-Publication Data
Nicholls, David, 1936–
The pluralist state : the political ideas of J. N. Figgis and his
contemporaries / David Nicholls. — 2nd ed.
p.   cm.
Includes bibliographical references and index.
ISBN 0–312–12163–6
1. Pluralism (Social sciences)—Great Britain—History.
2. Political science—Great Britain—History.   3. Figgis, John
Neville, 1866–1919—Contributions in political science.   I. Title.
JC330.N5   1994
320.941—dc20   94–1157
                                                CIP

For Gillie, with love

'God himself would admit a figure of society, as there is a plurality of persons in God, though there be but one God; and all his external actions testify a love of society and communion. In heaven there are orders of angels, and armies of martyrs, and in that house many mansions; in earth, families, cities, churches, colleges, all plural things; and lest either of these should not be company enough alone, there is an association of both, a communion of saints which makes the militant and triumphant church one parish.'

— JOHN DONNE (1624)

Contents

Preface

I wish to thank the Community of the Resurrection, Mirfield, Yorkshire, for allowing me to use their library, and for their hospitality on a number of occasions. This monograph has benefited greatly from criticisms and suggestions at various stages of its development. Ernest Thorp, David Price and Martyn Thompson, have made very useful criticisms and I should particularly mention the help given to me by Alec Vidler.

The second edition has involved extensive rewriting and additions. Not only have I added a new Introduction, but there is much additional material in a number of chapters. The chapter on the ideology of a pluralist state (Chapter 6) is almost entirely new, growing out of some brief and inadequate paragraphs in the first edition.

I am grateful to Geoffrey Marshall and Tunku Varadarajan for advice on legal aspects of sovereignty and group personality, to Paul Hirst for encouraging me to do a revised edition, to Jonathan Chaplin for advice on certain aspects of Catholic social thought, to Archie Brown, and once again to David Price and Ernest Thorp for their helpful criticisms and suggestions. I have not always taken their advice, so any errors which remain are only partially their responsibility! I am grateful to my sister Sara May for reading the proofs.

For permission to reproduce as appendices the articles by J. N. Figgis and H. J. Laski I am grateful respectively to the Community of the Resurrection and to the editor of the *Philosophical Review*.

Littlemore, Oxford   DAVID NICHOLLS
St Nicholas Day 1993

Introduction

Since the first edition of this book in early 1975 significant developments have occurred which have brought into prominence many of the themes with which Figgis and other British political pluralists were concerned. These changes have occurred both at the level of political theory and of institutions. The early 1970s were the halcyon years of bipartisan welfare-statism. Apart from the apparently marginal activities of 'right-wing' think-tanks like the Institute of Economic Affairs, and sectarian groups on the 'left', there was a general consensus on the role of the state in the economic and social life of the country. There were some disagreements between the two main parties about the future of road transport or steel, but there was a widespread accord on the major part that must be played by the state, not only in the general control and supervision of the economy but in the ownership and management of several industries and most public utilities. The idea, for example, that in twenty years' time HM judges would be committing convicted criminals to privately owned prisons which are profit-making business enterprises would have seemed like something out of space fiction. No one in the mainstream of the Conservative Party would have so much as entertained the idea. The Labour Party was not even prepared to take seriously a suggestion by one of its MPs that council houses might be sold to their occupants, with the proceeds going into a fund for building more houses. The state (with its local government arm) remained supreme. Labour politicians appeared to give little priority to the importance of freedom and choice, whether of the individual citizen or of the group.

A reviewer of the first edition of this book claimed that its themes 'do not strike the modern reader as questions of immediate note'; among these he cited:

> the nature of state sovereignty, the limits of moral obligation to the state, the nature of law in society, the nature and role of groups within society ... the relationship of groups to the state, the question of authority and democracy within groups.[1]

Whatever might have been true in 1975, this is evidently not so today. These issues are among the most salient topics of debate and contention in contemporary British politics.

I

The 1980s witnessed a tidal wave of privatisation, which has not only changed the institutional structure of the country, but has swept away a whole collection of assumptions about what is possible. The state has, in many spheres of its activity, been discredited and much of the 'family silver' has been sold. With a few exceptions, however, the industries and public utilities have come under the control of huge financial conglomerates, and the new small share-holders have no real say in the running of the companies.

The Thatcher regime of the 1980s purported to be critical of state bureaucracy and in favour of decentralisation in a number of spheres. The claim was that devolution and the introduction of so-called internal market mechanisms would bring more 'customer choice' in such matters as education and health. What in fact has happened is that small units have indeed been given more powers but so has Whitehall; it is the middle levels of county, municipality and region which have been throttled. School governing bodies have been given more 'powers', but not much more power, owing to the constraints of a very tight budget. Those of us who have been involved with school governing in the past will be aware of the need to liberate schools from the tentacles of local government bureaucracy. Not every aspect of LMS (local management of schools) is bad. But in its assault on local government the Thatcher regime established a dangerously centralised system of domination by the ministry of education. Continual interference by central government in the financial affairs of local authorities has deprived them of the right to spend their money in the way they choose. A recent example in Littlemore well illustrates the situation. For many years the governors of a local school have been hoping to sell a part of the school land in order to raise money to improve accommodation for pupils. Government regulations, however, restrict the right of the County Council to spend more than 50 per cent on new buildings, despite the unanimous wish of the education authority, the school governors and the trustee.

Again, hospital trusts have fallen under the immediate control of Whitehall, and – like individual schools under LMS – are too small to assert a position contrary to central policy or in any effective way to resist the decisions of central government, as the regional health boards or county education authorities were able to do in the past. The composition of regional police authorities is also to be brought more under central control.

Other institutions which have been deliberately weakened in different ways have been the trade unions, and such public corporations as the BBC, whose boards have been packed with political appointees sympathetic to the government's programme. Even devoted supporters of Margaret Thatcher became alarmed when her cabinet turned its attention to their cherished institutions. This happened particularly in the reaction to government plans for imposing its ideology on the legal and education establishment. A conservative like the late Professor Elie Kedourie of the London School of Economics resented government intrusion and the introduction of business techniques into universities, as leading to a centralised absolutism.[2] Keith Joseph and Rhodes Boyson, among others, voiced alarm at the imposition of a national curriculum in schools.[3]

Whether the state is more or less powerful than it was in the pre-Thatcher era may be debated, that its role has changed is incontrovertible. Equally apparent is the decline in power and independence of the various intermediate institutions in the country. In certain spheres individuals may have been given increased choice, and liberals would willingly concede that this is good, other things being equal. For this freedom to be significant, however, people must have the *means* to make these choices effective. Even so these changes may give them more power at the micro level but less power at the macro level, owing partly to the fact that they are unorganised and unco-ordinated in their actions. The pluralist writers whom we shall be considering in this book would generally have viewed these current trends with dismay.

II

Not only have the past two decades seen an assault on the managerial and welfare role of the state in Britain and other parts of Western Europe but, more dramatically, recent events in the former Soviet Union and eastern Europe have led to havoc – not only at home but among their sympathisers in the west. Though marxism, as a theory, is fundamentally anti-state – committed to its ultimate 'withering away' – those countries which fell under communist control witnessed the development of a gargantuan bureaucratic brontosaurus, combining ruthless power with monumental inefficiency. With the collapse of communist dictatorships thinkers on the 'left' have been looking to cooperative or associative forms of socialism, such as those advocated by nineteenth century writers like Pierre-Joseph Proudhon or Peter Kropotkin and to movements like syndicalism or guild socialism. They have been looking to the ideas of William Morris and away from Fabian statism.[4]

These changes also put the ideas of the British pluralists once again on the political agenda.[5] Even under the communist regimes of eastern Europe some thinkers had pointed to an associative tradition in socialism, calling for a revival of worker self-management and co-operative ownership.[6] At the level of political theory and analysis the concept of pluralism has increasingly been applied to these east European states.[7] Some earlier writers had noted that even under communism significant elements of pluralism were to be found in these countries, often despite the efforts of their governments. These assertions led to a spirited debate about whether the concept of pluralism could usefully be employed in the analysis of the Soviet and east European political systems in the 1960s and 1970s.

Many political scientists believed by the mid-1960s that the concept of totalitarianism was unsatisfactory in the way it was applied to Soviet and east European states. On the one hand it was thought to be tainted with ideological positions adopted by such cold war critics of the Soviet Union as Carl Friedrich and Zbigniew Brzezinski,[8] and on the other that it concentrated attention on the implementing of centrally made decisions rather than looking at the process by which these decisions were made. In the jargon of the time it attended to 'outputs' of the political process at the expense of 'inputs'. Political scientists were keen to indicate the existence of numerous pressure groups and other associations in the Soviet Union exercising effective influence on the decision-making bodies, thus playing a major role in the political, social and economic dynamics of the country.[9] In order to accommodate this changing emphasis in Soviet studies Jerry Hough and others began to speak of a Soviet pluralism, sometimes qualified by the adjectives 'institutional' or 'bureaucratic'.[10] Another author was prepared to speak of 'pluralistic trends' in Czechoslovakia in the mid-1960s, but in doing so wished to distinguish the situation there from that in the Soviet Union.[11] Nevertheless in a volume on *Pluralism in the Soviet Union*, Hough defended his use of terms like 'pluralism' and 'corporatism' in discussions of Soviet politics, insofar as they direct attention to certain important questions – rather than supplying a wholly satisfactory framework for analyzing the political system.[12] In the same volume Archie Brown maintained that use of the term 'pluralism' in this context involved a 'conceptual stretching' (a phrase used by Giovanni Sartori), which renders the term practically meaningless; almost all regimes would qualify.[13]

This raises the question whether the notion of pluralism which was discussed by these writers is basically the same as that used by Figgis, Laski and their contemporaries. As will become evident from the body of this book, there is little similarity between them. No one would suggest that the political system in the Soviet Union of the 1960s and 1970s bore the slightest resemblance to the notion of a pluralist state in the understanding of these British theorists. The groups had no real 'personality' or autonomy from the state nor was the idea of state sovereignty questioned. Brown suggests that in the first edition of this book I am 'inclined to stretch the concept [of pluralism] unduly by playing down or ignoring the element of *autonomy*'.[14] But I stated clearly that in Figgis's theory, 'The state recognises groups because they exist; they do not derive their existence from being recognised.'[15] They should, he maintained, be largely self-governing. Indeed, the whole idea of group personality, outlined in Chapter 4, implies a considerable degree of autonomy from the state. Curiously, Susan Solomon, in the same volume, asserts that the British pluralists, so far from ignoring the element of autonomy, 'failed to raise the crucial question of state activity' and 'never considered that such groups, once accorded autonomy, might operate at cross purposes and that the state might have to act as arbiter'.[16] Figgis in fact made it perfectly clear that the state must 'control and limit within the bounds of justice' the activities of groups, whose activity 'may be restrained in so far as it interferes with others'.[17]

Whether or not political scientists may appropriately use the concept of pluralism in discussing the politics of the Soviet Union, the use of the term by the Czech reformers during the 'Prague Spring' of 1968 rendered it anathema to the Soviet Communist Party itself for two decades. Only when Gorbachev used the term 'socialist pluralism' in 1987 did the term begin to be acceptable. By 1990 Gorbachev was speaking of 'political pluralism' and in the same year the 28th party congress advocated 'the free competition of socio-political organizations within a constitutional framework'.[18] Even with the collapse of the USSR and the radical reforms which have taken place in Russia, the situation in 1993 hardly resembles anything at all like a pluralist state in the sense which the British pluralists understood it.

III

Developments in the European Community, towards closer union, have increasingly raised questions about the relevance of the concept of sovereignty – both national and parliamentary sovereignty. Talk about losing sovereignty to Brussels and of handing over bits of sovereignty, have suggested considerable confusion about the concept. At the level of legal theory too there is disagreement about the full implications of Britain's accession to the Treaty of Rome in 1972, some of these developments will be discussed in Chapter 3.

The well-established concept of 'subsidiarity', or 'subsidiary function', in continental Catholic social thought has also, during the debate on ratification of the Maastricht Treaty, entered the vocabulary of British politics. The idea, going back into the nineteenth century and formulated by Pope Pius XI in his 1931 encyclical *Quadragesimo Anno*, involves the devolution of decision-making and management to the smallest unit which can competently perform the task. After criticising the tendency to devalue all social groups leaving only the individual and the state, the encyclical maintained that 'it is an injustice, a grave evil and a disturbance of right order for a larger and higher organization to arrogate to itself functions which can be performed efficiently by smaller and lower bodies'.[19]

The cavalier way the British prime minister has used the term 'subsidiarity', to mean merely the devolution of decision-making from the European Commission to the House of Commons or the Cabinet, led some of his critics to believe that the principle itself was a modern invention, cooked up to justify British ratification of Maastricht. For John Major, subsidiarity, it seems, stops at Whitehall. In fact the subsidiarity principle together with the institutional structure set up under the Treaty of Rome may provide the framework for the solution to more than one British malady. Any hope for a just and peaceful settlement in Northern Ireland, for example, must be seen in the context of a limited devolution of power to the province within a larger European setting.

IV

Pluralists have been concerned not only with the structure of authority in the state, but also, by analogy, with authority in those groups and associations which compose the state. Recent centralising tendencies have not been restricted to the state. The determination of the Labour Party leader, John Smith, and his supporters to alter the position of the trade unions in the governing structures of the Labour Party is no doubt due primarily to a belief that the unions are generally unpopular and that their present relationship with the party constitutes an electoral albatross. However, the campaign to do away with block votes is conducted in the name of 'democracy' and 'one person one vote'. From its beginning, however, the Labour Party has been a coalition of groups and individuals and the campaign has radical implications for the structure of the party. The semi-autonomous role of trade unions with their block votes may have had some unfortunate consequences in the past. I well remember an observer describing a union delegation during a snap vote at the party conference. There had been no opportunity to discuss a common position and one delegate raised his hand in favour of the resolution and others were pulling it down. Hundreds of thousands of votes were going up and down, while the tellers were trying to count.

There is nothing undemocratic about recognising the reality and semi-autonomous status of groups within a larger whole. It is an aspect of the federal system in the USA where, in a presidential election, each state votes in the electoral college as a single unit, with a block vote. The attempt to break down the Labour Party into a collection of private individuals, making decisions on the basis of one person one vote, must be viewed by pluralists with suspicion. This is not, of course, to say that constructive reforms are not long overdue in the constitution of the party, or that constituency groups should not be given more power.

The issue of authority within associations has also recently been sparked by the Church of England General Synod's decision to accept the ordination of women to the priesthood. It brings up two matters related to the theme of this book, and to the position maintained by Figgis, as discussed in Chapter 7. The decision, to become binding, must first be accepted by Parliament. A rejection by Parliament would have raised in an acute form the future of church-state relations, leading to vigorous demands for disestablishment. The second issue is perhaps more fundamental: the spiritual authority of national churches and synods. Practically all members of the Church of England would agree, on the one hand, that a national church does not have authority to change (in a more than verbal manner) the ancient creeds of the church or the structure of the sacraments, and on the other, that it does have authority to decide on less basic matters, such as the marriage of clergy and the use of the vernacular in worship. Disagreement occurs on whether the ordination of women raises fundamental doctrinal issues, which would require a much more general consensus among christians. I shall discuss this matter briefly in Chapter 7.

V

In Britain, as elsewhere, ethnicity has become increasingly salient in social and political life. In the 1950s and 1960s migrants from the Caribbean and the Indian sub-continent in Britain were generally concerned to become accepted by the 'host' communities and tended to keep a low profile. They were often officially encouraged to come and were welcomed, being willing to take jobs which the natives were unwilling to perform in a climate of economic growth and full employment. Competition for a decreasing stock of public housing, increased unemployment and economic decline have contributed to a growing hostility to ethnic minorities which has been dialectically related to a rise in ethnic self-consciousness on the part of these groups. In the last twenty years muslim organisations, in particular, have become more active and vociferous in their demands for separate facilities and for a recognition of their corporate rights. Pluralist reaction to these developments will be discussed in Chapter 5.

Recent decades in western Europe and the USA have seen the growth of a huge number of new social movements, bringing together a wide cross section of people – from different classes, ethnic identities and religious beliefs – to promote particular causes or interests. Pressure and interest groups have existed for a long time, but such phenomena as the green movement, gay rights and feminist groups, manifest something relatively new in the nature of their membership and in their mode of operation – by direct action and by popular demonstrations; in this respect they are following a path trodden by the Campaign for Nuclear Disarmament. Furthermore many of these groups have formed international alliances, like 'Kairos Europa', which comprises about 500 groups and networks of poor and marginalised people principally in countries of the European Community. Members of these social movements are generally suspicious of established political parties and represent a challenge to traditional procedures of government. Political theorists must take them seriously, but too often continue to think of politics in terms of the individual and the state. In a new book Paul Hirst writes:

> We have entered an era when the old certainties of politics have dissolved, in which politics and society are more pluralistic and less capable of being dragooned by the ideological programmes of left and right.[20]

He rightly argues that this situation ought not simply to be celebrated as the end of ideology (Bell) or the end of history (Fukuyama), but that it raises certain fundamental issues which cannot be ignored.

VI

My interest in British political pluralism goes back to the late 1950s when I began work for a PhD at Cambridge University, under Alec Vidler. The thesis, 'Authority in Church and State: Aspects of the Thought of J. N. Figgis and his Contemporaries', was submitted to the History Faculty in 1962. The first edition of this book was a drastically compressed version of the thesis; in fact one of the comments most frequently made by friendly critics was that it needed filling out at a number of points. In revising the material for the second edition I have expanded on certain themes. This edition is more clearly focused on the ideas of J. N. Figgis himself, who was perhaps the most original and interesting writer among the British political pluralists, and certainly the least known. The few paragraphs devoted to the idea of a secular state in the first edition have been expanded into a new chapter, focusing particularly on the question of the ideological foundations of a secular state. More space has been devoted to a discussion of the institutional working out of pluralist theories in such movements as syndicalism, guild socialism, distributism, corporatism and various schemes for functional representation.

The idea of a pluralist state has much similarity to what Michael Oakeshott has called 'civil association'. His masterly essay 'On the Character of a Modern European State',[21] was published in 1975. It appeared too late for me to refer to it in the first edition of this work, but as an undergraduate in the Government Department at LSE it was difficult not to gather intimations of the distinctions he drew in this essay.[22] His contribution to political thought is difficult to overestimate but by no means carries with it all the consequences which his admirers imagine. Pierre-Joseph Proudhon, for example, emerges as one of the heroes in the epic struggle between *universitas* and *societas* as appropriate models for the modern state.

The political pluralism of Figgis and Laski was particularly concerned with a search for constitutional norms and institutional structures within which individuals and associations could pursue ends and purposes of their choice. The terms and conditions governing this enterprise (to use an Oakeshottian term) should be distinguished as clearly as possible from the substantive ends which are pursued. The search for such a structure should be based not on the particular ends favoured but on formal criteria of justice which might be acceptable to all (or as many as possible) of the groups and individuals who make up the state. This search manifestly has something in common with the monumental attempt by John Rawls to describe and defend a system of justice as fairness in *A Theory of Justice*, and in his recent work on *Political Liberalism*. In this latter he explicitly recognises the plural (he uses the term 'pluralist') nature of the modern state, and modifies his earlier theory to confront this less abstract understanding of political reality. I shall refer briefly to this matter in Chapter 6.

With respect to the question of a constitution it is one of the more baleful aspects of recent British politics that successive governments appear to regard the British constitution as a more or less pliant instrument with which to forward their own policies and interests. There has been an increasingly arrogant attitude towards the rule of law and the notion of ministerial responsibility. A home secretary has continued to serve after having been convicted of contempt of court, a chancellor of the exchequer failed to resign after having admitted that public funds were spent on legal fees in connection with litigation to secure the eviction of an occupant in the basement flat in his private house. Ministers appear to take responsibility for almost nothing that happens in their departments. The constitution is held in contempt and sacrificed to the interests of party or faction; this has been evident in party policies on proportional representation and in the demand for (and opposition to) a referendum over ratification of the Maastricht treaty. The interests of party have in turn taken second place to personal ambitions. This trend is not the responsibility of one party, nor is it new for improprieties to occur in British politics. What is remarkable is the refusal to resign when corruption has been publicly revealed. This is in striking contrast to the practice of, for example, the Attlee government of 1945–51, and does something to explain the contempt in which politicians are generally held. It was amusing to hear the leader of the Liberal Democrats, in a recent BBC interview, remarking on the low esteem enjoyed by 'politicians', implicitly excluding himself and his party colleagues from this category, when what in fact distinguishes them is merely that the low esteem of which he spoke is more graphically reflected in their general election results! Pluralists are particularly disturbed by these constitutional developments, for they see governments as properly concerned with procedural rather than with substantive issues. Their legitimacy depends not on their passing legislation to forward some supposed common good, but on their maintaining of a structure within which disputes between their various constituent groups may be settled in a predictable and fair way.

In the Conclusion to the first edition I alluded to the pluralist theories of contemporary American political scientists, which may be traced back through David Truman to A. F. Bentley.[23] I argued that the pluralism advocated by these writers was quite different from the pluralism of Figgis and his contemporaries. The former saw the plethora of social and political groups as attempting to influence the substantive policies being pursued by governments. Against the 'power élite' theories of C. Wright Mills and his followers, they rightly maintained that the decision-making process in the USA is influenced by a whole series of different and distinct élites. Edward Shils, Robert Dahl and Nelson Polsby were among the leading American pluralists of the period.

Since that time, Dahl has somewhat modified his position in *Dilemmas of Pluralist Democracy*. While defending himself against misrepresentation by Kenneth Newton, he seems to accept the criticism of having paid too much attention to the decision-making process and failing to emphasise the power which certain groups possess in determining the agenda of politics.[24] In his later book Dahl accepts the possibility of particular associations distorting 'the public agenda', and thereby threatening the 'final control of the agenda by the citizens' (or *demos*).[25] He also stressed the importance of group autonomy in limiting the power of governments, thus permitting a 'mutual control', whereby the state and the associations restrict each other's power. Among the 'dilemmas' of pluralism, there is the danger of a conservatism where an elite consensus among acceptable groups prevents structural reforms which might redistribute resources in an egalitarian direction.[26] He further asserts that membership of these associations might undermine 'civic consciousness'.[27] Despite this shift in emphasis in his later book, Dahl's concept of a pluralist state remains basically the same as in his earlier writings. The model is one of a number of associations of different shapes and sizes competing with each other in their attempts to influences governments in their pursuit of substantive goods. The primary role of groups is that of persuading or cajoling governments to pursue policies which are thought to be in the interests of their members.[28]

This is very different from the model of a pluralist state envisaged by the British pluralists, where the role of government is to to maintain in existence a structure of rules and practices within which associations will, as far as may be, pursue their own goods; it is not the proper function of governments to impose some supposed substantive common good on the country. The only kind of 'civic consciousness' which such a state assumes is, as I have argued below in Chapter 6, a willingness to live and let live on the part of groups and individuals, and an acceptance, for whatever reason (often for purely pragmatic reasons) of a set of procedures – a constitution – which permits such freedom and acknowledges the need for institutions to settle disputes and draw the line in conflicts. Even this acknowledgment will be provisional; groups will always reserve the right to resist governmental decisions when they believe their very existence or integrity are at stake. Pluralists thus recognise a 'contingent anarchy' at the basis of a political order.[29]

It should be observed that although governments are concerned with procedural and structural matters, allowing groups to pursue their own visions of the good life, this does not mean that governments are merely passive. They may properly see their task as one of encouraging and facilitating the foundation of groups and the growth of associative life. I remember being approached some years ago, in the weeks prior to a general election, by a television producer who was planning a programme on christianity and politics. He asked me about the points of contact and I mentioned the importance, for a Christian understanding of human nature, of freedom and the ability to make responsible choices. He clearly believed that the Labour Party scored better on the criterion of 'love your neighbour', and was pleased to hear my response, which he interpreted as a theological defence of Thatcherism. In the course of the TV interview I stated that in my view it was important for the state to allow people to make decisions for themselves, as individuals and as groups, and to encourage the formation of co-operative enterprises within which people may pursue common ends. The producer asked me to concentrate on the duty of the state to allow individual choice, assuring me that someone else would deal with matters of group life and co-operation. Having cast me in the role of a defender of *laissez-faire*, the producer manifestly felt that the other matters would only confuse the viewers. A refusal to accede to his request led to my being excluded from the programme!

Pluralists refuse to accept that politics is a matter of the individual and the state. A false individualism and a mechanical collectivism are, they believe, two sides of the same coin. British pluralism of the early twentieth century developed out of a reaction to these connected tendencies. They argued that a true understanding of human nature recognises individuality indeed, but as manifesting itself and maturing within the context of a multitude of different associations and communities, families, churches, sporting and cultural societies, trade unions, civic associations, universities and schools.

1 Parentalism and Pluralism

This book is about the political thought of a group of British writers, active in the first two decades of the twentieth century.[1] They were all either historians or writers strongly influenced by historical method. They were responding to certain tendencies apparent in their day and were aware of the relative nature of all political thinking. Although their ideas were frequently presented in the context of historical treatises or essays, they were addressed – at least in part – to problems of their own day. In reacting vigorously against the growing power of the state and against certain political theories which justified the omnicompetent state, they responded not only by appeals to the past, but by enlisting the support of contemporary intellectual currents. Figgis, in particular, appealed to writers like Henri Bergson, Rudolf Eucken, William James and even to some themes in Friedrich Nietzsche to defend a pluralist model of political order and the role, in particular, of churches in the modern state.

I

This volume is focused on the ideas of John Neville Figgis (1866–1919), who was in many ways the most interesting and least understood of the British political pluralists. Born in Brighton, the son of a minister in the calvinistic sect known as the Countess of Huntingdon's Connexion, he went to St Catharine's College, Cambridge, to study mathematics and later history. He rejected the faith of his family and was for a time an agnostic. However he came under the influence of the professor of ecclesiastical history, Mandell Creighton, who later became Bishop of Peterborough then London. He decided to be ordained in the Church of England and worked as a curate in the parish of Kettering. He returned to Cambridge in 1896 as a college lecturer at St Catharine's and chaplain of Pembroke College. It was at this period that he wrote *The Theory of the Divine Right of Kings* (1896) and gave his Birkbeck Lectures, which were later published under the title *Studies of Political Thought from Gerson to Grotius, 1414–1625*.

Figgis left Cambridge in 1902 to become Rector of Marnhull (a Dorset village made famous by Thomas Hardy, as 'Marlott', the home of the tragic heroine of Tess of the d'Urbervilles). While in the parish he underwent what amounted to a religious conversion. Gone was the optimistic humanism of his Cambridge days; he became, at once, more evangelical and more catholic in his theology. In 1907 he left Marnhull to join the Community of the Resurrection at Mirfield, an Anglican monastic community founded by Charles Gore. Figgis's Hulsean Lectures, given at Cambridge in 1908–9, shocked his former colleagues. 'Why,' he demanded from the pulpit of the university church, 'are we to suppose that there is more risk in believing too much than too little?'[2] The gospel is a message of human sin, divine forgiveness and of the need for redemption. He pointed, almost with relish, to the otherworldly and mysterious aspects of the Christian faith which give it a distinctive appeal. He firmly rejected liberal attempts to present a gospel shorn of the supernatural, in order to make it compatible with the prejudices of nineteenth century materialism – prejudices which he claimed were in any case being abandoned by contemporary intellectuals. While at Mirfield he published his most important contribution to political thought, *Churches in the Modern State*. In addition to a number of religious works, he wrote a book on Nietzsche, and *The Political Aspects of S. Augustine's 'City of God'* (published posthumously in 1921). His health being weakened, so it was said, by a pendulum movement from Mirfield fasts to Cambridge feasts, he never fully recovered from the trauma of being torpedoed in January 1918. He became increasingly subject to acute depression, which had threatened for some years. He died in 1919 on Palm Sunday, that most ambivalent of christian festivals, aged 55.

Figgis's theory of the state was strongly influenced by a number of earlier writers, in particular by Otto von Gierke (1844–1921) and F. W. Maitland (1850–1906). Figgis helped Maitland to translate part of Gierke's great work *Das deutsche Genossenschaftsrecht*, which was published in 1900 under the title *Political Theories of the Middle Age*. Gierke recognised the close connection between social reality and legal practice in the past, and insisted on bringing sociological perspectives to bear in his understanding of legal theory in his own day. Maitland was perhaps Britain's greatest legal historian; nor was he reticent in relating the fruits of his studies of the past to his analysis of contemporary legal and constitutional problems. From these two legal historians Figgis derived his belief that law must respond to changing social realities if it is to be an effective instrument of social control. As we shall see in Chapters 3 and 4 this was particularly true with respect to group personality and the concept of sovereignty.

Two other principal influences on the ideas of the young Figgis were Mandell Creighton (184–1901), the ecclesiastical historian, and Lord Acton (1834–1902), the formidably learned liberal catholic historian, who was Figgis's senior colleague at Cambridge. Together with R. V. Laurence, Figgis later edited several volumes of Acton's letters and essays. Acton's almost fanatical belief in liberty infected his younger colleague, and this belief lies at the very foundation of Figgis's political pluralism. Creighton was influential as a scholar and a teacher. His respect for learning and his suspicion of following the latest intellectual fashion were communicated to his younger pupils. It was Creighton's understanding of the Church of England in the context of the idea of national churches and the position stated by conciliar theorists of the fourteenth and fifteenth centuries that most influenced Figgis.[3]

I shall also examine the ideas of Harold J. Laski (1893–1950), G. D. H. Cole (1889–1959), Bertrand Russell (1872–1970) and other writers who shared pluralist ideas. Laski, in particular, was considerably influenced by Figgis. It was somewhat perplexing for Laski's American friends to find an agnostic Jew so taken up with the problems of christian church conflicts, and writing about such topics as the political theory of the Oxford Movement and of the Scottish Disruption. Oliver Wendell Holmes indeed lamented the influence of Figgis on the young Laski. The focus of his interests was, however, rather different from that of Figgis, and he became increasingly concerned with questions of administrative law and governmental accountability. His *Grammar of Politics*, first published in 1925, despite his claim that it 'completes an effort, begun in 1915, to construct a theory of the place of the State in the great society',[4] marks the start of a decisive break with his early pluralism. In 1926 he succeeded Graham Wallas as professor of Political Science at London University, based at the London School of Economics. A brilliant teacher and stimulating lecturer, he inspired generations of students, and his many publications spread his influence far beyond the university. In the 1930s he was much influenced by marxism, and became a controversial figure in public life as chairman of the Labour Party in the mid-1940s.[5]

Cole was significant as a guild socialist but, as we shall see, was hardly a pluralist at all. He believed, throughout the tergivisations of his early work, in functional representation at a central parliament or assembly of some kind, either supplementing or replacing geographically based representation. In this respect he recognised the importance of groups in the state, but he sometimes put forward a Rousseauite theory of popular sovereignty, diametrically opposed to the ideas of Figgis and Laski on this issue. He also manifestly attached little importance to group personality and to the need for groups to manage their own affairs and live their own lives. He was for most of his life an Oxford academic and a prolific writer. He retained a suspicion of the centralised state and always felt uneasy with the statist policies of the Labour Party, though in 1928 he rejoined the Fabian Society.[6]

II

As we shall see, these writers did not always agree with each other, but I shall suggest that their pluralist theories share a number of features and were proposed in the context of, and with reference to, a common social and intellectual climate. Figgis in particular was acutely aware of the collapse of the great nineteenth century holistic systems. The mechanistic materialism of the mid-nineteenth century had passed. No longer was physics seen as the model to which all sorts of human knowledge must conform. As a historian he rejected the causal model, which was unable to accomodate notions of human intention and choice. Absolute idealism, though still powerful in the universities, was increasingly being challenged. A new philosophical scepticism embodied in the words and works of Arthur Balfour, was in evidence. Although professing to admire the attempt of German idealists and their British disciples to construct a coherent system, he remarked wryly, 'my small philosophical barque attempts its explorations in shallower waters'.[7] His astute critique of 'naturalism' and of idealism, particularly in his popular work *Foundations of Belief* (1895), had considerable impact on the intellectuals of his day. F. C. S. Schiller also assailed the rationalism of an earlier era.[8] Even an idealist like F. H. Bradley could write, 'though I am willing to concede that my metaphysics may be wrong, there is, I think, nothing which could persuade me that my instinct is not right'.[9]

Gone were the days of the static monism of many neo-Hegelians. The new philosophical movements sweeping the western intellectual world were dynamic and pluralistic. The 'activism' of the German Rudolf Eucken and the 'creative evolution' of Henri Bergson in France shared a rejection of rationalist philosophical systems. Knowledge of the world is achieved not by detachment, but by active involvement in life. This they had in common with a philosophical tradition that was in many ways quite different, the pragmatism of William James.

William James used the term 'pluralism' to describe his own philosophical position, distinguishing it from the monism of contemporary idealist philosophers. While the monist philosophers insisted that the universe is a single, interrelated and coherent totality, which can be known properly only in its totality, radical empiricism and pluralism stand out, he claimed, for the legitimacy of the notion of *some:* each part of the world is in some ways connected, in some other ways not connected with its other parts, and the ways can be discriminated.[10] The world of the pluralist, he asserted, is more like a federal republic than an empire or a kingdom. There is always some self-governed aspect remaining, which cannot be reduced to unity.[11] It is likely that a monist in philosophy would reject political pluralism and would hope that the coherence characterising the whole universe might become concrete in institutional form. Nevertheless, as we shall see, Hegel's social and political thought has certain definite pluralistic elements as, indeed, does Aristotle's. Nor is it necessarily the case that a philosophical pluralist must be a political pluralist. Yet Figgis and Laski referred occasionally to the pragmatism of James and to the intuitionalism of Bergson in support of their political theories. Philosophical pluralism certainly rules out particular kinds of political monism.

The emphasis upon *action* found in James, Bergson and Eucken was, as we have noted, drawn upon by Georges Sorel, the French revolutionary syndicalist, and also by Léon Duguit, the legal theorist and by some of the philosophers of Italian fascism. Coherence was not, these men claimed, a feature of the real world, nor could it be appealed to as a criterion of truth. Reality contains many loose ends. So the political pluralists rejected attempts to subsume the whole of social life under the state, even when – as in Hegel himself, or in some of the British idealists – a certain social pluralism and hostility towards centralisation were evident.[12]

It was Friedrich Nietzsche who administered the *coup de grâce* to the comfortable liberal humanism of the previous century. Those who had rejected the christian religion were confident that they could retain a broadly christian morality. Nietzsche said no. There was a close link between them, and both must go, to be replaced by a philosophy of life based on the will to power. In a number of his works Figgis pointed to the significance of Nietzsche's diatribes. In the past, christians had been condemned for not living up to their ideals, now the ideals themselves were under attack. The German prophet symbolised for the Anglican monk a coming crisis in civilisation of cataclysmic proportions. Well before the Sarajevo assassination Figgis declared from the pulpit:

> The forces of civilisation are imposing; but apart from Christ they are visibly dissolving. Its tall towers are shaking, and the splendid spires of the edifice of the western world are crumbling. Catastrophe is threatening. We can almost hear the thunders of the avalanche of war – war on a scale unknown. Hardly does the world even look stable any longer. It is not like the forties of Victorian complacency, but looks all tottering – tottering.[13]

III

If the negative liberalism of Jeremy Bentham, John Bright and Herbert Spencer had been the ideology of a developing capitalism, the positive liberalism of T. H. Green, Henry Jones, L. T. Hobhouse and the Webbs became the ideology of established capitalism.[14] It is no accident that Joseph Chamberlain, a leading spokesman of the rising industrial interest in the midlands, should be one of the first politicians to recognise the need for a new theory of positive state action. In the first part of the nineteenth century the machinery of state – which was still largely controlled by landed interests – was likely to be used to hamper the development of industrial capitalism; the interests of the industrialists were best served by *laissez-faire*.

By the close of the century the most significant challenges to capitalism were coming, not from the old entrenched agricultural sector, but from trade unions and other groups which refused to accept the new social order. Herbert Spencer, who was so eager to welcome almost every kind of voluntary association, was suspicious of trade unions; perhaps he could dimly see that they provided a potential challenge to the new order. The state was falling increasingly under the control of the commercial and industrial élite, who clearly recognised the positive role which the state itself could play in preserving the economic and social structure which they had done so much to build. Not only was a strong state needed in order to prevent violent uprisings from working-class groups – the negative liberalism of an earlier generation had insisted that the state should retain this function – but it was increasingly acknowledged that capitalism could survive only if positive action were taken to mitigate some of the harsher features of the new industrial order. This positive action could more efficiently be undertaken by the state than by private agencies. In one western European country after another the state began to take upon itself the role of an anxious parent.

Functions previously performed by families, trade guilds, friendly societies, local voluntary groups or civic associations increasingly were taken over by central government. They were either directly managed or closely regulated by government. Many of these functions were delegated to municipalities, but the system of local government itself came under increasing control from Whitehall and Westminster. This growing power of the state was graphically reflected in the national insurance legislation of Asquith's Liberal government. Rather than attempting to strengthen the old friendly societies and voluntary agencies, and filling the gaps which they had left, these new schemes followed the German pattern, entirely superceding the partial system which was in place and setting up a centralised, state-run programme.[15]

Legislation had already been passed, restricting hours of work, prohibiting the employment of children, enforcing safety regulations, providing unemployment pay and old age benefits. This 'new Toryism', as Spencer called it, was justified by modifications in the theory of liberalism and in the concept of liberty. In providing the means of a better life, the state is increasing the *liberty* of the mass of the people. A sustained campaign by philosophers and social theorists to modify the concept of liberty prepared the way for a significant change in Liberal Party policy. What happened at the end of the nineteenth century to the concept of liberty is an interesting example of how conceptual modification may be related to political exigencies.[16] In the mid-nineteenth century 'freedom' or 'liberty'[17] had meant an absence of restraint or interference (particularly by government). As members of the Liberal Party responded to demands for increased governmental intervention, particularly in the welfare, industrial and economic fields, philosophers of a liberal persuasion began to modify the concept of liberty and to assert its positive aspects. To be free to do something includes having the means or the power to do it. By supplying these means the state can take positive action to increase human freedom. Furthermore, by restricting certain powerful private individuals or groups, it could liberate those who were being oppressed by them. Other philosophers went further and claimed that to be free means to follow a rational way of life; to be able to choose what is bad or irrational is not true freedom. So the way was open for paternalist coercive legislation to be justified under the principle of liberty.[18] Pluralists regarded these developments with some dismay.

So successful were the positive liberals in transforming liberalism from a doctrine of *laissez-faire* to a doctrine of positive state action, that some present-day writers regard the advocacy of this kind of positive state action as the very essence of liberalism. T. Lowi writes of interest group liberalism in the following terms:

> It may be called liberalism because it expects to use government in a positive and expansive role, it is motivated by the highest sentiments, and it possesses strong faith that what is good for government is good for the society.[19]

The positive liberals certainly did a thorough job.

The new positive role adopted by the state threw socialists into confusion. Only the bourgeois socialist prophet, from the snug security of his study, could possibly argue that the labour movement should oppose or reject the benefits which were being offered by the state. No one involved in the daily struggle of the movement could realistically think in these terms. Yet it required a William Morris in England and a Rosa Luxemburg in Germany to warn socialists against believing that social reform can properly take the place of social revolution, and that the capitalist state can gradually evolve into a friendly society. The warnings were not heeded. In Germany revisionism carried the day. Its leading theorist Eduard Bernstein had come under the influence of British Fabians, during his time in England, though he remained enough of a marxist to criticise the 'eternal heaping of duties on the state'.[20]

Fabians, largely unencumbered by marxist preconceptions, found no problem in welcoming the 'new Toryism'. It was the aim of social democrats, in the words of Bernard Shaw,

> through Democracy to gather the whole people into the State, so that the State may be trusted with the rent of the country, and finally with the land, the capital, and the organization of the national industry – with all the sources of production, in short, which are now abandoned to the cupidity of irresponsible private individuals.[21]

Sidney Webb wrote complacently of 'our irresistible glide into collectivist Socialism',[22] and was unashamedly élitist in his attitudes. Beatrice used to say that she and her husband were 'benevolent, bourgeois and bureaucratic', in contrast to the guild socialists who were 'aristocratic, anarchist and arrogant'.[23] Robert Michels observed how most British socialists thought of democracy in terms of a benevolent despotism.[24] With the defeat of William Morris and his supporters, at the famous debate of the Fabians in 1886, British socialists moved towards bureaucratic parentalism, taking over much of the ideology of the positive liberals. Nothing was to stand in the way of the state. The new leviathan, however, was to be democratically controlled; the will of the people is the will of God. 'Lewis was shocked,' wrote H. G. Wells of a liberal politician, in *The New Machiavelli*: 'A "Mandate" from the country was sacred to his system of pretences.' It is hardly surprising that Shaw welcomed the advent of Mussolini in Italy, and that the Webbs in their old age became admirers of Stalinism. Curiously, in a recent book, P. P. Craig follows Stanislas Ehrlich by writing of the Fabians as attacking the unitarist state and referring to 'pluralist traits within their work'.[25] Most pluralist and guild socialist theory was, however, directed precisely against the kind of collectivism advocated by the Fabians. Although they did make grudging concessions to functionalism in some of their writings, this is very different from pluralism.

The action of the state in exercising compulsion against people for their own good came to be justified in terms of helping them to live the life that they would really like to live, if only they were provident enough; it is one of the rights of the citizen to be protected against his own weaknesses. Those who did not justify the positive actions of the state as directly contributing to an increase in human freedom, defended these actions as promoting the general happiness or realising the common good, a happiness and a good which were thought in some way or other to be willed or desired by 'the people'. The paternal state imposes sanctions upon people in order to compel them to act in accordance with their own interests, or to refrain from acting against these interests. The maternal state goes further; by anticipating the needs and desires of citizens, it makes provision for them in such a way that they do not even want to act in a manner incompatible with the 'general interest', with which their own interests are said to be inextricably involved. Paternalism employs the harsh external method of physical sanctions, maternalism adopts a more gentle means of moulding character and of taking away those nasty, awkward, 'anti-social' traits which lead people to question, to challenge and, like the prophets of Israel, to disrupt the comfortable complacency of their neighbours (not by interfering in some direct manner, but merely by being what they are, and by speaking the truth as they see it).

The late nineteenth century was characterised by a growth in nationalism and by governmental insistence that all loyalties must be subordinated to the claims of the national state. Germany and Italy had been united on the basis of nationality, and conscious efforts were being made, particularly in the former, to enlist the support of all subordinate groups and to weld them into a coherent whole. Those groups which insisted on maintaining independence from the government were regarded as subversive, hence Bismarck's attacks on the Roman Catholic Church during the so-called *Kulturkampf*. The dynamic nationalism of a youthful Germany led to demands in other European countries for a more unified state. The virulent anti-clericalism of Emile Combes in France sprang from the same root. Economic policies were adopted in order to strengthen national unity – protection became the order of the day. In the field of education there was the demand that developments were required in order to serve the needs of the state. In Britain a new emphasis was placed upon technical subjects and upon the natural sciences; these were thought to be more useful than the humanities, and would strengthen the power of the state; the example of Germany was pointed to. The state was seen to be the only really important group to which the individual belongs. Nationalists endeavoured where ever possible to draw state borders according to the boundaries of nations.

The First World War reinforced the claims of the state. Lesser loyalties were forgotten in the patriotic struggle. The duty to make 'the supreme sacrifice' was given religious sanction. Even pluralist writers, like Figgis, who had warned against the inordinate claims being made by the state, saw the war as a kind of crusade. Ernest Barker, in an extraordinary note appended to his article on 'The Discredited State' (which had been delivered as a lecture in May 1914), remarks on the changed situation and its effect upon his own understanding of the state. 'It is curious how differently one would have written in January 1915,' he wrote, 'We have forgotten that we are anything but citizens, and the State is having its midsummer of credit.'[26]

The majority of social thinkers of a 'progressive' tendency happily piled more and more duties on central government. Not only was government to be concerned with regulation but increasingly with the provision of services. Groups like the Christian Social Union urged state participation in more and more spheres of social life. Canon Henry Scott Holland wrote of the people of London, 'The State, in some far golden day yet to come, may be to them as a home ... . Its eye will be on them, its arm about them.'[27] The chapter on 'Christianity and Politics', in the influential collection of essays, *Lux Mundi*,[28] had maintained that 'the State is sacred', and in doing so was only echoing the dictum of F. D. Maurice that 'the State is as much God's creation as the Church'.[29] I have argued elsewhere that this sacralising of a paternalistic state is closely related to a liberal theology of 'the fatherhood of God and the brotherhood of man' and to an unbalanced 'incarnationalism', which tends to play down the reality of sin and the need for human redemption.[30] Figgis was critical of both these tendencies in the theology of his day. Earlier, as we have noted, he had himself been influenced by these trends, but reacted sharply to them in his Hulsean Lectures. At the same time he became an outspoken adversary of the 'omnicompetent state'.

IV

It was against this background that pluralism developed. How can we expect this parental state to realise a common good when it is composed of social and economic groups whose interests are often incompatible? How can we expect the state to act in the real interests of the masses when its political and administrative machinery is effectively controlled by a small group of individuals whose interest it is to preserve the *status quo*, and above all to perpetuate and extend the power of the state itself? How can there be a general happiness which is anything other than the happiness of persons, and of groups of persons, pursuing some end which they choose to pursue? How can the state do anything to increase this happiness, other than by allowing people to live their lives as they choose as members of those associations which they desire to join and by providing a structure within which they may do so?

By the beginning of the twentieth century it had become clear to a number of thinkers that the only hope for freedom in the modern world was by attacking the growing power of the state and the outrageous claims being made on its behalf. The only factor uniting these thinkers was a refusal to pay homage to the established capitalist system of their day, and a recognition that the parentalist state was rapidly becoming the chief instrument for its preservation. Figgis saw clearly that the ascendancy of the absolute state in his own day was directly linked to 'the horror of that very economic and industrial oppression which is the distinctive gift of modern capitalism to history'.[31] In an Ash Wednesday sermon of 1912 he drew attention to the social conditions in which the working class lived. 'Most of us', he told his respectable congregation, 'live in a world of ideas in which we take the slums for granted.' 'The state of our cities,' he went on,

> the lives of the vast masses among the workers, are a disgrace to any civilisation, and ... in so far as this civilisation calls itself Christian, it is a lie; and our comfortable piety, and religious books and Church circles do but make the evil more glaring.[32]

Why, he demanded, were his fellow church people afraid of giving excessive support to the poor, while happily ministering to the materialism of the rich? 'If we are going to make mistakes, for God's sake let us make our mistakes on the side of the oppressed and not against them.'[33]

Many of these thinkers were members of groups whose existence was being challenged by the claims of the state. In France the government was committed to establishing a secularist state[34] where the corporate claims of the christian churches and of trade unions were alike rejected. 'There are and there can be no rights,' wrote M. Emile Combes, 'except the right of the State and there are and can be no other authority than the authority of the Republic'.[35] Monastic communities, like the one to which Figgis belonged, were the object of particular hostility from these French radicals, as constituting a state within the state.

In England the situation had developed rather differently. The Church of England was still seen as a national institution, and in exchange for the privileges involved in this status its spiritual independence in a number of spheres was limited. Trade unions, for their part, were treated with toleration and even with respect, so long as they concentrated on improving conditions for their members, and accepted the developing ideology of a welfare state. Nevertheless any action which was thought seriously to threaten the social and economic arrangements of the state was suppressed, while the very desire to make radical changes was eroded by the maternalistic actions of the state.

Elitist thinkers in Italy, France and Germany reminded their contemporaries at the turn of the century that large-scale organisation inevitably involves control by a small élite. But, on this question, Mosca, Pareto and Michels did little more than repeat in sociological jargon the perceptions of J. F. Stephen, Henry Maine and Arthur Balfour. Democracy would not mean, as J. S. Mill had imagined, the government of each by all the rest, but the government of each by a relatively small group of 'wirepullers'. The result of cutting up voting power into little bits 'is simply that the man who can sweep the greatest number of them into one heap will govern the rest'.[36] Many of these elitist writers believed that the 'iron law of oligarchy' was not only a fact but was a welcome fact. Stephen insisted that bureaucracy was the only hope for a country which paid lip-service to the notion of democracy. He attacked those who feared an increasing centralisation, and argued that we must choose the best servants that we can find and give them the power necessary to do their work. Not only was oligarchy inevitable in the state, but also in any large organisation. Maine and Michels applied the theory specifically to political parties.

Anarchists, of course, shared this perception with elitists; large-scale organisation necessarily involves oligarchy, particularly in the case of compulsory associations like the state. Instead of welcoming oligarchy, which is the invariable companion of organisation, they rejected both. Anarchists insisted that freedom can be preserved only in small voluntary groups, and that mass participation in the politics of a large state is an impossibility.

The pluralists – Figgis, Laski, Russell – accepted the main contention of the anarchists; they believed that people should in general be left to pursue ends chosen by themselves, in the context of voluntary associations. Yet Figgis argued that the state should remain as the society of societies, responsible for maintaining order among the groups within it. The state should not itself, however, pursue a goal or purpose other than that of maintaining a situation where people are able, as individuals and associated in groups, to follow paths which they choose for themselves. Figgis agreed with Rousseau's critique of representation. True participation can never be achieved through representative government. In the modern state, he insisted, the mass of people will have nothing to do with the law except to obey it, unless there exist strong local groups having real autonomy. 'The mere fact of a system of so-called representatives will not secure freedom.'[37] Participatory democracy is possible only in small groups.

If Maine and Michels were right in claiming that the iron law of oligarchy applies as much to large organisations within the state as to the state itself, did the pluralists not see that large groups like trade unions and churches constitute a potential threat to individual freedom in the same way that the state does? Many of them did recognise that any large centralised organisation would invariably be controlled by a small, often self-perpetuating and self-interested, oligarchy. These writers therefore extended their federal ideas to the larger groups which compose the state. Figgis, for example, was much concerned with the problem of authority in the church, and warned against the centralising tendencies of Rome. He saw in ultramontanism 'a theory analogous to that which we have been combating in the State'.[38] He argued in favour of power being dispersed within the church among semi-autonomous national churches, and to smaller units like dioceses and monastic communities, and was particularly insistent on stressing the role of *small* groups in the church. His interest in the conciliar movement of the fifteenth century was not simply in its claim that general councils have greater authority then the pope; these conciliar theories recognise the existence, and allow for the development, of semi-autonomous units within the catholic church.[39]

G. D. H. Cole and the guild socialists were suspicious of the large trade unions and argued for a system of industrial unionism, where much of the real power would be exercised locally. What most of the pluralists rejected was the idea that the state should interfere with groups in order to protect the interests of members, and impose upon the group the kind of polity which it thinks best. So long as people were free to leave, the state should not as a general rule interfere. The really effective claim for freedom and for a devolution of power within the large associations must come from within and not from outside. Only if it comes from the members themselves will it be likely to lead to a real change for the better; if it comes from the state nothing but state absolutism can result.

The attempt in the 1980s to impose upon trade unions a 'democratic' structure has dangerous implications. Does the state have the moral right to impose a supposedly democratic structure on groups within it? Can it properly insist that bishops be elected by 'one man [*sic*] one vote', or that the Nicene Creed may be changed by a simple majority of church members? May a future government legitimately turn the Conservative Party itself into a democracy? The political pluralists we are discussing would have replied 'no' to these questions.

The British pluralists envisaged a situation in which members of the state pursue their chosen ends in life, as individuals and associated in voluntary groups, with as little interference from coercive governmental authorities as possible in the context of order and peace. Figgis used the term 'state' to apply to this collectivity; it is the society of societies, whose purpose is to maintain some kind of order, and to adjudicate between the claims made by its members. Individual citizens will naturally join groups, for humans are social animals. These groups will develop a life of their own, which cannot be accounted for simply in terms of the actions and ideas of their individual members. The degree of unity attained by the group will depend upon the nature of the purpose pursued, and upon the loyalty manifested by its members. Pluralist writers believed that a permanent association, pursuing a definite purpose upon which its members are in general agreement, manifests a unity which enables us to treat it in certain respects as a 'person'.

Obviously there are important ways in which a group differs from an individual person, but there are certain common features which groups share with individuals. These groups have an existence which is not derived from the state. Certainly, they agreed, there must be some machinery for recognising and registering these groups, and for settling disputes between them. The law, if it is to be an effective instrument of social control, must recognise groups as real entities – as legal persons – but the life of groups is not derived from their having been recognised. Quite the reverse; the law recognises them because they exist as social facts, just as the law recognises individuals as legal persons. Individual citizens will often belong to a large number of groups, each pursuing different ends. Some of these associations will be formally organised, others will be traditional, informal groups governed, like the family, by custom rather than by written regulations. Some will pursue ends which are limited and specific, others will have a purpose wider and less easily specifiable. The British pluralists did not envisage these divisions reinforcing each other, but thought of them as cutting across one another, so that within a given state people of different social classes would join together in pursuing the same sport, and people of different religious persuasion would belong to the same trade unions. These theorists would have accepted T. S. Eliot's judgment that 'numerous cross-divisions favour peace within a nation, by dispersing and confusing animosities'.[40] A somewhat similar position has been defended by a number of American writers of recent years.[41]

There will certainly be occasions on which individuals will find themselves torn between loyalty to one group and loyalty to another. There will inevitably be friction in a pluralist state. People will have to make up their minds what they should do in cases of conflict. Perhaps the state will itself intervene, and side with one group against another on the particular issue; normally citizens will accept the decision of the state, because they accept the importance of there being some generally recognised machinery for maintaining order and settling disputes. But they may on a particular occasion refuse to accept the ruling of the state, and disobey, or even take to arms.

Sometimes the state may go beyond its role as the mediator, attempting to pursue some national goal which it will illegitimately impose upon its citizens. It will speak of a 'common good', or a 'general will', or a 'public interest', which is an all-embracing, substantive purpose to be followed by the state as a whole. In this case the state will sooner or later come into conflict with a number of the voluntary groups which are to be found within it. Forward-looking politicians dedicated to national objectives will anticipate the kind of conflicts which will arise and will set about under-mining the position of voluntary groups in the state. These groups will be called 'divisive', and their very right to exist will be challenged; they destroy the unity and coherence of the state. Discussing the means of preserving a tyranny, Aristotle wrote:

> One of them is the forbidding of common meals, clubs, education and anything of a like character ... . A second measure is to prohibit societies for cultural purposes, and any gathering of a similar character; in a word, the adoption of every means for making every subject as much of a stranger as is possible to every other.[42]

The British pluralist writers believed that individual freedom is most likely to be preserved when a large number of associations coexist in the state, and when the state does not itself pursue some national policy which purports to realise a common good. The state should concern itself with maintaining order and peace, by settling disputes between individuals and groups. So far as there is a common good worth considering, it is structural rather then substantive in nature. There will assuredly be tension and even friction between the groups, but this is not a wholly regrettable thing; in an imperfect world, freedom is more likely to survive in such a situation of friction. Furthermore it is in the context of conflicting claims made upon their loyalty that citizens develop their conscience and personality. Pluralist writers disliked coercive authority, believing that people should be encour-aged to form self-governing associations to pursue the ends which they think valuable, rather then waiting for governments to act. They agreed with Proudhon that government is at best a necessary evil. 'To be governed', wrote the Frenchman,

> is to be kept in sight, inspected, spied on, directed, law driven, num-bered, enrolled, indoctrinated, preached at, controlled, estimated, assessed, censored, ordered about, by creatures who have neither the right, nor the wisdom nor the virtue to do so.[43]

Political pluralism, then, emerged at a time when the state was becoming increasingly active and powerful. Politicians frequently made claims which were totalitarian in their consequences and the fashionable political theories of the day gave undue prominence to the role of the state. The pluralist emphasis upon the importance of groups within the state, and particularly upon the crucial role of small groups, was a protest against, on the one hand, individualism and its corollary collectivism, and on the other against philosophical idealism. It was a cardinal belief of the pluralists that individualism and collectivism were but two sides of a single coin. Individualism, which was based upon a false view of human nature and of human relationships, leads by easy stages to collectivism and to statism. Deny the political importance of the social life of citizens as it manifests itself in the family, the church, the sporting or cultural group, the civic association, and one is left with politics as a matter of 'the man versus the state'. Idealists, while they often recognised the importance of the role which groups play in life, usually failed to carry this recognition in to their political theories. They became either sponsors of state paternalism (often unwittingly), or of the individualistic ideology of 'self-help' along the lines recommended by the Charity Organisation Society.

V

Political pluralism was built upon a foundation of three pillars:

(a) an insistence that liberty is the most important political value, and that it is best achieved in a state where power is distributed and dispersed, rather than being concentrated at one point;

(b) a rejection of the idea of sovereignty: legal, political and moral;

(c) a notion of the real personality of groups.

One chapter will be devoted to each of these themes.

An accusation frequently levelled against pluralism is that the group can be quite as oppressive to the individual as can the state. I shall address this issue, in Chapter 5, which will consider the positive theories of the pluralists about the relationship between the individual, the group and the state.

When appraising pluralist ideas of the state a crucial question is: what social conditions are necessary for the existence and persistence of a such a state? Obviously an institutional structure is required. It is also alleged that there must exist among the population common 'values', a political culture of toleration (or even indifference) with respect to issues of ultimate truth. Some political theorists argue that every state must have the underpinning of some kind of 'public philosophy', 'civic religion' or 'national church', in order to maintain the political culture upon which a state can grow roots and flourish. Chapter 6 will attend to this problem.

In the seventh chapter I shall deal with the question of authority within groups, looking particularly at Figgis's ideas about authority in the church, which he saw in some respects as analogical to authority in the state. The final chapter will deal with certain institutional consequences of pluralism, considering such movements as guild socialism, distributism, syndicalism, functionalism and corporatism as attempts to embody in institutional form the main principles of pluralism. In conclusion I shall consider the coherence of pluralism as a general theory and its relevance to situations different from those in response to which it evolved.

2 Liberty and the Division of Power

The proper ends of political action are not self-evident. If there is one thing that a history of political thinking should teach us it is this: that there has been no generally agreed conclusion about what are the proper concerns of government. Some writers insist that the achievement of some kind of 'just society' is the end. Others claim that governments should be concerned with happiness; some think that equality must be achieved at all costs. Others again believe that so long as life is protected and order is maintained, a government may do as it will; or put in contemporary jargon, governments should be concerned with conflict resolution. In this chapter I shall attempt to clarify the belief of Figgis and other pluralists of his day about the status of liberty as a principal end in politics, to point to some of the ambiguities in their understanding of the concept of liberty, and to examine their conviction that the realisation of liberty in the modern state, depends upon the dispersion of power and on the existence of vibrant social groups and associations.

I

A number of political scientists writing in the early decades of the present century assumed that the role of the state is simply to resolve social conflicts and to use its power to impose a kind of amoral compromise upon the contending parties. They appear to have seen this role of the state as self-evidently true and to have denied that state policy can have any further moral purpose or that this conception of the state makes questionable moral assumptions.

Certainly major conflicts must be resolved, or contained, if a state is to continue; and it is clear that one of the jobs which a government must do is to control conflicts. But conflicts can often be resolved in a number of different ways. Totalitarian governments achieve this aim in one way, while liberal governments attempt to do so in a somewhat different manner. Governments can attempt to resolve (or rather prevent) conflicts by suppressing subordinate groups. François Duvalier and his son remained in power for twice as long as many American presidents or British prime ministers, and resolved conflicts in Haiti during that period. But the autocratic and ruthless method they chose to accomplish this purpose is not the only method open to politicians. There are other ways of going about things, and we need to have some idea of which method is best – if not the absolute best, then the best in the circumstances. Moral debate cannot therefore be avoided. Many political thinkers write as though the end which they happen to espouse is self-evidently the only possible end of politics, seeking to purge political theory of ethical content. We do not, they argue, need to justify, to give reasons for, or to defend, our view about the duties of government. Bernard Crick goes so far as to *define* 'politics' as the conducting of the affairs of government in a manner of which he approves. This understanding of politics has a respectable pedigree going back at least to Aristotle. Politics, Crick writes, 'can be simply defined as the activity by which differing interests within a given unit of rule are conciliated by giving them a share in power in proportion to their importance to the welfare and the survival of the whole community'.[1] Nevertheless, the very title of Crick's book, *In Defence of Politics*, makes it clear that if politics is defined in this way, the significant moral discussion is shifted to a defence of politics itself: why should we conduct the affairs of state in a *political* manner, rather than in any other manner? It is thus clear that Crick is by no means attempting to rid political theory of an ethical component.

Some writers claim that there are a number of values which a government should hold while conducting the affairs of state, and that it is impossible to reduce these to a single principle. Equality, freedom, justice, happiness, order, are all goods and may not be reduced to a single end. They cannot be so reduced, for they are inherently incommensurable. The pluralist writers we are considering would seem to believe that these political goods can at least be arranged in some kind of hierarchy, with liberty at the top. Even those like Karl Popper, who believe that it is more important to eliminate evils that to realise good in politics, must have some idea about what is evil and be prepared to defend this judgment in moral argument.

Closely connected to the idea that there are many political values none of which take priority over the others, is the doctrine that there can be no such things as a single *right* course of action for the individual in any concrete instance. There are, it is suggested, a number of 'goods' corresponding to the various roles the individual plays, but there is no single course of right action in a given situation. A prime minister may come to the conclusion that what is good for him as a husband, or as a property owner, conflicts with what is good for him as a statesman, and there is no satisfactory way of resolving the conflict. He has simply to select one of the goods or to work out what is essentially an amoral compromise between the conflicting claims, and to act accordingly. This ethical pluralism, as it may be called, is

closely connected to a particular sociological theory about the relation
of persons to the social groups to which they belong. This theory is
conveniently summarised by Walter Lippmann:

> the life of a modern man is not so much the history of a single soul; it is
> rather a play of many characters within a single body .... The modern
> man is unable any longer to think of himself as a single personality
> approaching an everlasting judgment.[2]

This notion has enjoyed considerable popularity among certain modern
American sociologists.[3] There can, according to this theory, be no course of
right action for the individual person, as such a person does not really exist
as a moral being. There is no 'self' distinct from its social relationships and
the roles these relationships imply. There is a plurality of goods for the
individual which are incommensurate. This is argued in two articles by
S. P. Lamprecht. For him, there is a plurality of ends and there is 'neither one
unified *summum bonum*, nor one single course of right conduct'. Not only
does this writer say that there are several goods, which few would deny, but
that 'there is a plurality of right conduct'.[4] The reason he gives for this latter
assertion is that, as 'right' means aiming at the good and as there are several
goods, there are thus several rights; which only shows that if you use words
in an odd enough way you can prove almost anything. Surely by 'right' we
normally mean that which ought to be done in any given situation. 'In the
recognition of conduct as "right",' observed Sidgwick,

> is involved an authoritative prescription to do it: but when we have
> judged conduct to be good, it is not yet clear that we ought to prefer this
> kind of good to all other good things.[5]

In an effort to show that there is no single right course of action in any
situation, Lamprecht presents the reader with a difficult moral problem,
regarding the number of soldiers a commander should sacrifice for the
safety of a cathedral in wartime. This is rather like presenting us with a difficult mathematical problem as proof that there is no solution. 'The practical difficulties in the application of a rule,' observed Walter Bagehot, 'do
not disprove its being the true and the only one.'[6] The fact is that com-
manders have to take some course of action, and have to do so on the basis
of some idea of right and wrong. According to the view of Lamprecht all
we can hope for in politics is a kind of amoral compromise between the
various possible goods pulling in different directions. Figgis certainly
allowed for a plurality of goods and of general principles calculated to
achieve these goods, but in cases of conflict applied the ultimate criterion
of love.

There is something of the same element of ethical pluralism in the thinking of A. F. Bentley. 'When we have reduced the legislative process to the play of group interests,' he wrote,

> then log-rolling, or give and take, appears as the very nature of the process. It is compromise, not in the abstract moral form, which philosophers can sagely discuss, but in the practical form with which every legislator who gets results through government is acquainted.[7]

While compromise is certainly an important aspect of politics, it is surely not the beginning and the end, as Bentley seems to assume. The political pluralists we are discussing rejected the 'role' theory of the individual and insisted that there is such a thing as 'right conduct' in politics; they maintained that the ends of politics must be ethically determined, and rejected the notion of the ethical pluralists that there can be no single right course of action in any situation, arguing that the maximisation of liberty should be the principal end of political activity.

II

Lord Acton's devotion to liberty is well known; much of his life was spent in collecting material for a projected history of liberty – 'the greatest book that was never written'. Acton insisted that liberty, or freedom (and I shall use the terms synonymously), is the highest political end, and that the important thing to discover is not what a government does but what it allows to be done. Figgis also believed that it is the prime duty of a government to ensure as much freedom as possible, maintaining that it is upon liberty that all the minor ends of the state depend for their stability. He asserted that freedom is good because it enables people to develop their personalities to the fullest extent. 'The theory of liberty,' he wrote, 'is always concerned at bottom with human character.'[8]

For Harold Laski, too, 'the emphasis upon freedom is made because it is believed that only in such fashion can the ethical significance of personality obtain its due recognition'.[9] The pluralist writers would have agreed with Gladstone that it is liberty alone which fits people for liberty. By being treated responsibly they develop a fuller sense of responsibility. All true liberals, Figgis insisted, must value human character above the efficiency of the state machinery. It is because the state is interested in human character that it should not attempt to mould character directly. A solid liberalism consists, according to these pluralist writers, in two propositions, (a) that the state ought to be concerned with the development of the personality of its citizens, and (b) that this personality develops best (as a general rule) when citizens are left as much choice as possible in determining how they should live their lives. If the first proposition were held without the second, the most extreme form of totalitarian paternalism might be justified. If the first proposition is denied, then the kind of liberalism which might be advocated would lack a solid basis. The proper role of the state is rather to provide a framework which will facilitate the foundation and growth of those groups and associations within which citizens are able to develop their personalities.

Many writers have attempted to defend liberalism on a sceptical basis, arguing or assuming that moral justifications of liberty are unnecessary. The Hobbes–Hume tradition of sceptical liberalism insists on seeing liberty as a residuum which governments may find it convenient to leave untouched by legislation. Although a wise government will avoid unnecessary meddling with the personal lives of its citizens, there can be no claim on the part of the citizens to freedom as a right. While Figgis and Laski insisted that governments have a moral duty to maintain the kind of structure within which as much freedom of choice is left to as many people as possible, the sceptics recognise no such moral duty. They therefore deny that citizens have a right to as much freedom as is possible in the situation. Certainly the pluralists acknowledged that there cannot be an absolute right to the same amount of freedom in all contexts. In a state of siege or during a war there can rarely be as much freedom as in peacetime. Nevertheless it is still a duty of governments to maximise freedom within a given context.

Some liberals, like Acton, believe that all political values can be subsumed under the principle of liberty. Limitations on freedom can, for them, ultimately be justified only by the claim that a greater freedom is guaranteed by the restriction than would exist without the restriction. How can this be? Surely restriction is the very opposite of freedom; the more restrictions one has in a state the less freedom there is. How is it possible then to say that restrictions can *increase* freedom? Bentham had asked a similar question – surely liberalism necessarily implies *laissez-faire*.

In his book, *Fear of Power*, Preston King makes a similar point. Although it may in certain circumstances be right to confine a man in prison, 'it seems something of an exaggeration to argue that such acts promote "freedom"'.[10] With Bentham, King agrees that the imprisonment may be justified, but on grounds other than the maximisation of freedom. Bentham admitted that although laws are an infraction of liberty, and therefore an evil, they may be justified in so far as they prevent a greater evil – in so far, that is, as they minimise pain. He does not seem to conceive of the possibility of laws increasing freedom in any way. Now although it is clearly false to suggest that the freedom of the man imprisoned is promoted by the action, it may very well be the case that the freedom of others (whom *he* had been restricting) is promoted by confining the man. As L. T. Hobhouse put it: freedom involves constraint, but it is constraint on something else, 'that which is free being in the respect in which it is free necessarily unconstrained'.[11] One would have thought that King, from the nature of his argument, would have been the first to agree that agencies other than the state may deprive people of liberty, and that the state, therefore, in restricting the activities of these agencies may increase the total freedom in a given situation. Yet he thinks otherwise: 'Where one assumes liberty (*qua* autonomy) to be an absolute or ideal good, one can only accept (in consequence) the legitimacy of very little or of no government at all – barring doubletalk.'[12] This would, however, be true only in the ideal situation when each person exercised liberty in such a way as to be compatible with the activities of every other person. Otherwise some limits on freedom will be necessary to keep in being a situation in which maximum freedom can be enjoyed by the bulk of the people. It is thus false to suggest that, in any situation other than the ideal, a belief in liberty as the chief end in politics implies the legitimacy of 'no government at all' (or of 'very little government' – how little? How does 'very little government' enter into the argument? If by 'very little' King means no more than is necessary to maintain an ordered and peaceful state in which freedom may meaningfully be enjoyed, the dogmatic liberal will agree with him – but this might be quite a lot of government in certain circumstances).

The pluralist writers, then, clearly recognised that some freedoms must be curtailed by government action if freedom is to be maximised in a state. It may be appropriate to mention here that they rejected J. S. Mill's attempt to draw 'a circle around every individual'[13] within which the individual must be left free to act as he chooses. Mill's distinction between self-regarding and other-regarding acts was scornfully discarded as indicating a misunderstanding of the nature of human relationships. 'Few persons', wrote A. D. Lindsay,

> would now endorse J. S. Mill's distinction between actions which concern only the individual who does them and actions which concern other people also, as though anything a man did, or thought, or was, could be without effect on his fellows.[14]

Figgis concurred; how could anyone seriously accept Mill's distinction between 'acts purely self-regarding and those which are not'? Laski agreed.[15] If Mill's critics had bothered to read the essay *On Liberty* with the same care that Mill wrote it, this kind of misrepresentation might have been avoided. He explicitly recognised that *all* actions may affect other people directly or indirectly; when he used the expression 'conduct which affects only himself', Mill went on immediately to qualify this: 'when I say only himself, I mean directly, and in the first instance; for whatever affects himself, may affect others through himself'.[16] Unfortunately this kind of carelessness is occasionally found in the writings of the British political pluralists. Ernest Barker also criticised Mill as the prophet of an empty and abstract individual, but happily avoided this kind of misrepresentation.

A more telling argument against the position of the dogmatic liberal would be to maintain that freedoms are incommensurate and that it is therefore impossible to argue that by restricting A and thus liberating B, C and D, one is increasing the total freedom in a state. There is, according to this objection, no meaning which can properly be attached to the term 'total freedom in a state'. There are only particular freedoms and it is impossible to reduce these to a single quantitative scale. There is clearly some force in this objection. Mr Jones is prevented by the law from the practice of his religion which involves performing certain noisy rites in the middle of the night, thereby depriving the Smiths, the Browns and the Percivals of the freedom to sleep (i.e. they are now obliged to stay awake during the period of Mr Jones's exercises, whereas before they were free either to sleep or to stay awake). Nevertheless who is to say that the freedom of religious expression which Jones claims is not more valuable than the relatively trivial freedoms of his neighbours? The US Supreme Court often seems to think that it is. If freedoms are not commensurate then it is certainly impossible to decide how governments should act by simply referring to a 'libertarian calculus'. There must be some idea of a difference in qualities of freedom, and there exist, therefore, significant political values other than freedom. There is hardly any case of freedom being extended to one group of people which does not involve some deprivation of freedom, however trivial and indirect, for other members of that state. This argument against liberty being the only political value seems to be fairly conclusive, but most of the pluralist writers we are here considering did not claim that it was the only value.

A solid liberalism must rely upon some conception of human nature. Acton's insistence upon the inviolability of conscience is well known. It was, in his view, the development of an idea of conscience which marks the greatest step forward in the history of liberty. 'The Christian notion of conscience,' he taught,

> imperatively demands a corresponding measure of personal liberty. The feeling of duty and responsibility to God is the only arbiter of a

Christian's actions. With this no human authority can be permitted to interfere.[17]

Tolerance of error, he observed, is necessary for freedom, and this tolerance is hard to defend in cases of *manifest* error except by a belief in the inviolability of conscience. The doctrine of the sovereignty of conscience promoted toleration, and 'all liberty is founded upon a belief in its infallibility'.[18] Acton held this latter principle in a radical manner, which could have anarchic consequences. Although it may be true that the individual has an absolute duty to follow his conscience, it may not be the case that the political authority is obliged in all cases to permit individuals to do so. In situations when someone's conscientious actions might have disastrous consequences for others, the state may surely restrain that person. This does not necessarily involve forcing the conscience of the person concerned, as when a magistrate over-rules the conscientious objections of Jehovah's Witness parents to a blood transfusion for their sick child. The life of the child may be saved, while the conscience of the parents is intact – as they never consented to the transfusion.

Figgis and Laski both agreed with Acton that a strong doctrine of conscience is a necessary part of a sound liberalism. Nevertheless there is a limit to the freedom which the state can permit to anti-social consciences, particularly in times of emergency. They would rather have agreed with Mandell Creighton's remark that:

> society cannot be altogether abolished to suit people's consciences. But I am bored with people's consciences. Let them be requested to leave off growing conscientious scruples, and grow cauliflowers, or some other useful product.[19]

Discussing the position of conscientious objectors in the 1914–18 war, Figgis wrote that in his judgment it was right to assure liberty to genuine C.O.s; but owing to its obvious abuse severe measures should be taken to test the reality of the conviction. Yet he believed that one has a duty to follow one's conscience ultimately, after having given due weight to the relevant authorities. Blind obedience to any authority, leads to a corruption of the conscience.

Harold Laski thought that J. H. Newman's discussion of conscience in his *Letter to the Duke of Norfolk* was 'the profoundest analysis of sovereignty the nineteenth century produced'.[20] There Newman replied to Gladstone's claims that, owing to the Vatican Council's definition of papal infallibility and universal jurisdiction, a Roman Catholic could no longer be a loyal citizen, and that the papal authority will always take precedence

over the claim of the civil government. Newman maintained that for the
Roman Catholic the papacy is indeed the supreme ecclesiastical authority,
but it is ultimately the conscience which recognises it as such:

> if either the Pope or the Queen demanded of me an 'Absolute Obedi-
> ence', he or she would be transgressing the laws of human nature and
> human society. I give an absolute obedience to neither.[21]

Acton had insisted that the first agent in the development of conscience
must be religious or quasi-religious. Though christianity has not always been
characterised by a belief in the freedom of conscience, it was in a christian
context that the belief reached its fullest and most adequate expression. It
was the doctrine of conscience which brought over religion to the cause of
freedom. Figgis believed that the notion of freedom is intimately connected
to a belief in 'the spiritual nature of men'.[22] The materialist doctrine that
humans are complicated machines hardly has a place for a high doctrine of
conscience, nor, therefore, for a solid conception of human freedom. Why
should too much fuss be made about civil liberty if the individual is simply a
lump of matter moved here and there by contending forces? 'The moment
you begin to examine what freedom means,' Figgis declared,'you find your-
self driven to a spiritual view of human life.'[23]

Laski agreed with Acton and Figgis that a strong doctrine of conscience
is an indispensable underpinning for a sound liberalism, and regarded his
own pluralistic position as taking away from the state and giving back to
the individual conscience that superior morality with which the former had
wrongly been invested. He did not, however, base his politics on a religious
foundation, but upon a humanist belief in the importance of individual
personality. Bernard Zylstra concludes from his detailed study of Laski's
political ideas that

> If there is a line of continuity in his thought from the very first of his
> publications to the end of his life, it should be sought in his insistence
> upon the central place of individual man.[24]

III

When pluralists argued that liberty is one of the chief ends of political
activity, did they think of liberty in the negative hobbist sense of an
absence of external impediments to action, or did they have a more positive
notion of freedom? The pluralists we are considering were not philosophers
and there is often, in their writings, a certain lack of precision in the use of

concepts. Acton defined freedom in various ways; he claimed that freedom is not the power of doing what we like, but 'the right of being able to do what we ought'.[25] This has definite traces of a rationalist notion of freedom, which pictures people as free when they live under the guidance of reason; though Acton here thought of a person as free when *able* to do as he ought (rather than when actually doing as he ought, which is the full-blown rationalist notion of freedom). In his later writings, however, Acton introduced a further subjective element. 'By liberty,' he declared in 1877, 'I mean the assurance that every man shall be protected in doing what he believes his duty.'[26]

Figgis recognised that there is a danger in speaking of freedom as the right to do as we ought; such a definition of freedom can easily lead to a justification of tyranny in terms of freedom.[27] Yet he seems to have put forward no satisfactory notion of freedom to take its place. Laski spoke of T. H. Green's concept of freedom as 'more valuable' than the negative empiricist position, and wrote of liberty as 'the positive and equal opportunity of self-realisation'.[28] He even stated in one place that to compel obedience to 'rules of convenience which promote right living' is not to make a person unfree.[29] Most of the other pluralist writers were in roughly the same position, acknowledging the inadequacy of the negative Hobbist or Spencerian concept of freedom as mere 'absence of restraint', and yet failing to work out a satisfactorily coherent alternative.

It is difficult to find in the writings of G. D. H. Cole a consistent notion of freedom. *In Social Theory* (1920) he put forward the following analysis: freedom can, in the last resort, apply only to the individual person – but it can apply to him directly in the form of 'personal liberty', and indirectly in the form of 'social liberty'. By personal liberty Cole meant the negative empiricist conception of freedom as 'being let alone':

it is simply the freedom of the individual to express without external hindrance his 'personality' – his likes and dislikes, desires and aversions, hopes and fears, his sense of right and wrong, beauty and ugliness.[30]

This, of course, is a definition with which neither Hobbes nor Spencer would wish to quarrel. Social liberty, on the other hand, is the freedom of groups – or to be more precise – the freedom of the individuals in so far as they are members of groups. This freedom has an internal and an external aspect. The latter is 'the freedom of the association from external dictation *in respect of its manner of performing its function*'.[31] He maintained that this external freedom 'implies' internal freedom, interpreted as the democratic organisation of the group itself. Why external freedom implies internal freedom he did not say; and it seems quite possible for a group to be free from external restraint and at the same time hierarchically or aristocratically governed within. Unfortunately, Cole also clouded the issue by trying to maintain that economic equality is implied in his notion of personal liberty. It is definitely not clear how the idea of 'being let alone' involves the introduction of social and economic equality. Certainly private agencies – groups other than the government – may interfere with individual freedom (as we have already had occasion to observe). State action may be called for to prevent such interference, and be justified in terms of the maximising of freedom; but it is not at all clear how economic *equality* is demanded by the notion of freedom which Cole put forward.

In 1918 Cole vigorously attacked the rationalist notion of freedom,[32] though in the previous year he seems to have defended a concept of freedom very similar to the rationalist notion; he wrote as follows:

> Freedom is not simply the absence of restraint; it assumes a higher form when it becomes self-government. A man is not free in himself while he allows himself to remain at the mercy of every idle whim: he is free when he governs his own life according to a dominant purpose or system of purposes.[33]

Cole changed his position with every book he wrote and it is quite impossible to derive a coherent theory from these early writings.

Bertrand Russell, on the other hand, seems consistently to have assumed an empiricist notion of freedom. 'Liberty in itself is a negative principle,' he wrote, 'it tells us not to interfere, but does not give any basis for construction.'[34] He nevertheless rejected the kind of 'negative liberty' which had been advocated by Herbert Spencer, arguing that by giving freedom to the strong to suppress the weak we do not maximise freedom in a state; it is possible to increase the total freedom by restricting the activities of a minority.[35]

Thus while they accepted liberty as one of the principal ends of politics most of the pluralist writers whom we are considering in this essay had not thought through the various complications in the notion of freedom. At times they used a definition of freedom which the most extreme empiricist could accept. Elsewhere they scornfully rejected the empiricist idea of freedom as unsatisfactory. They recognised that liberty must be limited by law if a state is to be maintained in which there is some semblance of order, insisting that unless such order be established, no freedom can meaningfully be possessed by the members of that state. The notion of freedom which they generally assumed was more than 'being let alone'. To be free to do something, a person must have the means or the power to do it. And this implies a situation where there is order and some approximation to social justice and the absence of huge economic inequalities.

I V

The Corrupting Influence of Power is the English title of a book by G. Ritter, and sums up in a phrase an essential aspect of pluralist thought. Lord Acton, whose dictum on the corrupting tendency of power is frequently quoted (and more frequently misquoted), had a considerable influence on the ideas of the British political pluralists. If we are to understand the pluralist movement properly we must see it as an adaptation to the conditions of the early twentieth century of the traditional whig distrust of power. This suspicion of power, with the demand for constitutional safeguards, virile groups and general decentralisation are traditional whig ideas. The separation of power is, for the whig, an essential prerequisite of a liberal state. This separation can be achieved in several ways.

During the nineteenth century, the whig was fighting a losing battle and often appears to have been a mere conservative. Yet it would be a mistake to think that writers like Tocqueville – who shared a whig approach to politics – were essentially conservative. Tocqueville was not averse to change in itself, but to change which abolishes local powers and group loyalties in favour of a centralised system of organisation. Centralisation, he argued, was already taking place during the *ancien régime*, but without the great success which accompanied it after the revolution. Before the revolution there were many old, and in themselves even vicious, institutions which acted as breakwaters, albeit irregular and ill-constructed, against the omnipotence of the state. The centralising tendencies of the old regime were best seen in the French administration of Canada and Algeria, where they operated unhindered by traditional vested interests. Some social power must, he held, predominate over other groups, but if this is unchecked it becomes dangerous; unlimited power is bad. Whereas a strong centralised administration can achieve great things in a short time, once it does break down, the whole state falls apart. 'When power is dispersed,' on the other hand, 'action is clearly hindered, but there is strength elsewhere'.[36] He saw the discussions on the new French constitution of 1851 as concerned primarily with the question of the limitation of power. One thing which the French could not establish, he pointed out, is a free government, and the one thing which they could not get rid of is centralisation. Napoleon Bonaparte had speeded up the centralising tendency of the *ancien régime*, while the restoration and the government of July were as absolute centralisers as Napoleon himself.

If Tocqueville can be said to represent the 'right-wing' revolt against the concentration of power, Proudhon played a similar role on the 'left'. He endeavoured to combat (as did the guild socialists in a later age) the centralising tendencies of socialism. Centralism is, he held, incompatible with liberty. He divided regimes into two sorts, authoritarian and liberal. The essential characteristic of the former is the concentration of power, while the latter are distinguished by a division of power. Centralisation not merely endangers the liberty of individuals and associations, but is not particularly efficient. '*Avec la centralisation,*' Lamennais had declared, '*vous avez l'apoplexie au centre et la paralysie aux extrémités.*'[37]

It was this aspect of the thought of St Thomas Aquinas that led Lord Acton to call him the first whig. 'My view,' he wrote in a letter to Figgis, 'is that the revolutionary doctrine goes back to St. Thomas, and it is he, and not the evil one, that I call the First whig.'[38] In an unpublished lecture on the political ideas of Aquinas, Figgis tried to show what Acton had meant by this. First, the whig regards freedom as the true end of politics. To this was added the sense, that freedom can be secured only by a careful distribution of power among different bodies checking each other.[39] Acton declared that the puritans of the seventeenth century believed that the sphere of government should be limited and that this would be achieved by a division of power. Others, however, like Carlyle and Froude believed the opposite doctrine; 'They hold,' wrote Acton,

> that great and salutary things are done for mankind by power concentrated, not by power balanced and cancelled and dispersed, and that the Whig theory, sprung from decomposing sects, the theory that authority is legitimate only by virtue of its checks, and that the sovereign is dependent on the subject, is rebellion against the divine will manifested all down the stream of time.[40]

The middle ages were seen as the period when power was dispersed and many semi-autonomous groups flourished. Absolute power was thought to be more intolerable than slavery. Yet Marsilius had sounded the trumpet of a new movement; with him, Figgis pointed out, there is almost no feudalism, no use of the system of estates which led to whiggery.

> nor is there any of that system of checks and balances which are the result of medieval life, and preserve freedom at the expense of efficiency – no it is the omnicompetent, universal, all absorbing modern

State, the mortal God, the great Leviathan of later teachers ... not power divided, but power concentrated and united.[41]

With the renaissance came a further concentration of power. In Venice, Acton lamented, power passed from the nobility to a committee, from the committee to a council of ten, from the ten to three Inquisitors in which form by 1600 it had become 'a frightful despotism'.[42] Yet there was a tradition of whiggery which carried through from Aquinas and the early Jesuit writers to Locke and Sidney. Acton's own position was clear. 'Suspect power more than vice,' he advised his history students at Cambridge.[43] The possession of unlimited power not only corrupts the people over whom power is exercised, but 'corrodes the conscience, hardens the heart, and confounds the understanding of monarchs'. 'Liberty,' he informed Mary Gladstone, 'depends on the division of power,' and he quoted with approval the dictum of Fénélon that power is poison.[44]

This administrative centralisation and concentration of power had continued throughout the nineteenth century. 'Some would warn us,' Maitland observed in 1900,

> that in the future the less we say about a supralegal, suprajural plenitude of power concentrated in a single point at Westminster – concentrated in one single organ of an increasingly complex commonwealth – the better for that commonwealth may be the days that are coming.[45]

How then are we to remedy this danger of power? Since the 'demon' of power can never be destroyed, our task, it has been argued, 'is to clip its wings'.[46] Power, the pluralists believed, is in itself a great danger, and must be checked: all people are, in part at least, wicked, and any ruler with absolute power is likely to misuse it. There is, believed Laski, a poison in power against which nations must be on their guard.[47] He agreed with Tocqueville that by limiting power we limit the ability to do good, but we also limit the chance of doing evil. Pluralists concentrated on avoiding the worst in politics rather than on trying to achieve the best. They rejected the hobbist notion that anarchy is the only great threat to the state, and that absolute power must be put into the hands of the rulers in order to avert this danger. The preservation of life at any cost was not for them the sole end of politics. The pluralists were pessimistic with regard to individuals and optimistic with regard to the mass; they trusted 'man' but distrusted 'men'. Things will be better – freedom will be preserved – Laski insisted, if we keep power from the few and spread it out among the many, dividing it 'upon the basis of the functions it is to perform'.[48]

It is the concentration of power to which they objected, and they aimed not at educating the despot, but at preventing the accumulation of power. They would have agreed with Sorel's criticism of the socialists of his day: '*Ils attaquent plutôt les hommes au pouvoir que le pouvoir lui-même.*'[49]. The pluralists did not claim that power is evil in itself, but that the evil results of power concentrated almost invariably outweighs the good consequences. By dividing power we encourage human responsibility. Russell agreed, and further argued that by preventing the concentration of power in the hands of 'officials and captains of industry', we diminish the opportunities for acquiring the habit of command, out of which the desire for exercising tyranny is apt to spring. Strong organisations like trade unions, churches, cultural associations, are to be welcomed as safeguards of liberty.[50]

There are various ways of decentralising power and many of these were advocated by the thinkers whom we have been discussing. Traditional groups should be preserved and must be regarded as bulwarks against the total state, while voluntary associations should also be encouraged. The totalitarian and the tyrant always aim at breaking down these groups and reducing their subjects to a mass of unassociated atoms. Burke thought that the French had,

> first destroyed all the balances and counterpoises which serve to fix the state, and to give it a steady direction ... and then they melted down the whole into one incongruous, ill-connected mass.[51]

Traditional groups should be maintained, and constitutional checks upon the central power should be in operation. Tocqueville held the same opinion on despotism; it seeks to rid a country of corporation, class and even of family ties, and isolates citizens from each other. In aristocratic states there are a number of powerful individuals and families who can check the claims of the central government. It is the role of voluntary groups and artificially created political divisions to stand in lieu of these in democratic states.

During the nineteenth century a tradition of Roman Catholic political thought grew up which emphasised the importance of groups. Baron von Ketteler, the Bishop of Mainz, who was one of the leaders of this catholic social movement, pointed back to the middle ages when a mass of autonomous groups flourished and when 'concentrated unlimited power in the hands of a single man was unknown'.[52] The right of local and functional self-government was held to be essential for a truly free society. There was, he argued, a dangerous tendency in his own day to break down societies into a mass of individuals. Having done this the autocrat has less powerful opposition and can do practically what he likes.[53] It was on the basis of such theories that the notion of 'subsidiarity' developed within catholic social thought.[54]

Lord Acton too was keen that the freedom of groups should be maintained and increased. He told Simpson that what was most needed for a theory of liberty was a right notion of corporations, and their place in society. The modern theory, he lamented, condemned all groups beside the state as subversive, and recognises only an atomic freedom for the individual. In his essay on 'Nationality', Acton argued that many national groups within a state would check the tendency to absolutism. F. W. Maitland pointed in horror to France, where

> we may see the pulverising, macadamising tendency in all its glory, working from century to century, reducing to impotence, and then to nullity, all that intervenes between Man and State.[55]

Figgis even more perhaps than his masters saw the liberty of groups as the essential element in a free state. 'The battle of freedom in this century', he declared from the pulpit, 'is the battle of small societies to maintain their inherent life as against the all-devouring Leviathan of the whole'.[56] Small groups in particular must be allowed to take their place alongside the larger associations if freedom is to be a positive thing. Toleration was achieved in England not by the mere assertion of individual rights, but it was 'the religious body, the sect with its passionate assertion of its own right to be, which finally won toleration from the State'.[57]

There are, however, countries such as the USA where traditional barriers do not exist in great number; what is to be done to secure liberty? The answer of the whig is federation. By separating the executive from the legislature, and the state governments from the federal government, the constitution of the United States enabled a free society to remain in existence. Acton regarded the distribution of power among several states as the best check upon popular democracy; a large democratic state cannot maintain the principle of self-government but by federalism of some sort. Tocqueville saw the separation of power among the states of the union, together with a myriad of voluntary groups, as a bulwark against absolutism. Proudhon too regarded the federal system as essentially opposed to centralised absolutism. As against the authoritative or monarchical principle, which had as its accompaniments the elimination of group loyalties and the concentration of power, Proudhon set the federal system, which carries with it local self-government, the separation of power and an agricultural/industrial federation.

The pluralist movement may then be regarded as an aspect of federalism, and it has been argued that 'The greatest contribution to the federal idea in

Great Britain is, without doubt, the rise of the pluralist theory of the state.'[58] Figgis spoke of the medieval principle behind the House of Commons as a 'semi-federalist polity', while the Council of Constance 'stands for an inchoate federalism ... as against a centralising bureaucracy '.[59]

It is therefore the case that the pluralist writers are the inheritors of a long tradition, which feared the concentration of power and sought to build and maintain strong barriers to stem its force. These barriers might be found in traditional groups and aristocracies, in voluntary associations, in national groups or in federal constitutions, but the purpose is always the same. It is perhaps true, however, that the pluralists failed to see the possible danger of strong groups; it is quite as conceivable for individual freedom to be infringed by group action as by the action of the state, and thinkers of this persuasion must always be on their guard against the possibility of group tyranny. To say that they ignored this potential danger of group tyranny would be wrong, and, as we shall see in chapter five, some insisted on the necessity of a strong state above the groups to control them, yet it may be true that they were not sufficiently alive to the danger. Thus, not only was it held by the pluralists to be the case that true freedom requires a recognition of the life of groups in a state, but also that the existence of groups helps to ensure freedom of thought and action for the individual.

V

'Liberty provokes diversity,' Acton pointed out, 'and diversity preserves liberty by supplying the means of organisation.'[60] That fact was used by Figgis to explain the rise of toleration in England. 'Political liberty', Figgis declared in a famous phrase, 'is the fruit of ecclesiastical animosities.' It was the claim of religious bodies to freedom of speech and worship that led to the tolerant state which we know today. The reformers were by no means in favour of religious liberty as such and the reformation so far from checking, actually developed and encouraged 'the orgy of State-autocracy which set in with the Renaissance'.[61] Only indirectly can we ascribe the development of toleration to the reformation – it stimulated the growth of autonomous religious groups, the struggle between which was to bring some measure of toleration, and freedom.[62] As Creighton had indicated, it is a great mistake to think that the English puritans were essentially in favour of religious liberty; they were willing to allow freedom only to those with whom they were in general agreement. 'Political liberty, *as such*,' observed Figgis, 'never was and never will be an ideal of Puritanism.'[63] Nor was toleration the result of religious indifference, as is sometimes suggested.[64] Much more is it true to say that religious indifference is the result of toleration.

Toleration, then, was not achieved by any single group, but by the failure of any group to predominate sufficiently to crush the rest; toleration was thrust upon us. It was, according to Acton, to the clash between the church and the state in the middle ages – or more accurately to the struggle between *regnum* and *sacerdotium* – that we owe the rise of religious liberty. In a situation where church and state are united under one head, as in England, there is a danger of this liberty disappearing. The gradual growth of religious sects, however, and their conflicts with the established church, replaced the medieval dichotomy and led to the evolution of religious toleration. Hardly any of these bodies valued liberty in itself, and, as Figgis pointed out,

> The two religious bodies which have done the most to secure 'the rights of man' are those two which really cared least about individual liberty, and made the largest inroads upon private life wherever they obtained the supremacy – the Roman Catholic Church and the Presbyterian.[65]

Bellarmine and Knox would have been horrified to be told that their ideas contributed in a significant way to the growth of toleration and of the secular state! It was not primarily the claim of individuals to freedom of speech which led to toleration, but the claim of groups to freedom of assembly. 'By himself apart from religious discords the individual would have secured no freedom.'[66]

Few, then, believed in liberty as a political end. Figgis mentioned the Benthamites and Hoadly; Acton added Socinus, the independent founders of Rhode Island and the Quaker patriarch of Pennsylvania – these dogmatic liberals were the true prophets of liberty. Things began to change though, and as Butterfield reminds us, toleration which had been a political necessity was turned into a religious ideal. Yet as late as 1893 Creighton could declare, in his essay on *Persecution and Tolerance*, that too often we were tolerant only because it happened to suit us to be so. But if religious liberty has come about almost by accident, we must, Creighton held, defend it dogmatically as the right thing. We have seen how Figgis was eager that liberty should be defended as a dogma rather than as a mere expedient, and how he regarded the tolerant state as the best state.

Bearing all this in mind, it is not at all easy to see what Harold Laski meant when in his post-pluralist period he criticised Figgis for failing to recognise clearly that,

(i) the concessions were always grudging because some religious group or other remained dominant and a religious group is *more suo* exclusive, (ii) that the concessionaire didn't care a damn about freedom for any of its rivals and, the Quakers apart, would probably have persecuted if it could.[67]

Figgis had made his position quite clear on this historical issue and it is astonishing that Laski was able to misrepresent him in this manner. 'This achievement of individual liberty,' Figgis had written,

> was never attained and except for the short period of the Benthamite movement never sought merely for its own sake. Its achievement became feasible only because it was connected with the recognition of the right to exist of some society usually religious, which the civil magistrate did not desire to exist. It is often agreed that religious differences are the ground of modern liberty. It is a mistake to suppose ... that this is because as a rule any or all religious bodies cared about such liberty. What they desired was the right to be, what they denied was the right of the State to suppress them as societies.[68]

VI

Liberty and toleration in England have, Figgis taught, come about principally through the struggle of religious groups to live. Virile groups will always provide a bulwark against statism and are to be encouraged by liberals. Yet a group can easily become too powerful and tyrannise over other groups and individuals. A strong state is needed which will be above the groups, whose purpose is to keep them within the bounds of peace and justice. Freedom is important because human beings are not mere machines, moved around by physical forces, but are spiritual beings. In making choices they develop their moral character. It is a necessary condition of becoming fully human that people engage freely in social life, in cooperation with others. The pluralist concern for liberty therefore had a moral, spiritual and, in some cases, a religious basis. If this is so, is it not essential that there exist agencies in the state for the purpose of maintaining this civic morality? But where does this leave the theory of a plural or secular state? We shall return to this issue in Chapter 6.

As historian and political theorist Figgis argued that human freedom is most likely to flourish when a large number of voluntary and traditional groups exist and where power is not concentrated at the centre, but dispersed throughout the body of citizens. Some restriction will be necessary to regulate the life of groups, guarding against those which endanger the liberty of their members or threaten the life of other groups. To this matter we shall return in Chapter 5.

Though Figgis's historical studies led him to see how the growth of toleration and civil liberty came about as an unintended result of conflicting group loyalties and counter-claims, with the groups themselves rarely interested in liberty for its own sake, he defended a policy of toleration as a matter of moral principle, which ultimately rests on theological foundations.

3 The Attack on Sovereignty

Doctrines of state sovereignty tend to become salient in periods of acute political conflict and of rapid social change. This is clearly evident in the attention given to the idea of sovereignty by writers of the sixteenth and seventeenth centuries. British political theorists and publicists of the eighteenth century, however, tended to concentrate attention on other issues and only towards the turn of the century did writers like Jeremy Bentham and James Mill turn once more to the concept of sovereignty. Francophone writers, in particular Joseph de Maistre, had paralleled this movement, in the wake of the French revolution. It is natural that, in an age of instability, the ruling classes, and even the rising middle classes, should look to some strong centralised body to maintain order and protect property. Such a body is immensely strengthened by its being endowed with legal, moral and indeed religious legitimacy. In volatile situations, like mid-seventeenth-century Britain, it became, in the words of A. J. Balfour, 'necessary to bolster up by argument the creed which authority had been found temporarily insufficient to sustain'. Consequently the two celebrated myths – 'both of extraordinary absurdity'– were propagated: social contract and divine right.[1] These formed, in turn, a basis for theories of practically unlimited state sovereignty.

Political pluralism, as we have noted, rests upon three pillars; the second is the denial of state sovereignty, in almost any sense which that term can have. Pluralists believed ideas of sovereignty to be in most cases incoherent, but none the less dangerous because of this. Myths and slogans about sovereignty have in the past deceived the very elect! Before outlining the nature of the pluralist attack upon state sovereignty it is necessary to draw some important distinctions. This clarification will be attempted by outlining the development, in Britain, of the idea of sovereignty during the nineteenth century. Unfortunately we must traverse what James Bryce called, the 'dusty desert of abstractions through which successive generations of political philosophers have thought it necessary to lead their disciples'.[2] I shall begin by stating the theory of John Austin, and consider the modifications which were introduced into it by A. V. Dicey, D. G. Ritchie and James Bryce.

I

An independent political unit, for Austin, is one where there is a determinate person or body of persons which, while not obeying habitually

38

the will of another, itself is habitually obeyed by the bulk of the people. This body is the sovereign. It should be emphasised that Austin did not believe that this body is *always* obeyed by *all* the people. Laws are the commands of this body which is 'incapable of legal limitation', and is thus 'legally *despotic*'.[3] The body which is habitually obeyed is not entirely free from limitation, either political or moral; it must consult the opinions of the people, and is limited by positive morality and by the law of God. He thought that the sovereign in Britain was the Monarch, the House of Lords and the House of Commons, or, 'speaking accurately', the electors of the Commons. Thus there was, for Austin, one sovereign, who was, while in the legal sense unlimited, in the political and moral sphere limited by public opinion, positive morality and the law of God. In Britain the power which is habitually obeyed by the bulk of the people is the Monarch in Parliament (with the proviso that at the time of an election the persons enfranchised take up active participation in sovereignty); this body is legally unlimited.

Austin suffered much illegitimate criticism at the end of the nineteenth century. Sir Henry Maine informed the world that the assertion that in any society 'the irresistible force' was stored up in one man or body of men was not so much false as 'only verbally true', and went on to point out that,

> the vast mass of influences, which we may call for shortness moral, perpetually shapes, limits or forbids the actual direction of the forces of society by its Sovereign.[4]

But this Austin never denied.

Then a distinction was drawn between the legal and the political sovereign. A. V. Dicey declared that, in England, Parliament is sovereign legally, and that there is no legal appeal from its commands. On the other hand the political sovereign, 'the will of which is ultimately obeyed by the citizens of the state', is, 'in strict accuracy', the body of electors, whose will 'is sure ultimately to prevail on all subjects to be determined by the British Government'.[5] D. G. Ritchie distinguished, in addition to the legal and political sovereigns, a nominal sovereign, in whose name executive acts are performed; this is the Monarch in Britain. The legal sovereign must be a definite body or thing and is 'the authority behind which the lawyer *qua* lawyer will not and cannot go'.[6] With regard to a political sovereign, Ritchie believed that there is in any society a 'power which is ultimate', although this does not reside in any person or body. James Bryce accepted this distinction between legal and political sovereignty. In addition to the legal sovereign,

There is in every State a Strongest Force, a power to which other powers bow, and of which it may be, more or less positively predicted that in case of conflict it will overcome all resistance.[7]

The residing place of this force is the political (or, as he calls it, 'practical') sovereign. Later, however, he maintained that the practical sovereign does not enjoy 'utterly uncontrolled power'.[8]

The essence of this criticism of Austin is that there are two sovereignties, the political and legal. While the latter is conceived to be in the hands of a definite person or body of persons, the former is in the control of 'the electors', or 'public opinion'.[9] If we were to ask Dicey, Ritchie and Bryce to be more specific, they would, I think, refuse to help us. In the thought of Ritchie, the only way to specify this 'power' which will ultimately prevail is to see what *does* ultimately prevail. It is in the hands of no determinate person or body. Ritchie tells us nothing about the political sovereign except that it is the (indeterminate) body which controls the power which ultimately prevails in a dispute. As there is rarely such a thing as a *power* which prevails in social disputes, but a situation which results, the whole concept of political sovereignty is somewhat vacuous.

Dissatisfied with the obvious inadequacy of the Austinian notion, these thinkers have so widened the concept of sovereignty as to make it meaningless. Instead of telling us, as Ritchie at first appears to, that there is a body that exists somewhere which we can, perhaps, consult, and whose will always prevails, he merely says that 'whatever will be will be', and invents a fictitious thing – a political sovereign – which is supposed to have willed the situation which prevails. The same might be said of Dicey, though he appears to be more specific, when he declares the 'electors' to be sovereign. Does he mean the majority of the electors? Most British governments come to power with the support of a minority of electors. Also it is quite possible to indicate situations in many countries where a tiny minority of the electors with the support of troops and police could hold down a majority. If Dicey were to reply that it is difficult to know what the electors will on a particular occasion until after the event, then his statement that the will of the electors ultimately prevails, is perilously near to a tautology.[10] We may agree with Henry Sidgwick's typically restrained comment, that the effort of Dicey and others to put forward a theory of a political sovereign divorced from the legal sovereign 'seems to me highly dubious'.[11]

W. J. Rees tried some years ago to rehabilitate the notion of what I have called a political sovereign.[12] He distinguished two kinds of political sovereign: a coercive and an influential sovereign. He further divided the former into an institutionally coercive sovereign, and a socially coercive sovereign. Rees's whole essay is characterised by a somewhat barren conceptualism, and little attempt is made to apply the concepts which he distinguishes to the realities of political life. His question 'Where is the influential sovereign located?' betrays a serious misunderstanding of the nature of political decision-making. We are rarely, if ever, able to point to one person or body of persons whose actions by themselves determine a particular decision. Decisions are made in the context of a number of different groups and individuals each attempting to bring various pressures and influences to bear on the situation, including at times the threat or actual use of force. The alliances between the associations themselves, and between individuals, are often shifting, and may change as the issue to be decided changes. It is obviously the case that some groups will have more influence or more power than others, but there is probably no country where a single identifiable group is able unilaterally to determine all political decisions, without reference to the interests and opinions of other groups. There is in addition the fact that only certain issues reach the decision-making process. Others may be filtered out or suppressed by powerful groups or individuals, or just may not arise due in part to a dominant ideology.[13]

There is however, another alleged type of sovereignty which we cannot ignore. This is what may be called 'moral sovereignty' – the claim that there is in the state an authority to which obedience is due whatever it wills, a body whose commands are morally binding in all circumstances. This conception of sovereignty distinguishes Austin (who rejected it) from Thomas Hobbes and from Thomas Hill Green (who accepted it – though in radically different senses). A person can be obliged to do something, so the theory runs, only if he has in some way willed it himself. For Hobbes, we desire order above everything except life itself, and so long as the sovereign keeps order and protects life, citizens are morally obliged to obey him. This obligation proceeds not from fear, but from a promise to obey (though fear is, of course, among the most significant psychological causes for persons making and keeping the promise, and is therefore vital in making the promise an effective act). There is, insisted Hobbes, 'no obligation on any man, which ariseth not from some act of his own'.[14] The moral sovereignty of Leviathan stems from the consent or promise of the citizens – this can, for Hobbes, be the only possible source of its authority.

Kant also believed that an action can be a duty for me only if it is in accordance with a principle to which I consent – a principle which is self-imposed. A person, Kant maintained, 'is bound only to act in conformity with a will which is his own'.[15] Rousseau too insisted that a form of society must be evolved in which each obeys himself alone. He developed the notion of a general will which always wills the common good, and therefore represents the real will of all citizens. Thus when people are forced to do something which they do not want to do, they are being helped to do what they *really* want. Green believed that Rousseau's concept of a general will distinguished him from all previous political thinkers, and constituted his great contribution to political theory. The true sovereign, according to Green, embodies the general will, which is my will, and the citizen is thus obliged to obey the state (in so far as the actual state approaches the idea) because he has willed (perhaps unconsciously) the laws which it commands. Moral obligation, Green asserted, must be self-imposed and the laws of a state are binding only because they are thought to have been willed by the subjects. Will, rather than force, is the basis of the state. Thus by a fiction of consent, made plausible through the distinction between a real and an apparent will, a halo is placed above the state, which is given an authority that is absolutely binding upon the consciences of citizens.

The fallacy that duty can arise only from consent, thus unites thinkers as different as Hobbes and Green, Kant and Rousseau. Although certain writers try to draw liberal conclusions from this principle, the natural consequence is authoritarian and potentially totalitarian, laying all the emphasis upon *who* commands and paying little attention to *what* is commanded. An example of this type of political theory can be seen in a little book by Joseph Tussman, *Obligation and the Body Politic*. There he writes as follows:

> 'I have a duty to ...' seems to follow from 'I have agreed to' in a way that it does not follow from 'I am forced to' or 'I am in the habit of'. This is sometimes expressed as the view that obligations are, or even must be, voluntarily assumed.[16]

It is not quite clear how Tussman believes that duty 'seems to follow from' a promise, but even if the relationship is as strong as implication (which it is not; if I promise to kill my parents today in a fit of rage, it is by no means clear that I have a duty to kill them tomorrow), this is very different from saying that obligations must be assumed voluntarily. He gives us no indication as to why obligations must be undertaken voluntarily. Later in his essay he truly says that there is nothing inherently authoritative about a majority, but goes on to assert that minorities are bound by the decision of the majority only if they 'consider the decision as *theirs*'.[17] Surely the minority is bound by the majority decision if it considers that decision to be right, or if it thinks that the mischief done by resisting would be greater than the mischief done by complying. Why must they consider the decision as 'theirs'?

How is it then that so many thinkers have believed that duty can arise only from promise or consent? It is certainly true that we can hardly *blame* a man for acting in a way which he believes to be right. We cannot condemn him for not acting in accordance with a rule that he does not recognise, for not following a law of right conduct which he does not accept. Nevertheless there is surely a distinction between recognising a rule of right conduct as binding upon me, and my promising to follow such a rule. I may believe that wanton cruelty is wrong without having consented or promised not to behave cruelly. Certainly promises create a *prima facie* obligation; but they are not a source of absolute obligation, nor are they the only source of obligations. I can therefore properly be blamed for an act only if I see it to be wrong – but I need not have promised or consented not to act in this way. We may, of course, want to go on to say that, although the person is not to be condemned or blamed for an action which he believes to be in accordance with a criterion of goodness which he accepts, the act (considered as an act) is wrong, owing to the fact that either (a) the criterion he accepts is faulty, or (b) he is mistaken in believing that his particular act is in accordance with that criterion. On the utilitarian model, then, I could recognise, by reason, that the greatest happiness principle is binding upon me, without ever having promised or consented to behave in accordance with it. On the intuitionist model I could believe that something is right, by intuition, without having by an act of will promised in any way to do it.

II

Pluralist writers were critical of all these notions of sovereignty distinguished above: legal, political and moral. They attacked the idea of state sovereignty from the standpoint of the doctrine of the inherent rights of groups which they had derived largely from Gierke. Figgis has been accused of misinterpreting Gierke, who is said to have been a believer in the sovereign state. By sovereignty, however, the German theorist meant something very different from the 19th century British idea of sovereignty. He referred to the relationship between the state and other powers external to it. He meant that the state should be subject to no superior human will. 'The state alone,' he wrote,

> cannot be subordinate as sovereign collective person to any organised will-power external to and above it, and consequently it cannot be limited in its will and action by a higher community participating in its decisions.[18]

This does not, however, imply that the state is above law, which it creates (i.e. the state is not legal sovereign in the Austinian sense). The state is, in Gierke's thought, morally as well as legally bound to recognise the rights and personality of groups and of individuals. It is thus not moral sovereign. Like his hero Althusius, Gierke saw the state as enshrining the general will in some of its manifestations, and what distinguishes the state from other groups is its possession of sovereign power.[19]

In his Introduction to a translation of parts of Gierke's *magnum opus*, Ernest Barker declares that Figgis's theory 'which runs counter to the idea of the unitary State' is 'alien to the logic' of Gierke's general position.[20] This is true insofar as Gierke, as a typical German political theorist, subscribed to a mystical notion of the unity of the state. He was an idealist in philosophy and saw the state, in its idea, as a moral unity, in a way Figgis would have found hard to accept; it was indeed very different from the pragmatic approach of the British pluralists. With respect to the way that actual states operate, Gierke was, however, a pluralist.[21] I shall consider in due course whether and to what extent Figgis's theory can be said to be inconsistent with the idea of a unitary state.

If there is one thing which united the British pluralist thinkers it is the rejection of the state as *moral sovereign*. The theory of Hobbes, which was for Figgis 'the meanest of all ethical theories',[22] based an immoral doctrine of omnipotence upon a false view of human nature. So far from being a creation of human will, social life is in fact a natural and necessary aspect of human nature. It is no artificial creation of individual choice. Figgis attacked the hobbist idea that citizens can have no rights against the state. This view was, he claimed, not merely some dead theory lost in the pages of seventeenth century English texts, but was alive and well, and being practised in his own day. M. Emile Combes, the theoretician of French secularism, had declared that the only rights there can be are state rights, and that the only authority which is legitimate is that of the republic. Here we have a totalitarian theory being put into practice in the legislation of a country. This theory, in Figgis's view, denies the fact of conscience, the legitimacy of religious and other groups, and the reality of family life.

In Britain the situation was less clear, but Figgis and other pluralists saw tendencies at work which pointed in the same direction. Figgis quoted an astonishing statement by Mr Justice Darling to the effect that the law of God can be altered by an Act of Parliament, as evidence that this Hobbist way of thinking was widespread. 'For my part,' declared the judge,

I am of the opinion that this marriage, which before was contrary to the Law of God merely because the statute condemned it as such, is so no longer, and that by virtue of the statute which legalises it.[23]

Figgis insisted that moral sovereignty (the idea that any person or body of persons ought to be obeyed whatever it commands) is false in theory and dangerous in practice. Yet he believed it to be widespread in his own day. 'Can you,' he demanded,

take up a liberal paper to-day without finding appeals to that general will, statements about that popular source of all power, defiance of every person or body of persons who dares to throw his puny ... preferences against the ungovernable right of the people's will and to stem, as they say, the tide of progress and democratic enlightenment with the obsolete pretences of vested interest?[24]

Theories of natural rights were, Figgis thought, misleading but had developed in reaction to the ascription of absolute moral supremacy to the state. If this unwarranted claim to moral sovereignty were to be relinquished, then the notion of natural and imprescriptible rights, which arose in opposition to it, would go too.

The conception of objective right, of a higher or natural law, is one which Figgis did not accept in some of his early writings, but his increased fears regarding the claims made on behalf of the state convinced him that there must be some objective standard which secures the liberty of individuals and groups. When he published his first book he wrote as an historian, and was impressed by the relativity of political theories. He rejected concepts of natural law as involving a utopian attempt to find absolute principles in politics. It is, he maintained, impossible to discover an immutable basis for politics and to lift it above considerations of mere expediency. But why is it impossible to discover political principles which are universally applicable? This is not the same as a belief that all nations must be reduced to the same uniform level, but it is merely to state that there are certain values which it is the duty of all states to encourage as best they can in the situation in which they find themselves. This notion of objective right forced itself upon him more and more as he thought about politics. 'It is this notion of a higher law,' he wrote in an unpublished paper,

which is the basis of all constitutionalism and is one of the legacies of the Middle Ages to the modern world. It provoked and eventually secured the victory of Parliament in the XVIIth century – after, indeed, when the victory was won ... Parliament took over from the other side the doctrine of an omnipotent sovereign and Whigs like Charles Fox were imbued completely with the notion[25] (which among other results lost us America). In the XVIIth century, however, the contest as far as it was political and not religious was directly between those who claimed for law a supreme place – and those who were obsessed with the new conception of an omnipotent sovereignty.[26]

Other pluralists were equally keen to deny moral sovereignty to any determinate body, although in an early paper G. D. H. Cole differed from the rest by talking in terms of a general will residing in the people. In so far as the state represents the will of the people, the state is, according to Cole, sovereign.[27] Bernard Bosanquet congratulated Cole on this fundamentally Rousseauite position, which is totally opposed to pluralist theory.[28]

Cole translated this theoretical position into institutional form with his conception of a court of functional equity, which would represent citizens in the fullness of their social relations. Full sovereignty, however, was thought to lie in the 'complex of organised associations' within the state, and he thought that we cannot get more specific without handing it over to a body of which the function is partial rather than general.[29] As the individual can never fully be represented by associations, not even the most representative body will be completely sovereign. If there is no possibility of finding out where the sovereignty lies, is there much point in talking about it at all?

Ernest Barker, too, thought that sovereignty is not indivisible but is 'multiple and multicellular'.[30] Does this solve the problem of sovereignty? Is it not, on the contrary, true to say that as soon as the concept of sovereignty becomes indeterminate and divided, it ceases to perform any useful function in political and legal theory? Perhaps Charles Benoist was wisest when he declared, 'As for sovereignty, let us without remorse drop it from our political vocabulary, for time has set about to erase it.'[31]

One of the thinkers who most emphasised the conception of objective right in politics and law, which we are opposing to the notion of moral sovereignty, was Léon Duguit. For him, it is the possession of force which distinguishes the state from other groups. There is no obligation to obey the state as such; its commands are obligatory only when they are just, and when the consequences of obeying them will be better than the result of disobedience. Sovereignty is an attribute of will, and will is a faculty of persons, and as the state is not regarded as a person in Duguit's system, the problem of sovereignty evaporates – there is no such thing as sovereignty. 'We no longer believe,' he wrote,

in the dogma of national sovereignty any more than in the dogma of divine right. The rulers are those who actually have the power of compulsion in their hands ... power is not a right but simply an ability to act.[32]

Harold Laski was considerably interested in and influenced by the thought of Duguit and Figgis in this matter of sovereignty. Barker tells us that it was Figgis, and through Figgis, Maitland and Gierke, who were the chief influences on Laski in his New College days. Laski in effect reversed the famous dictum of R. L. Nettleship that 'will not force is the basis of the state'.[33] What characterises the state is its possession of force and this gives it no inherent right to be obeyed in all matters. Pluralism, he insisted, denies ultimately 'the sovereignty of anything save right conduct'.[34] It is a false theory which would suggest that the will of any person or body of persons is unconditionally binding on human consciences. This is why Laski valued Newman's remarks on conscience and sovereignty so highly. Laski and the pluralist writers with whom he was associated were more concerned with discovering *what* ought to be done than with finding out *who* has the right to make political decisions. The state is characterised, then, by the fact that it is the organ which possesses preponderant force, but the pluralist denied the rightness of force and rejected the idea that 'the pursuit of evil can be made good by the character of the performer'.[35]

In later life Laski saw the essence of the pluralist position as including a belief that the state's title to obedience lies in what it wills rather than in the fact of its willing. What is needed, Laski maintained, was a new theory of a flexible natural law or objective right, which does not lay down any immutable laws to be applied automatically in all circumstances. He thought that an effort to develop the ideas of the medieval schoolmen on this matter was needed in order that a satisfactory theory of the state should be evolved. It was, in his view, the decline of natural law theories which had led to the rise of ideas about the sovereignty of Parliament. Even such an acute theorist as Morris Cohen apparently failed to grasp, or at least refused to accept, this theory of objective right. His belief that there must always be some body which draws the line in disputes, would have been acceptable to the pluralists, or at least to Figgis and to the majority of British pluralists; but Cohen went on to say that 'the state cannot give up its reserve *rights* to limit any form of conscience which it *deems* a nuisance'.[36] Surely the state has only the right to limit forms of conscience which *actually are* threats to the security of the nation or to the liberty of others, not any form which *it deems* a nuisance. If by 'rights' Cohen meant simply legal rights, then there would be little to quarrel with but the context implies moral right.

Figgis and Laski would have agreed with L. T. Hobhouse when he declared that the essential mistake of some idealist political philosophers –

and, we might add, of Hobbes who wrote of Leviathan as the 'mortal god'
– was that they regarded the state 'as a kind of divine institution'.[37]

III

The conception of *political sovereignty*, as we have defined it, was also
rejected by Figgis. He thought that any talk of a person or body of persons
possessing a supreme power which will on all occasions triumph is false,
misleading and perhaps dangerous. In addition to rejecting the moral theory of sovereignty, as a political philosophy, he refused to accept the
popular idea that there is or must be in every state a body which is politically or practically supreme. It is not the case that in any dispute the
state, in Britain, would be sure to prevail. It is possible that a church or
important trade union could fight successfully against a decree of the state.
Whether there are rights against the state or not, as Figgis pointed out,
people think that there are. There is always the ultimate possibility of civil
war, and it is a false social theory which ignores this fact. There is no single
identifiable body in Britain which can get its way whatever it commands.
Does it solve the problem by saying that 'the people' or 'public opinion'
are sovereign? We have seen that it can hardly be said to do so.

Laski also attacked a concept of political sovereignty, which insists that
there must be in every social order some single centre of ultimate
reference, some power that is able to resolve disputes by saying a last word
that will be obeyed.[38] He regarded 'society' as a parallelogram of forces in
which different elements prevail on different occasions. Ernest Barker also
found the conception of political sovereignty unacceptable. On one
occasion this group or interest would prevail, on another that; there is no
body which can be relied upon to win in all circumstances. MacIver
observed that the opposition of large groups to government policy can in
many instances prevent the carrying out of that policy. A. D. Lindsay also
asserted that the state has control over the activities of groups and individuals only in so far as the citizens are prepared to give it this power; and this
willingness is always limited:

> Wherever, therefore, men's loyalty to a non-political association, a class,
> or a church, or a trade union is greater than their loyalty to the State, the
> State's power over the trade unions or churches or classes within it is
> thereby diminished.[39]

G. D. H. Cole again differed from the pluralist writers in this crucial matter.
'There clearly must in the end,' he stated,' be somewhere in the society an

ultimate court of appeal, whether determinate or not.'[40] What an indeterminate court might be like he did not say! He wrote of the sovereignty of the whole community, and believed that this sovereignty could be represented – though imperfectly – by a federal body, including the state (as the association of consumers) and other functional associations. He even wrote of an 'ultimate body' which everyone but anarchists must believe to be sovereign.[41]

IV

The problem of *legal sovereignty* is a complicated one. Figgis never appears to have wished to challenge the doctrine that the enactments of the British Parliament are not normally to be questioned in the law courts. In his early pre-pluralist writings he had been prepared to accept the idea of the supremacy of Parliament as a legal theory, as well as a practical guide to lawyers. He declared that Coke, with the common law theorists,

> had not really grasped the conception of sovereignty; he maintained a position, reasonable enough in the Middle Ages, but impossible in a developed unitary State.

He believed that Locke was guilty of a confusion between natural law and positive law, and praised theorists of the divine right of kings for a deeper insight into the nature of law than their opponents, who were 'ever haunted by the vain illusion of placing legal limits on the sovereign power'.[42] The Jesuit and whig theorists, asserting that law which is not just is not really law and ought not to be obeyed, were thought by him to be of little value, and the idea that contracts could be binding apart from the positive commands of the sovereign 'seems nonsense to us, as Austin showed'.[43]

Soon, chiefly under the influence of Maitland, Figgis began to doubt the value of the Austinian theory. Even at the time of his first book he confessed that it would be difficult to fit the feudal system of law into Austin's idea of sovereignty. Gradually he came to doubt the whole of Austin's theory. If we take it as it stands, when the sovereign is one – political and legal – it is, as various thinkers have pointed out, impossible to apply to the real world. When all the substance has been taken out of the theory, by writers like Ritchie, Dicey and Bryce, who separated the political sovereign from the legal sovereign, with the former evaporating into indeterminacy, the conception becomes theoretically useless. If in fact the legal sovereign is politically impotent and dependent on external forces then as a theory of law it is

valueless. A legal theory which does not apply to the world as we know it is
not a useful one. 'It is,' Figgis declared of the Austinian theory,

> either fallacious or so profoundly inadequate as to have no more than a
> verbal justification. One begins by thinking Austin self-evident, one
> learns that many qualifications have to be made, and finally one ends by
> treating his whole method as abstract and theoretic.[44]

If the theory of legal sovereignty simply means that judges in Britain
ought not normally to question an Act of Parliament, then there can be little
objection to it. If, however, we define law as merely the command of a sovereign Parliament, it fails to cover a large number of laws, which are not
commands in any sense, but hypothetical regulations governing certain
procedures (if you want to draw up a valid will, this is how you do it). We
have to introduce qualifications such as 'what the sovereign permits it
commands' and that the state itself only submits to the process of law by
the courtesy of autolimitation. In fact it is not a question of Parliament's
deciding to permit certain things, but of its not being able to do anything
else.

The idea of state sovereignty (meaning the absolute supremacy of the
legislative branch of government, represented in Britain by the Queen in
Parliament) has also led to a belief that the executive branch of government
(represented by the Crown) should not be subject to the authority of the law
courts. There is no necessary connection between these two principles, but
it was thought demeaning for 'the sovereign' to be sued in the law courts.
As Duguit saw, the whole modern conception of the administrative state
demands also that the executive be responsible in the law courts for its
actions. The Crown Proceedings Act of 1948 belatedly recognised the need
for government departments to be legally responsible for their actions.
Prior to this, redress could be sought only by a Petition of Right, which
could be turned down by the executive itself, with no right of appeal.[45]
Only recently Kenneth Baker, as home secretary, was found guilty of contempt of court for ignoring an injunction restraining him from deporting a
foreign national.

Laski was in substantial agreement with Figgis on this question;
'Legally,' he stated, 'no one can deny that there exists in every state some
organ whose authority is unlimited. But that legality is no more than a
fiction of logic.'[46] Yet, as we have seen, even this approach to the question
is flawed. He recognised that although this theory, speaking of law in these
terms, is of purely formal interest, it is likely to lead the unwary into
dangerous waters. Legal absolutism, he acknowledged, passes easily into
political absolutism. The term 'right' can be, and is, used in both legal and

political contexts. Lawyers of his day, however, were loathe to abandon the idea of legal sovereignty, as they found it useful in practice.

Oliver Wendell Holmes thought that 'from a (sound) legal point of view' the ideas of Figgis and Laski were false.[47] He and Pollock spilt much ink lamenting the influence of Figgis on the young Laski. 'It was', thought Pollock, 'an ill day for him when he fell into the hands of Figgis.'[48] Yet the Austinian theory of sovereignty could never be made to apply to the United States. There was no person or determinate body of persons whose commands could not legally be questioned. If we say that the constitution is sovereign, even this can be amended. If we then say that the body which can change the constitution must be the legal sovereign, this is hardly a determinate body issuing commands habitually obeyed by the people, and furthermore there are two ways of changing the constitution. In the case of India and Germany the irrelevance of Austinian theories of sovereignty are even more palpable. By 1958 Professor H. L. A. Hart declared that

> the general acceptance of the authority of a lawmaking procedure, irrespective of the changing individuals who operate it from time to time, can be only distorted by an analysis in terms of mass habitual obedience to certain persons who are by definition outside the law.[49]

Recent developments in connection with British membership of the European Community raise a numbers of important issues about sovereignty. In 1972 by the Treaty of Brussels Britain, with two other countries, became members of the Community, itself founded under the Treaty of Rome of 1957. This was ratified by Parliament in the same year under the European Communities Act. 'United Kingdom law,' writes A. W. Bradley,

> now recognises that Community organs have the right to make decisions and issue regulations, which may have the effect of overriding legislation by Parliament.[50]

Judges have sometimes attempted to maintain Dicey's principle that no person or body outside Parliament 'is recognised by the law of England as having a right to overtide or set aside the legislation of Parliament,'[51] by arguing that they are merely *interpreting* Parliamentary legislation subsequent to 1972 in a way consistent with European law, thereby following the intentions of the legislature, made clear in the act of that year. If the conflict is explicit the situation is more complicated. In the case of *R. v. Secretary of State for Transport, ex p. Factortame Ltd*, the owners of some fishing vessels asked the courts to set aside certain regulations made under the Merchant Shipping Act (1988). The Divisional Court applied to the European Court for a ruling, but as this would have meant a delay of two years the court granted interim relief to the shipping company and instructed that the Act should be disapplied in the particular case. This was reversed by the Court of Appeal and the House of Lords, who declared that as a matter of *English law*, the act takes precedence; the Lords, however, considered that there might be an overriding principle of *Community law*, and referred the matter to the European Court for advice. In the meanwhile the European Commission asked the European Court of Justice to declare that, in passing the offending clauses of the Merchant Shipping Act, the United Kingdom had failed in its obligations under the Treaty of Brussels and should suspend the application of these parts of the act. The British government complied and in a debate in the House of Commons the solicitor general made the enigmatic remark that 'This case involves no erosion of sovereignty over and above that which we accepted in 1972–3.'[52]

There is, of course, no act of Parliament, establishing Dicey's principle of Parliamentary sovereignty; it would involve a *petitio principii*. If it is indeed a principle it must be a principle established by common law. In recent centuries judges appear to have accepted it, but common law can change, and also it is not obvious that it would be applied in the case of Parliament passing legislation which was grossly immoral or manifestly inhuman. In the case of a virulently racist party achieving a majority in the House of Commons and passing an act involving the extermination of black people, it is perfectly conceivable that the courts would refuse to uphold this legislation by maintaining that the principle of 'parliamentary sovereignty' is not absolute.

V

The Austinian theory of sovereignty is today a mere historical relic, but that it is so is due partly to the attacks on it made by the group of thinkers we have been discussing. We may say with Gierke, that the state is the authority in the modern world which has the duty of formulating laws, and that the law courts must recognise this. But law, Gierke argued, is not the creation of a sovereign state, it is merely formulated and rationalised by the state. Both law and the state emanate from the life of the community; the state is not the offspring of law (as in the natural law theories) any more than the law is the child of the state (as in the Austinian conception). A more radical view was maintained by Duguit, who put law above the state, and found Gierke's position untenable. 'It attempts on the one hand', he said, to reconcile the autonomy of the individual with the omnipotence of the State and, on the other hand, to subordinate the State to law, while maintaining that it is omnipotent.[53]

It is certainly difficult to see how Gierke's theory would work out in practice; as an idealist he would probably have said that in so far as the state is a true state it will enact true law. The state is not even in law free to command just what it likes. There are occasions on which the state is forced to accept certain facts and to recognise them legally (as in the case of the personality of groups which will be discussed in the next chapter).

It may be agreed that so far as the state attempts to force upon the law courts a system which is unworkable, as the non-recognition of group personality would be, it is not merely making bad law, but is not making law at all. It is essential to the concept of law that it be applied (imperfectly perhaps, and with interpretation) in the law courts, and in so far as the state ignores social facts and forces an unworkable system upon the courts it is to that extent not making law. If the system of statutes were to become so out of touch with social reality as we know it, were ignored by the people, and were incapable of enforcement by the courts, would it fall under our conception of law at all? It is at least plausible to doubt it. If it is in fact impossible to divorce law from social reality and from politics, then a concept of legal sovereignty and a command theory of law are liable to lead to a political theory which denies the rights of individuals and groups. It is not merely a confusion of language that is responsible for ideas of legal, political and moral sovereignty being called by the same name. Unless legal theory is to be divorced from social and moral theory, a concept of legal sovereignty will lead people to talk and think in terms of moral and political sovereignty. This fact may be illustrated by the language of a fairly liberal Austinian: 'The state's will is sovereign, and therefore subject to no regulation from above; its powers over members are numerous, indefinite, and irresistible; and its purposes, general rather than special, touch human life at every point.'[54]

It was the political and moral implications of the concept of legal sovereignty that led Figgis and the pluralists to attack it. If we were to adopt the Austinian criterion of law, we would have to deny that international law is truly law; many legal theorists have been led on from this to deny any role to a judicial or quasi-judicial system of international control. This is one of the reasons why Figgis thought that the Austinian theory was dangerous; it amounts to what some philosophers would call a persuasive definition.

I shall sum up Figgis's conception of law by quoting a fairly lengthy passage from an unpublished lecture:

One school represented by John Austin fixes upon the coercive element in all positive law and ... makes of law above all things a command – and grounds it in some way or other on force. The other school looks at the objects of law, its universality, its aim, its connection with the State ... and fixes its thought on its content. It sees in law the sacrament of justice, the symbol of something beyond and above human affairs, an attempt of a human society to conform to the eternal principle of right. This school is represented by what Austin had the impertinence to call the 'fustian description' of law in Hooker. ... The [former] is expressed in the famous lectures of Austin on Jurisprudence and gives the definition of law as a command set by a person or persons politically sovereign to a person or persons politically subject. Even Austin had to go beyond a mere command – for he includes the conception of generality, and will not admit a mere particular command to be a law, probably not a tax. Austin's definition was practically the notion of law which came from the Renaissance lawyers and political philosophers – represented by men such as Bodin and Hobbes – and has reference to a fully developed compact State with an irresistible government. No one can deny that it has in it elements of truth – or that it describes one aspect of law – but it is not all. It lays too much stress on one element, that of command with its corollary force. It has in practice a very evil political reaction – for it tends to foster the notion, that not merely legally but morally the sovereign may do whatever he pleases.

Both doctrines can be traced back to the Roman jurisprudence – the latter [i.e. the command theory] to the idea of imperial power – to the maxims *quod principi placuit, legibus solutus* and so forth. The former to the notion of law as *ars aequi et boni*, to the conception of equity and the dictates of natural law, which may explain and if need be override the positive.[55]

VI

Thus Figgis and the pluralists were dissatisfied with the theory, or rather theories, of sovereignty which had support in their day. So far as the moral, political and legal sovereigns were united in one person or body (as in Hobbes) the theory was immoral; so far as the political and legal sovereigns were united (as in Austin) the theory was untrue to the facts, unless made tautological; and any theory which separated all three tended to be so empty that – apart from the assertion that the law courts in Britain cannot go behind Acts of Parliament – it was misleading and even dangerous.

Once the idea that will is the basis of obligation be rejected the theory of sovereignty collapses. The rejection of state sovereignty was an essential preliminary to the formation of a political philosophy of pluralism. If the state is morally sovereign, then groups and individuals can never have rights against the state. A notion of political sovereignty will undermine the sociological idea of group personality, and the whole possibility of pluralism is called into question by state omnipotence. A narrow construction of legal sovereignty removes from the sphere of law the system of common law which is the basis of most of the guarantees of group life, while construed widely the statement of the theory is analytic, though still perhaps misleading. It is thus clear that a demolition of the notion of state sovereignty was a necessary preliminary to the setting forth of an adequate theory of political pluralism.[56]

4 Group Personality

Political pluralism, as set forth by the group of thinkers we are considering in this essay, is essentially bound up with the idea of group personality. It is convenient to discuss this idea first in its sociological, and then in its legal aspects. The order is important for, as we shall see, those theorists who spoke of the real personality of groups in law insisted that their legal ideas were rooted in social facts. Figgis, Laski and Cole, following Gierke and Maitland argued that social groups are real entities which have a life and being which is something more than the sum of their individual members. As living entities they are able to 'grow' and to develop their original purpose, in relation to the changing world in which they live. Furthermore these theorists maintained that the legal system should recognise groups as entities, having these characteristics and deal with them as legal persons as 'real' as individual persons. On the complex question of legal personality, F. W. Maitland wrote,

> If once you become interested in the sort of history that tries to unravel these and similar problems, you will think some other sorts of history rather superficial. Perhaps you will go the length of saying that much the most interesting person you ever knew was *persona ficta*.[1]

I

By the end of the nineteenth century the individualism associated with such writers as Jeremy Bentham and J. S. Mill was being vigorously attacked from many quarters. Philosophers, sociologists and social psychologists joined forces to discredit individualism. Perhaps the most telling criticisms came from sociologists, like Emile Durkheim, whose very discipline depends upon the denial of at least some forms of individualism. Herbert Spencer is an interesting case of radical political individualism combined with the belief in 'society' as an organism that has grown and developed in the same way that a biological organism develops. Society, for Spencer, is not to be seen as a collection of individuals, but as an organic whole of which the 'large divisions' are families, trade organisations and other groups. These display a life which is something more than a sum of their constituent parts, and statements about them cannot be reduced to statements about these individual members.[2] An association becomes more and

56

more complex as it develops and as the inter-dependence of the parts increases. In his influential work on *Ancient Law*, published in 1861, Henry Maine also wrote of a society as an organism, and pointed out that human social organisation did not originate in a series of contracts between isolated individuals, but began as a closed hierarchical structure based upon status. In early societies a person's position is determined by his place in the complex of traditional groups into which he has been born, and history shows humanity gradually emancipating itself from this closed society, its members placing themselves in associations and relationships of their own choice. Maine regarded groups as of primary importance, being the cells out of which the body politic is formed.[3]

Curiously, neither Spencer nor Maine carried the conclusions of their social theories into their political theory. Both *The Man vs the State* and *Popular Government* fail to take seriously the organic nature of human associations and the importance of groups in the state. They are individualistic to the point of absurdity.[4]

Among sociologists, Durkheim played a vital role in the increasing recognition of group life. It is through membership of groups that individuals develops their personality. Perhaps Durkheim went too far in his attempt to explain all social phenomena in terms of the group, playing down the importance of individual psychology. This is particularly evident in his study on suicide. Durkheim insisted that the group is an entity distinct from its members, with a will of its own. The group thinks and behaves quite differently from the way in which its members would if they were isolated. It must, therefore, he insisted, be treated as an entity *sui generis*. Durkheim claimed to have come to this conclusion not by means of idealist metaphysics but as a result of his attempt to pursue the study of societies in a scientific and empirical manner. Durkheim is particularly significant from our point of view because he saw some of the political implications of his social theories. In a penetrating criticism of collectivism he pointed out that merely for the state to take over the means of production would solve none of the deeper social problems. 'Where the state is the only environment in which men can live communal lives,' he wrote,

> they inevitably lose contact, become detached, and thus society disintegrates. A nation can be maintained only if, between the State and the individual, there is intercalated a whole series of secondary groups near enough to the individuals to attract them strongly in their sphere of action and drag them, in this way, into the general torrent of social life.[5]

Durkheim can certainly be regarded as one of the precursors of syndicalism in France, though he would by no means have accepted the more extreme varieties of this theory.[6]

The revival of philosophical idealism in the last half of the nineteenth century in Britain, associated with the names of T. H. Green, F. H. Bradley, B. Bosanquet, James Seth, D. G. Ritchie and the Caird brothers, also contributed to the decline in individualism. In his *Ethical Studies* (1876) Bradley assailed the idea that society is nothing but an artificial collection of isolated individuals, and that these individuals are the only 'real' entities. In fact people owe their very identity to their membership of groups which have an existence just as real as that of individual persons. He went on to point out that

> there are such facts as the family, then in a middle position a man's own profession and society, and, over all, the larger community of the state. … That objective institutions exist is of course an obvious fact; and it is a fact which every day is becoming plainer that these institutions are organic, and further, that they are moral.[7]

Green also emphasised the importance of group life, and spoke of the state as 'a society of societies', a phrase later to be used by some of the pluralists.[8]

From a quite different, and indeed hostile, philosophical tradition, sociologists like L. T. Hobhouse, and social psychologists like W. McDougall, agreed that groups must be studied as entities in themselves and not broken down into their component individual members. The former maintained that it is fallacious

> to deny the reality of the social group, refusing to conceive it as a distinct entity, insisting on resolving it into the component individuals as though these individuals were unaffected by the fact of association.[9]

Most pluralist writers agreed with the sociologists in their criticism of 'methodological individualism', as Karl Popper would call it, and insisted that groups must be studied as entities in themselves. Further, they went on to argue that personal categories may properly be applied to them.

It was Otto von Gierke, interpreted and presented to the English reader by the legal historian F. W. Maitland, who most influenced the pluralist writers in their notions of group personality. Gierke was essentially a legal theorist, and his ideas will be examined in more detail in a later section of this chapter. His legal theories, as we shall see, were based upon sociological conclusions about the nature of group life. Maitland reminded his readers that we speak of 'the will of the nation, the mind of the legislature, the settled policy of one State, the ambitious designs of another'.[10] The best proof for Maitland that the realists mean business was that they took their groups into the law court and the market place and made them stand up to the wear and tear of legal and commercial life. Group personality was for Maitland no mere legal fiction. The 'morality of common sense' recognises the group as a moral entity.

Following Maitland and Gierke, Figgis too insisted on the real personality of groups. 'What do we find as a fact?' he demanded:

> Not, surely, a sand-heap of individuals, all equal and undifferentiated, unrelated except to the State, but an ascending hierarchy of groups, family, school, town, county, union, Church, etc., etc. ... In the real world, the isolated individual does not exist; he begins always as a member of something, and, as I said earlier, his personality can develop only in society.[11]

Figgis laid special emphasis on the 'small associations which mould the life of men more intimately than does the great collectivity we call the State'.[12] But at the same time he warned against any tendency so to absorb individuals into the group that they lose their distinct personalities. In one of his last books, *The Will to Freedom*, he saw this danger more clearly than in his earlier works.[13] Mandell Creighton had distinguished between an 'individualism', which narrows life 'to the limits within which self-assertion is possible', and the principle of 'individuality', which develops by 'growing into a widening circle of relationships'.[14] We shall consider in a later chapter the possible role of the state in protecting individuals from group oppression and encouraging individuality while rejecting individualism.

In *The Fellowship of the Mystery*, Figgis related these sociological observations to the christian belief in the church – not as an accidental collection of individuals – but as a central aspect of the gospel. We are not saved as isolated individuals but as members of a divine society. The church is not a collectivity of like-minded individuals; it is through their membership of the 'Body of Christ', that christians are able to share in the life of God.

What Figgis and these other theorists of pluralism were concerned to do was, in the first place to emphasise the social fact of group life, and only then to argue in favour of legal and political recognition of such groups. Addressing the Church Congress of 1905 Figgis declared,

> We say that the world is *not*, as a fact composed of a few vast entities known as States set against crowds of isolated individuals; but is a society of societies, each and all with rights, liberty and life of their own. ... The fact is that to deny to smaller societies a real life and meaning, a personality, in fact, is not anti-clerical, or illiberal, or unwise, or oppressive – it is *untrue*.[15]

Following Gierke he saw this fact of group life particularly manifest in the middle ages with its 'teeming clubs, its organic and historic divisions, parish, borough, hundred, county, and each with historic life and an individuality of its own'.[16]

The group, then, is an entity just as real as its individual members, and has an 'inherent life', not depending upon the state, and thus has the power of developing and growing. Figgis's insistence upon the right of a group to develop, and change its purpose, has important legal implications which I shall consider in due course. Although he was himself particularly concerned with religious groups, he insisted that his theory applies to all groups, and that it does not make a special case of the church. In fact, he claimed that his social theory should be acceptable to liberal-minded secularists for this very reason: it does not demand special treatment for religious groups. In this, Figgis differed from a writer like P. T. Forsyth who, although claiming to have derived his ideas partly from Figgis, made a special case of the church, the personality of which is 'a gift and moral prerogative from God'. A religious group is not, he went on to say, 'a member of the State in any such sense as a municipality is'.[17] Figgis, in contrast, believed that, sociologically, religious groups must be regarded in basically the same way as secular groups. As will be made clear in a later chapter, he did not conceive of the state as another group alongside trade unions, churches and commercial enterprises. He did not think of the state as possessing a personality. It was conceived rather as a structure or assemblage of structures within which groups and associations of various kinds can flourish.

Harold Laski maintained that a group possesses personality in the sense of being 'a binding together of its individual parts to certain modes of behaviour deemed by them likely to promote the interests with which they are concerned'.[18] Societies, he wrote, are persons just as individuals are persons, having a character, ethos and identity of their own; they therefore are morally responsible for their actions.[19] Some critics of the pluralists attack them for not recognising that the state has a right to claim personality just as much as any other group. As we have noted, Figgis did not think of the state in these terms; the state is a collection of groups. Laski, however, differed from Figgis on this matter, maintaining that states, as well as other associations, can be spoken of as persons. 'The reality of the State's personality,' Laski asserted, 'is a compulsion we may not resist.'[20] Many writers, however, did resist the compulsion and, later, Laski himself joined them. He gradually came to reject this 'realist' conception of group personality, partly after having considered the powerful arguments of Morris Cohen, in his article on 'Communal Ghosts'. In his *Grammar of*

Politics, an earlier realism was modified and later it was completely rejected. By 1948 Laski could declare: 'A group of human beings is not a person, in the sense that each member of the group is a person ... the corporate "person", in short, is not a person over and above its members.'[21] Yet even in his earlier writings he had interpreted the concept of a 'group will' or a 'group mind' in an individualist sense. The group mind is the mind 'of a number of men who, actuated by some common purpose, are capable of a unified activity'.[22]

G. D. H. Cole also moved away from his early insistence on group personality. In 1914 he had claimed that social science and social philosophy are basically concerned with 'the phenomenon of collective personality', and was even prepared to use the term 'group soul'.[23] Later, however, Cole came to reject the idea of group personality; personality belongs only to the individual man or woman. In his essay on *Social Theory* (1920) he insisted that the only kind of personality which a group possesses is legal personality, and that here the concept is a purely technical one. He claimed that although the analogy of a person is nearer to the truth than the mechanical or organic analogies, the ascription of personality to a group is likely to lead to confusion and to obscure the difference between individual and associative actions.

Thus we see in Laski and Cole a gradual move away from the notion of group personality. A suspicion of the concept was earlier voiced by Ernest Barker. He was himself considerably influenced by the ideas of Maitland and Figgis, but warned that 'to talk of the real personality of anything, other than the individual human being, is to indulge in dubious and perhaps nebulous speech'.[24] Barker suggested that the pluralism is not ultimately constituted by a plurality of groups but by sets of *ideas*. The struggle is between competing 'schemes in which real and individual persons and wills are related to one another by means of a common and organizing idea'.[25]

Figgis and the other early pluralists could hardly have accepted this theory of Barker. Trade unions, clubs, families and churches are tied together by bonds more powerful than 'organizing ideas'. The struggle between Bismarck's Germany and the Roman Catholic Church, known as the *Kulturkampf*, was not a struggle between two sets of organising ideas, but between two very concrete groups, each claiming the loyalty of its members (many of whom belonged to both bodies). Much of the anti-clericalism in France in the early part of the present century was not so much the result of a dislike of religious *ideas*, as an objection to the very concrete claims which a religious group was making on the loyalty of its members. It was these groups to which people like Emile Combes objected, owing to the challenge which they were thought to present to the state. Many have died for family or friends, for church or for nation, but who would be willing to die for an 'organizing idea'? Barker's position is surely less tenable than that of the pluralists on this matter of group personality.

The idea of group personality, or the belief that group life is 'real', was then central to the ideas of the British political pluralists. When Laski and Cole moved away from a belief in group personality they moved away from pluralism. The controversies between the pluralists and their adversaries about the nature of group life continues in our own day. There are those still who believe that the way to understand the life of a group is to understand the individual components and to see how they interact. This individualist approach is adopted by H. Simon and C. I. Barnard in organisation theory. In social and political philosophy one could mention Karl Popper, F. A. Hayek and Isaiah Berlin. John Wisdom put the individualist, reductionist, position as follows: 'to say anything about a nation is merely to say something (though not the same thing) about its nationals'.[26] Susan Stebbing has told us that we can talk about 'Germany', 'Great Britain' or 'Italy' if we like, so long as we recognise that these are only 'abstractions', and that it is dangerous to 'take these names for single entities'.[27]

Although these writers would claim to be 'empiricists', we look in vain for empirical support for these assertions. If it is true that to say anything about a group is merely to say something about its individual members, is it also true that to say something about individual persons is to say something about their limbs, and that to say something about their limbs is simply to say something about their cells? Surely we may say that groups are as 'real' as individuals. The physicist would see people as composed of atoms or electric charges, which for him are the 'real' units; the biologists talks in terms of organs which are 'real' for him. For the preacher or the moralist the individual person may be the basic unit; the social worker might think in terms of families or other social groups. None of these entities is any more real than the other.

Most social and organisation theorists today recognise the validity of the group as an entity *sui generis*, and are opposed to the reductionism of the individualists. Writers like Elton Mayo, Kurt Lewin, E. W. Bakke, G. Homans and P. Selznick reject reductionism. Selznick puts his own position as follows:

> Day-to-day decisions, relevant to the actual problems met in the translation of policy into action, create precedents, alliances, effective symbols,

and personal loyalties which transform the organisation from a profane, manipulable instrument into something having a sacred status and thus resistant to treatment simply as a means to some external goal.[28]

This methodological realism with respect to groups has certain important political and legal implications. Politically, we recognise that the group has an existence which is not derived from the state, just as the life of individuals is not thus derived. We conclude that the group should be treated as a 'person' in law, with duties and responsibilities which cannot be resolved into the duties and responsibilities of individual members of the group. The group has a developing life of its own, with the possibility that it may acquire new objectives, thus modifying its original purpose.

I I

The idea of group personality advocated by political pluralists had important legal aspects. It carried with it the rejection of the 'fiction' theory of legal personality, and the 'concession' theory which usually went with it. I shall first deal with the fiction theory and its consequences, and then look at the alternative 'realist' theory as put forward by Otto von Gierke and his followers. The pluralists with whom this monograph is particularly concerned were not primarily legal theorists, but we shall see how they took sides on these issues of group personality, owing to the social and political consequences which follow from the legal disputes. The legal arguments on the question of group personality have been extremely complicated, and at times confused. Considering the problem of corporate personality, Dicey wrote in 1904: 'If, then, the law be confused, it all the more accurately reflects the spirit of the time.'[29]

The fiction theory was formulated in the early nineteenth century, by Savigny who declared it to have been the theory which was orthodox in Roman law. According to this theory the only jurally capable person is the individual; only he can, under the perfect system, be the subject of rights. He is the only real entity recognised by law. Yet some modifications needed to be made in this theory for the sake of convenience. 'Nevertheless,' he wrote,

> this original idea of a person may undergo a twofold modification by Positive Law ... by being restricted or expanded. A Jural Capacity may, for instance, in the first place, be either wholly or partially denied to many individual Men; it may, in the second place, be transferred to

something external to the individual Man, and thus a Juristical Person may by this means be artificially created.[30]

The fiction theory thus assumes that the individual is in some way a real person in law, while the group is a fictitious person. Gierke traced the theory back as far as Innocent IV, though this has led to some controversy.[31]

There is some evidence that the fiction theory was assumed by many English lawyers before being explicitly set forth by Savigny. Thus in the famous *Sutton's Hospital Case*[32] Coke stated that corporate personality 'rests only in intendment and consideration of the law', while Blackstone referred to groups as artificial persons. Sir Frederick Pollock, however, in an essay presented to Gierke on his eightieth birthday, argued skilfully that the English common law has never accepted a clear theory of legal personality. He pointed out that the word 'artificial' does not necessarily mean 'fictitious', but merely 'in accordance with the rules of art'.[33] The fiction theory, as set forth by Savigny, gained considerable popularity in the nineteenth century, however, and usually carried with it the corollary that if groups are merely fictitious then they must be given their personality by some body, and this body is the state. Groups receive their personality as a concession from the state.

Otto von Gierke began in earnest the assault upon the fiction theory and the concession theory of group personality.[34] He denied that all law originates with the state. The state has no logical priority over the law; state and law are interdependent. He therefore looked critically at the concession theory of group personality. Gierke's sociological presuppositions were sympathetic to the idea of the real personality of a group. He argued that a group has a real existence which is more than the sum of its parts, and believed that groups possess many of the same characteristics as individuals. 'We find above the level of individual existence', he declared,

a second, independent level of existence of human collective associations. Above the individual spirit, the individual will, the individual consciousness, we recognise in thousandfold expressions of life the real existence of common spirit, common will, and common consciousness.[35]

He maintained that sociological investigation confirms what we know by common sense: that we do not live as isolated individuals, but that we find our fullest development in a vast number of associations and groups, culminating in the state. If the life of groups is a sociological phenomenon, Gierke argued, then the law should recognise this fact. 'Is it not, however, possible', he demanded, that law, when it treats organised associations as persons, is not disregarding reality, but giving reality more adequate expression? Is it not possible that human associations are real unities which receive through legal recognition of their personality only what corresponds to their real nature? I, with many others, answer, Yes.[36]

We have here, then, a legal theory that is closely connected to a sociological theory. When it burst upon England in 1900 with Maitland's translation of part of *Das deutsche Genossenschaftsrecht*, its assumptions were not always very well understood. Gierke's ideas, however, seem to have had a double effect in England. In the first place the purely legal conception of the personality of groups was already changing, and the fiction theory in its old formulation was being found increasingly unsatisfactory. Judges more and more found themselves treating groups as legal entities which could not be reduced to their individual members, and legal theorists were searching for a more adequate understanding of legal practice than was furnished by the fiction theory. Gierke's ideas helped to supply this need. Secondly, Gierke's theory, as interpreted by Maitland, provided material for the development of political pluralism.

By the beginning of the twentieth century there was considerable dissatisfaction with the fiction theory of group personality. Coke's dictum that 'none but the king alone can create or make a corporation'[37] was, strictly speaking, untrue even in his own day. There are and have been recognised for many centuries corporations in common law and corporations by implication. Also, by the first decade of the twentieth century, it was clear that the rigid distinction which many people had maintained between corporate and unincorporated bodies was breaking down. In the *Taff Vale* case a trade union, though not an incorporated body, was treated for legal purposes as a person and was sued by employers for damages incurred during a strike which had been organised by the union. Trade unions, declared Lord Atkinson, in a later and equally celebrated case,

> are, when registered, quasi-corporations, resembling much more closely railway companies incorporated by statute than voluntary associations of individuals merely bound together by contract or agreement, express or implied.[38]

By 1924 Sir Paul Vinogradoff was able to declare that there is no clear distinction between corporations and other permanent groups and that they shade off into one another.[39] Thus, construed narrowly, the statement that legal personality is a gift of the state is patently false. Construed broadly, it is true, necessarily true. If we include in 'the state' the common law and the activities of the law courts – if we say that legal personality is bestowed upon groups and upon individuals by legal practice – then we are right, by definition, for that is what legal personality means.

Legal theory is based upon legal practice, and it is worth looking at the way in which groups are treated in English and American law. It was generally agreed, and the House of Lords confirmed quite clearly in a celebrated case, *Salomon* v. *Salomon*, that a corporation is a person distinct from the individual persons who compose it. But it was generally held that corporations, unlike individual persons, could not commit torts which require a guilty intention, nor crimes which require *mens rea*. In 1854 Lord Alderson held that an action for malicious prosecution cannot be brought against a company, because a corporate person does not have a will and is therefore incapable of malice (*Stevens* case). Later, in the same century, Lord Bramwell declared: 'I am at a loss to understand how there could be corporate malice' (*Henderson* case). Nevertheless with the increased numbers of corporations and quasi-corporations, and with the obvious injustices that individuals suffered at their hands, some modification in legal practice was demanded. In a series of cases in the 1880s and 1890s the civil law was modified on this matter (*Edwards* case, *Kent* case, *Cornford* case, *Barwick* case). 'It is obvious', declared Judge Fry in the first of these cases,

> that great evils would arise if, on the ground that a corporation can have no mind, and therefore can have no malice, a corporation were able to escape from that liability which if they [sic] were not incorporated they would have to bear.

Thus by the end of the nineteenth century legal practice in civil law had moved away from some of the worst consequences of the fiction theory.

It was also held by many fictionists that corporations cannot be guilty of criminal offenses which demand a *mens rea*. In *R.* v. *Cory Bros.* the court found that a railway company was not guilty of a criminal offence if it erected an electric fence against which an employee fell and was killed; a company cannot have a *mens rea*. Nevertheless, things have changed; in a later case, *I.C.R. Haulage*, Justice Stable commented on the decision in *Cory*:

> If the matter came before the court today, the result might well be different. ... this is a branch of the law to which the attitude of the courts has in the passage of time undergone a process of development.

So another plank in the fiction theory gave way. In the same year (1944) Lord Caldecote said:

> the real point which we have to decide ... is ... whether a company is capable of an act of will or a state of mind, so as to be able to form an intention to deceive or to have knowledge of the truth or falsity of a statement.[40]

Legal practice can therefore be said to have moved away from the dogmas of the fiction theory, which as Maitland saw in 1900 had received notice to quit. The theory was practically unworkable as well as being logically untenable.

One question which particularly concerned Figgis was whether the law should recognise the right of a group to develop and change its purpose. If the group is sociologically a real entity, with a life of its own, then surely it will grow and develop. If the law is going to recognise this fact of the real personality of groups, then the law must, according to him, recognise the right of groups to develop and to determine for themselves the limits of this development. It was the *Free Church of Scotland* case which brought this issue to a head for Figgis. In 1843 the Scottish Church had split; almost a third of the Church, led by Thomas Chalmers and others, severed its connection with the state to form the Free Church of Scotland. The Disruption, as it was called, was mainly caused by demands for a change in the patronage system, so that more power in the selection of ministers would be given to the local congregation. The Free Church, however, believed strongly in the establishment principle, and was Calvinist in theology.

In 1900, after many years of discussion, the Free Church, under Principal Rainy, combined with the United Presbyterian Church, which had been formed in 1847 by a union of the United Secession Church and the Relief Synod. The United Presbyterians were somewhat more liberal in their interpretation of Calvinism than were the founders of the Free Church; nor did they accept the principle of church establishment. The union was approved by 643 votes to 27 in the Assembly of the Free Church, but the dissidents (popularly known as the Wee Frees) took the case to court claiming that the action of the majority was *ultra vires* and that they were themselves the true successors of the Free Church. The case eventually reached the House of Lords which, after wallowing in questions as unfamiliar to them as the development of doctrine and the meaning of the Westminster Confession, decided that the action of the majority had contravened the original trust and that all the property of the Free Church must go to the Wee Frees. The main point at issue was whether the two principles – establishment and the Westminster Confession's interpretation of Calvinism – were fundamental in the original trust, and in the minds of the founders of the Free Church. The church itself, through its constituted government, had declared by an overwhelming majority that they were not fundamental; but the Lords decided otherwise. The Free Church (i.e. the majority who wished for union) argued that any person joining the church thereby submitted to its organ of authority, and that this authority had decided that these matters were not fundamental to the church.

As Figgis saw, certain important issues were at stake here. Were the courts incapable of conceiving the development of purpose within a living body? Was it right for the courts to go behind the constituted authority of the church in deciding what is fundamental to that body? How strict should the courts be in their application of the doctrine of *ultra vires* and of the binding nature of trust deeds? These were some of the questions raised in the case and discussed by Figgis in *Churches in the Modern State*. 'This work,' wrote F. Hallis, 'is one of the most valuable treatises on many of the problems discussed' in his book on *Corporate Personality*.[41]

The doctrine of *ultra vires* in corporation law is a difficult one to apply. If a body which was founded to provide old ladies with radios suddenly decided to spend its money on Rolls Royce cars for its staff, the courts would declare that this was illegal. A railway company cannot (or could not) apply its funds to purposes other than those specified in the act of incorporation, 'If the great body of shareholders,' said Kindersley V. C.,

> agree to carry on a business different from that for which the company was constituted, a single shareholder has a right to say that it shall not be done, and may apply for and obtain an injunction.[42]

In the case of unincorporated bodies the trust deeds form a similar limit. With regard to *ultra vires* in company law, the Cohen Committee reported in 1945 that:

> we think that every company, whether incorporated before or after the passing of a new Companies Act, should, notwithstanding anything omitted from its memorandum of association, have as regards third parties the same power as an individual.[43]

This clear-cut solution, of eliminating the whole concept of *ultra vires* in this context was not, however, accepted. Section 5 of the Companies Act 1948 greatly extended the power of companies to alter their memoranda, though as one authority on the subject has remarked, 'the *ultra vires* doctrine seems to have outlived its usefulness'.[44] But the case of a church is somewhat different from that of a company, and if the law on this question has liberalised with regard to the memoranda of the latter, it should have liberalised all the more with regard to the trust deeds of churches. Is it not possible to treat a religious body more like an individual with powers of development, than like a dead thing, tied to the exact formulation of a document, as was done in the *Free Church* case? It was, as Maitland observed, an unfortunate day when this case was decided and the 'dead hand fell with a resounding slap upon the living body'.[45]

Figgis was thus demanding that the doctrine of *ultra vires* and the interpretation of trust deeds should be applied in a much more elastic way, and that the courts should be more willing to recognise the facts of group life than they had up to his time. He recognised that his position in this matter was consistent with theological notions of the development of christian doctrine, similar to those set forth by J. H. Newman. 'Belief in the Catholic Church,' wrote Figgis, 'is belief in development; and this means a creative evolution.'[46] The courts should normally be prepared to accept the decisions of the constituted authority within a group about the kind of developments which are desirable. This position agrees in substance with that which was later maintained by the Cohen Committee with respect to company law.

A later case in the United States brought out the issue once more. In the *Kedroff* case there was a dispute between the majority of the Russian Orthodox christians in the USA who had severed communion with the Moscow patriarchate, and the body which was still in communion with Moscow, regarding the possession of St Nicholas Cathedral in New York. A law was passed in New York State which had the effect of giving the cathedral to the dissident body. The Supreme Court found this statute to be contrary to the Fourteenth Amendment, and decided that the cathedral should be returned to the body which was in communion with Moscow. This was in many ways a more difficult case than the *Free Church of Scotland* case. Although the majority of church members were in the dissident body, the Russian church is not ruled by majority government. The constituted authority was not an elected body. Justices Reed and Frankfurter insisted that the court does not have a right to impose upon a religious society a form of majority government. As one writer commented:

> Figgis and Maitland would surely have applauded the opinion of Mr Justice Reed in the *Kedroff* case, for it seems to apply the principle of pluralism to the relationships of Church and State in just such a way as they had urged.[47]

It is interesting to note that one of the judges in this case, Felix Frankfurter, had been a close friend of Harold Laski, who had been considerably influenced in this matter of group personality by Maitland and Figgis.[48]

Figgis did not, however, make it clear what his position would be in a situation where the constituted authority of the religious body decided on one course of action and the 'real life' of the group continued along another course. Should the courts never look behind the constituted authority? In his discussion of the *Free Church* case, Figgis spoke of the rights of the 'overwhelming majority'. In that particular case the two, of course, coincided, but they need not always do so. Discussing whether the changes in church order at the time of the English reformation were legally valid in the sense of being 'the work of the hierarchy, and conformed to the legal traditions of the church', he declared,

> Suppose they did not, which seems to me much more probable, irregularities of procedure do not of themselves determine the life of a society. It is not easy to destroy a living society.[49]

Here, he would seem to be arguing that it might be right to look behind the constitutional fasçade at the real life of the group.

As might be expected, Figgis welcomed the *Taff Vale* decision which treated trade unions as legal persons, despite their unincorporated status. The fact that the Trades Disputes Act of 1906 declared them immune for certain purposes did not destroy the force of the decision. L. C. Webb wrote of 'Figgis's failure to see that the *Taff Vale* decision, which he welcomed enthusiastically, ... was bitterly resented by the whole trade union movement and was ultimately reversed by legislation.'[50] If Webb had read *Churches in the Modern State* more carefully, he would have seen that Figgis was fully aware of both these things. The decision, he wrote, 'showed that Trades Unions were personalities, *in spite of their own wishes*'.[51]

It is true to say, then, that by the period of the First World War the fiction theory of group personality had been thoroughly discredited. 'We have heard,' remarked Pollock,

> certainly that fictions may pass for facts on the strength of their antiquity, but it would be rather novel to say that facts, when they have existed long enough, become legal fictions, abstractions, *entia rationis*.[52]

Maitland, Figgis and Laski attacked the idea that group personality in law is a mere fiction; they insisted that behind the legal person lay a real entity, and that the law must recognise reality if it is to be an effective instrument of social control. They denied that this legal personality was arbitrarily conferred by the state (i.e. the government or parliament). Yet in their more clear-sighted moments they saw that *all* legal personality (including that of the individual) is 'artificial', and that it is created by being recognised in legal practice. Laski wrote that the group has 'an interest to promote, a function to serve. The State does not call it into being. It is not, *outside the categories of law*, dependent upon the State.'[53] In his earlier years Laski was torn between the realism of Gierke and Maitland who believed that groups including the state were real persons, and the positivism of Duguit who rejected the whole idea of real personality.

III

Many criticisms have been directed against the political pluralists' idea of group personality. It is sometimes suggested that the whole controversy was simply about words, and that there was no substantial issue at stake between the realists and the fictionists. I have already noted that there is some ambiguity in saying that legal personality is the concession of the state; nevertheless, there were significant differences between the realists and their adversaries. The patronising attitude of Glanville Williams is misplaced:

> A vast and fruitless controversy has raged over the question whether cor-porations aggregate are 'real' or 'fictitious' persons. ... It is submitted that the question is a spurious one and that there is no issue of fact between the two sides. The 'realists' say that an association of men is 'real', but this the 'fictitionists' do not deny. The 'realists' say further that an association of men is itself a 'person'; but this is simply an assertion of the determination of these writers to use the word 'person' in a certain way, not a proposition of fact relating to associations. ... In any case it is submitted that the controversy has no legal significance.[54]

Most disputes are about words, but not merely about words. Williams might say of an assertion that there is a wild bull and not a tame cow in the neighbouring field, that it is simply an assertion of the speaker's determina-tion to use the words 'wild' and 'bull' in a certain way. Nevertheless, the belief might well lead to a practical policy being adopted which is different from the one which would be pursued by a person who rejected the usage. As we have seen, a judge's attitude towards the question of group personal-ity is likely to determine the way he treats a group. Austin Farrer has remarked in connection with this method of philosophising: 'Metaphysical argument may be the grand cause of logical mirage; but linguistic conjur-ing is unrivalled for vanishing tricks.'[55] Should corporations and other associations be liable for crimes which require *mens rea* and for torts which need a guilty intention, or should only individuals be liable for such legal action? Should the former property of the Free Church of Scotland belong to one ecclesiastical group or to another? These are very practical questions, and it was issues such as these which principally concerned the 'realists'.

Legal practice has changed during the last hundred years, and no one would today hold the fiction theory in its strict form. This is not to say, however, that there was *never* a real issue at stake. H. L. A. Hart states that we should stop thinking of 'personality' as a set of qualities. All that group persons and individual persons have in common is the word 'person', signifying the determination of lawyers to deal with them for some purposes in a similar way.[56] But the reason lawyers have become increasingly determined to deal with groups in a manner similar to that adopted with respect to individuals is that they have something *else* in common. Otherwise we are forced to conclude that lawyers behave in a quite arbitrary manner; in which case the whole discipline of jurisprudence is misconceived. No doubt there are cases when the only relation existing between two entities having the same name is a verbal one, but equivocation (even in law) is the exception and not the rule. Groups are treated as persons in law because this corresponds to a social fact about groups; groups and individuals are treated as persons in law, because the way in which they act is in some respects similar. We do not, as a rule, call two things by the same name unless they have something in common.

The notion of real personality was perhaps the aspect of pluralist theory which has been most harshly criticised. Earl Latham, for example, while being generally sympathetic to the ideas of Laski, Figgis and Cole, attacks the concept of group personality. He maintains that the pluralists, after having taken away personality from the state, err by bestowing personality upon other associations.[57] Yet some of the pluralists did not deny that the state has a 'personality'. Gierke certainly did not deny personality to the state, nor did Laski. Figgis indeed adopted this position, on the grounds that the state is a structure and system of rules within which associations pursuing substantive purposes can exist. Not itself pursuing a substantive purpose, the state is different from those groups that compose it, and is more similar to a mechanical device than to an organic body with a 'personality'. Some of Latham's other criticisms of political pluralism will be looked at in a later chapter.

L. C. Webb accuses the pluralists of deducing the sociological idea of group life from the fact that groups have a legal personality. He writes as follows,

The doll so perfectly articulated that it is mistaken for flesh and blood is a familiar theme of classical ballet. Something of the same sort of illusion gave rise to English political pluralism. The group person as it exists within the universe of the law is a creation of art, a fictitious person. The English political pluralists were persuaded that the group person was real in the sense of existing independently of legal art.[58]

As we have seen, the British pluralists did not argue back from the fact that the courts recognise group persons to the reality of group life.[59] Quite the reverse; they argued that groups were social facts and that the law in their day inadequately reflected the reality of group life, and ought therefore to be modified. The pluralists certainly believed that groups exist as entities independently of legal art, but they did not argue in the way Webb suggests. Webb also states that Figgis failed to understand 'the significance of the Companies Act of 1862 and of later legislation providing an easy means of incorporation for non-profit associations'.[60] Yet we have seen that the position of corporations was not very different from that of unincorporated bodies with respect to the question of *ultra vires* and the right to develop. If the Free Church of Scotland had been a corporation, there is little reason to think that it would have been in a stronger position.

The pluralist writers did not deny that there should be some machinery for recognising groups as legal persons, as long as it is realised that this is a matter of recognising something that really exists, rather than of inventing something which does not exist. D. Lloyd seems to have believed that the realists denied the need for any kind of recognition.[61] We have already seen how Gierke wrote of associations that they 'receive through legal recognition of their personality' that which corresponds to their real nature. 'Spectacles are to be had in Germany,' declared Maitland,

> which, so it is said, enable the law to see personality wherever there is bodiliness, and a time seems at hand when the idea of 'particular creation' will be as antiquated in Corporation Law as it is in Zoology.[62]

Nevertheless the spectacles are necessary. The pluralists generally accepted that some kind of procedure is required for the recognition of associations.

I V

We may perhaps best conclude this chapter by a brief summary of Figgis's ideas about group personality. Within the state there are many associations of various sorts, often acting with a kind of unity which allows us to use personal language normally reserved for describing the activities of individuals. Furthermore, the activity of groups cannot meaningfully be reduced to the actions of their individual members. Through the interaction of the individual members of the group new ideas are evolved and the group moves in new directions. These sociological facts ought to be recognised by the law, if we wish the law to remain an effective and realistic instrument of social control. These groups do not derive their social existence from being recognised as legal persons; rather they ought to be recognised as legal persons because they are social entities. The courts should also recognise the right of groups to develop and grow, and thus to modify their original purpose. These were some of the substantial points which the pluralist writers made about group personality, and they form one of the foundation stones upon which their political theory was based.

5 The State, the Group and the Individual

In the preceding discussion I have maintained that the British pluralists structured their political theory on a foundation of three pillars: a belief that liberty is a fundamental political value and is best preserved by a dispersion of power, a denial of state sovereignty, and some notion of the 'real personality' of groups. The present chapter is concerned with their theories of the state, and with their ideas about the proper relationship between the state, the group and the individual.

The theories we are considering in this essay were put forward by historians. Figgis was primarily a historian who made significant contributions to our knowledge of political thought in the period from the renaissance to the reformation. His two most important academic works *The Divine Right of Kings* and *From Gerson to Grotius* have been republished in recent years. His three principal teachers, Acton, Creighton and Maitland were also historians.[1] Laski and others who contributed to pluralist theory also adopted a historical approach to the subject. These men looked at developments in their own day with a historical eye and were fully aware that their own political theories were in certain respects historically conditioned.[2] They were reacting against the growing power and scope of central government in their day, and were acutely aware of the need to prescribe limits to these activities and to protect the life of semi-autonomous associations. They saw a growing tendency on the part of governments to recognise only individuals, viewing groups as at the best an inconvenience and at worst a threat to national unity. In Germany, France and Britain the state was taking over welfare functions previously performed (often inadequately) by voluntary bodies. A militantly secularist and anti-clerical movement in France attacked the legitimacy of religious groups, as anything more than collections of like-minded individuals. Trade unions and other bodies were seen as challenging the 'sovereign rights of the state'. At the level of theory as well as practice there was a tendency to glorify the state and so to emphasise the need for national unity that groups and associations were denigrated.

Although British pluralist theory developed in a particular social context, its principal normative assertions may legitimately be applied to situations other than the one within which it evolved. The concluding section of this chapter will look at the relevance of political pluralism to situations where ethnicity is a salient factor, where social and cultural divisions are superimposed and 'segmentation' has occurred.

Before examining the theories of the state held by the leading pluralists of the period, I shall, however, glance briefly at the notions of the state against which the pluralists were reacting.

I

Many of the world's leading political philosophers have regarded groups as either irrelevant to political theory or, if relevant, then grudgingly to be recognised as significant but unwelcome intruders on to the political stage. Politics has often been seen as essentially a matter of the individual versus the state. An obvious example is Thomas Hobbes. Groups do not play an important part in his theory, although they are not ignored. In chapter 21 of *Leviathan*, groups are divided into two kinds: regular and irregular, and both are regarded with some suspicion. Hobbes found it necessary to accept the family, but he objected to what we would call political parties, describing them as 'cabals' or 'factions'. Lawful systems were thought of as in some ways analogous to muscles in the human body, while unlawful ones are like 'wens, biles and apostems'. Yet he regarded corporations in general as tending to the dissolution of the commonwealth, and if there are a large number of them in existence they are like 'worms in the entrails of a natural man'.

Rousseau recognised the existence of groups within the larger political unit, each with its own interests and rules of conduct. With respect to their members they are able to express a common will, but with respect to the state of which they are a part they represent a particular interest which is likely to be opposed to the general interest. In his *Contrat social*, groups are said to break up the unity of the state, and to that extent are thought harmful. If the general will is perfectly to express itself, individuals should be members of no partial societies or groups within the state, and each must think as an isolated individual citizen.

For a final example from the school of individualist thinkers we shall take the prophet of late nineteenth-century British rationalism, Henry Sidgwick. Cambridge was very much affected by what Sidgwick said and thought, and his influence was alive there at the time Figgis wrote. In *Elements of Politics* he dealt with the relationship between voluntary societies and the state. The whole tone is one of suspicion towards groups; they are assumed to be potentially dangerous, and the author's aim seems to have been to discover a means of suppressing as many of them as possible without violating the canon of individual liberty. 'Minor fragments' of governmental power can occasionally be conferred upon corporations and other groups,[3] but generally speaking they are thought of as private rather than public institutions existing strictly by permission of the state. Groups increase the danger of 'obstinate and systematic disobedience to Government'. The more force a 'recalcitrant element' can rely upon, the more the peril of disorder, though he graciously allowed that 'this is not a decisive argument for discouraging such associations'. Groups constitute a great danger to the individual whom they are liable to coerce, though the state should not necessarily intervene in all cases to stop this.[4] Unlike Hobbes, he thought that a large number of religious bodies was less dangerous to the state than one single church. Religious groups proved a special problem for Sidgwick. The results which religious bodies achieve were thought by him to be in general useful, and for various reasons the state would find it inexpedient to take them over. So the state must get the church, or churches, into its power by offering various bribes, and should attempt to gain control of the finances of churches. Bequests to religious organisations are

> liable to supply a dangerously strong inducement to the conscious or semi-conscious perpetuation of exploded errors, which, without this support, would gradually disappear.[5]

This somewhat quaint example of individualist collectivism which Sidgwick stood for is relevant for our purpose, as this was just the kind of political theory against which the pluralists strove.

In the late nineteenth and early twentieth century the most influential political philosophers in Britain were inspired by the idealist metaphysics of Hegel and the moral theories of Kant. Writers like T. H. Green, B. Bosanquet and Henry Jones derived certain of their ideas also from Rousseau, believing that the notion of a general will could be applied to the large modern state. They realised, however, that this meant recognising the important role which groups play. At this point it was Hegel who helped them most. Sociologically we may call Hegel a pluralist. Civil society, according to him, was made up, not primarily of individuals, but of groups, membership of which binds together individuals into the larger unity of the state. It is only through the existence of groups that a dangerous atomism can be avoided. The weakness of the French system of government was, according to Hegel, partly due to the virtual absence of such associations. He was critical of the tendency to concentrate power in the central government, attacking that illiberal jealousy which attempts to restrict the freedom of subordinate groups to manage their own affairs.[6] He insisted that 'dissimilarity in culture and manners is a necessary product as well as a necessary condition of the stability of modern states'.[7] Hegel, thus, believed in social diversity, and maintained that foreign affairs and national defence are the only things that must in all circumstances be controlled by the central government. Although he insisted that the interests of groups and associations 'must be subordinated to the higher interests of the state',[8] he did not mean by this that they must necessarily be subordinated to the interests of the central government, but to the common interest of the whole people.

Green also saw that the national state can exist only on the basis of other forms of community life; it was for him 'the society of societies'. Bosanquet too recognised that, generally speaking, the public affairs and social life are carried on by persons arranged in groups. All these writers admitted the possibility that the central government might on certain occasions be in the wrong, and that some other group might be right. Was not Hegel recorded as speaking of 'the heavenly Antigone, the most glorious figure ever to have appeared on earth' – Antigone who is the personification of civil disobedience? And did not Green urge that in certain situations there is a positive duty to disobey? Nevertheless it is true that Hegel's British disciples did believe that politics consists in the search for a substantive common good in which the true interests of all individuals and associations would be included. The idealists have had many critics, and have been accused of propagating a variety of conflicting errors. Earl Latham is apparently under the impression that 'the idealists' (which idealists?) postulated the state 'as a colossus of unity, a monolith, an absolute, a total system swallowing and assimilating all personal beliefs, attachments, obligations, and relations'.[9] From what has been said above, we may conclude that Latham is talking alarmist nonsense here. Despite, however, the pluralist element in the thought of many of the idealist writers on politics, G. D. H. Cole felt that he was living in a climate generally hostile to pluralism. 'The whole tendency of nineteenth century philosophy,' he wrote,

> was to regard the association as, at the most, a necessary imperfection, to be tolerated rather than recognised, with no rights beyond those of expediency, and no powers beyond those conferred expressly by statute. From this point of view we are now struggling slowly back to a saner doctrine.[10]

II

Pluralist writers like Figgis argued that the state is, as a fact, composed of a number of associations and groups, and that failure to recognise this will lead to disaster. Persons are by nature social, and their interests are plural. Any attempt by the central government to suppress groups will lead to resistance and eventually to violent upheaval. A wise government will not, therefore, attempt to eradicate group life. Pluralist writers also believed that a multiplicity of groups is beneficial to the state; that associations should be not merely tolerated but encouraged because (a) active participation in group life on the part of the individual leads to a healthy development of human personality, and (b) lively groups provide a bulwark against the totalitarian state. But how precisely did these pluralist writers see the state in its relationship with other groups and associations? It will become clear that there is no generally agreed theory of the state among these British political pluralists. Furthermore it is sometimes difficult to discover a coherent view in the writings of any single thinker. Cole in particular tended to write too much and too rapidly; he seems very often to have published the first half-baked idea which came into his head.

I shall begin by looking at Figgis's view of the state. For him the state is a group which is composed of groups, rather than of individuals. The individual is a member of the state, according to this view, *through* membership in subordinate associations. So the state is a 'community of communities', and it has a formal structure which culminates in central government. The term 'state' was used by Figgis to mean (a) the collectivity of groups forming a single political unit, and also in a narrower sense to mean (b) the formal organs of government by which the collectivity acts as a single entity. It is because Figgis thought of the state as a community of communities that he wrote of churches *in* the modern state rather than churches *and* the modern state, as one critic says he should have done.[11] He followed the usage adopted by Pope Leo XIII in his celebrated Encyclical *Rerum Novarum*, where he stated that

> Particular societies, then, although they exist within the State, and are each a part of the State, nevertheless cannot be prohibited by the State absolutely and as such. ... If it forbids its citizens to form associations, it contradicts the very principle of its own existence.[12]

The state is not, for Figgis as it is with Laski, MacIver and even in some places with Maitland, merely another group, alongside economic, cultural, civic and ecclesiastical groups. It is the community of communities, whose prime duty it is to maintain order among its members. Although Figgis wrote of the state as a 'community', it is evident that the state is not thought of as a community in the sense that a family, a monastery or a small village is. It is not a *Gemeinschaft*, but an association whose sole purpose is to provide a structure within which its various component groups might pursue their respective ends. The state is no more a community in the traditional sense, than is 'the international community', to which the various factions in ethnic conflicts appeal (a usage that would laughable if it were not so tragic), or the 'community' into which luckless mental patients are sent to live. Anything less like a *Gemeinschaft* is hard to imagine.

H. M. Magid criticises Figgis's theory of the state as a *communitas communitatum*, arguing that his view that people are concerned with the affairs of the state only in so far as they are citizens, implies that the state is 'a *communitas* of the citizens for the regulation of the *communitates*'.[13] This criticism, however, ignores the oft repeated view of Figgis that citizens are members of the pluralist state only *through* their membership of societies like churches, the trade unions or families. Figgis normally used the term 'society' to refer to any one of the particular groups which compose the state. He did not therefore make that distinction between state and society which one recent author believes to be fundamental to political pluralism.[14] In fact, Figgis did not see the totality of groups which make up the state as constituting anything like a single society. The only thing binding this collectivity together is the civil or political bond. We do not therefore find Figgis writing of the personality of the state, as Laski did; the state is, for him, a very different kind of association from the trade union, the church or the sports club, which are bound together by a common substantive purpose. The state exists simply to maintain some kind of order among contending groups.

Much popular writing, however, assumes that the state should constitute a single community or society.[15] Nationalism goes one step further in maintaining that the only politically significant community is the nation, and that state borders should follow those of nations (insofar as they can be said to have territorial borders). The term 'self-determination' is frequently used, when what is meant is that each nation should constitute a self-governing and 'sovereign' state. This dogma is at the very basis of most violent struggles over the past century and a half in Europe and beyond. Each nation and tribe is encouraged to demand such an independent status, rather than being content with a degree of autonomy within a larger whole.

Figgis insisted that citizens belong to various communities and associations and that it is the function of the state to regulate and control the life of its member groups. But first of all the state must have some machinery for recognising groups. The state has to play an active role in deciding which groups it should recognise as valid expressions of social life. The recognition of the legal personality of the individual citizen does not raise any great problems for the state, but the recognition of the legal personality of groups demands more positive action. However strongly we may believe in the naturalness of groups life, he asserted, it is the duty of the state to demand proper guarantees that a permanent group is being formed. Furthermore, he maintained, it must clearly be within the province of the State to prevent bodies of persons acting covertly and practically as corporations, in order to escape rightful government control.[16] If it is going to control the groups successfully, the state must require certain marks of group personality, such as registration, before it recognises the personality of associations.

The job of the state, then, is to maintain a situation in being where groups can pursue their several purposes as far as may be; conflict will arise, and in order to cope with these conflicts the state must have some machinery for registering and recognising groups. Although the state can withdraw recognition from a group, it ought not, in the nature of things, attempt to destroy a group. A group may continue to exist, and to manifest a social personality, even though it is unrecognised or even banned by the government. The group might indeed die if, for example, all its members died or if they disbanded the group for lack of a common purpose, or partly as a result of the withdrawal of state recognition, but it is not created or destroyed by the state. This may seem like a mere quibble over words, but the point which Figgis was trying to emphasise was that groups do not owe their existence to state recognition. The state recognises groups because they exist; they do not derive their existence from being recognised. Christian churches existed for centuries without such recognition, and yet remained social entities with a personality.

Michael Oakeshott has distinguished two ideal types with reference to which the modern European state may be understood. He uses two terms from medieval Latin, *societas* and *universitas* to describe two forms of association. The former is a non-voluntary association which exists to provide a structure within which people may pursue their own substantive interests and purposes, as groups or as individuals. The *societas* pursues no substantive purpose of its own. The *universitas*, on the other hand is a corporate association uniting its members in the attempt to realise some common purpose or good. In the former

> The persons associated are not joined in the pursuit of a common substantive purpose or in seeking the satisfaction of their individual wants. *Cives* and subjects are recognized and recognize themselves to be related in respect of their acknowledgement of the authority of a system of *lex* composed of conditions to be subscribed to in self-chosen conduct.[17]

The state seen in terms of *societas* 'is persons, families, groups, corporate associations, etc., each pursuing its own distinct and different purposes and

all related to one another in the recognition of a sovereign authority. It is
not one more grouping of operative persons.'[18] Those, in contrast, who
understand the state in terms of *universitas* believe that there must be some
common end to which the state aspires, a general interest which its government seeks to realise, welfare, happiness, the good life, economic prosper-
ity or development. Such a state will see voluntary groups within it as
rivals and as constituting a threat to the end pursued by the state itself.
Oakeshott's preference is clearly for the state to be seen in terms of
societas, or civil association, and this understanding has much similarity
with the ideas proposed by Figgis in his pluralist conception of the state.

As we have noted, Figgis asserted that although groups have rights,
these are not absolute rights. He praised the puritans of the seventeenth
century for denying that all rights are derived from the civil power, and for
asserting the right of religious groups to exist in the state.[19] Groups have
rights, but not unlimited and absolute rights. The state exists

> to control and limit within the bounds of justice, the activities of all
> minor associations whatsoever. The point at issue is not whether
> Churches can do anything they choose, but whether human law is to
> regard them as having inherent powers, rights, and wills of their own –
> in a word, a personality. If they have, their activity might be restrained in
> so far as it interferes with others – thus, they would not be allowed to
> persecute, and ought not to be allowed.[20]

The state does not create the groups, but recognises and controls them; they
have, so far as they are permanent, a personality and inherent rights. 'Is the
civil society,' he demanded,

> a single power from which all rights proceed by delegation? In this case
> there is no real check upon tyranny, however democratic the form of
> government. Or is the state merely the final bond of a multitude of
> bodies, Churches, trade unions, families, all possessing inherent life, a
> real thing, recognized and regulated by the government, but no more the
> creation of its fiat, than are individual persons?[21]

Just as the right of individuals to do as they like is limited, so is that of
groups; they are more powerful than individuals, and there is always the
danger of their demanding more than is just. The more exalted the object of
the group, the more likelihood there is of its getting out of hand, and the
greater is the need of governmental control. Thus the main job of the state
is to reconcile conflicting claims made by its members, allowing them as
much scope for development and expression as is possible within the limits
of order and peace. To control the groups, 'a strong power above them is

needed' and it is largely in order to regulate such groups and keep them in order that the coercive force of the state exists. In another place he wrote of 'the Christian idea of the State as the controlling power', which guides but does not create groups.[22] Thus, as for John Dewey,[23] the state controls but does not create groups and individuals.

These pluralist writers agreed with Hegel that the assumption by the state of managerial responsibilities – the transformation of states into enterprises – obstructs their vital functions of defending, governing and controlling the groups which comprise them. 'If both the necessary and the more arbitrary are alike in the power of the centre of the public authority,' wrote the German philosopher,

> and if they are both demanded with the same strictness, as by the government, the citizens may confuse both things together, become as impatient with the one as with the other, and bring the state, as regards its necessary claims, into jeopardy.[24]

Figgis was opposed to the conception of an omnipotent and omnicompetent state set against a mass of individuals who are its members – '"the great leviathan" made up of little men, as in Hobbes's titlepage'.[25] St Thomas Aquinas, in contrast did not set the state against a mass of isolated individuals, but rather saw the family and other social institutions existing in their own right and not by *fiat* of the state.[26]

Figgis argued that individualism and collectivism are but different sides of the same coin; a political atomism which sees a state simply as a collection of isolated individuals leads very easily to the doctrine of an omnipotent state. 'The truth is,' he declared, 'that both the State and the individual as commonly envisaged are not facts but fictions.'[27] Any attempt to base a system of politics upon these fictions is, he thought, likely to lead to tyranny in the end.

One matter on which Figgis's theory is not sufficiently detailed is the extent to which the state is justified in intervening in the affairs of a group to prevent the persecution of individuals, or to maintain justice. He does not seem to have been fully aware of what A. V. Dicey called 'the paradoxical character' of the right of association.[28] He would certainly have said that the presumption is always that the individual has freely chosen to join the group, and however absurd its rules may appear to the outsider, the state should not, under normal circumstances, intervene. It can do so, though, when there is definite evidence of persecution. As the whole purpose of politics is thought to be the development of character by encouraging the faculty of free choice, there must be occasions when the character of individuals is being warped by a group to which they belong; should the state intervene to protect them? Figgis does not tell us on what occasions this might be justified. Presumably he would allow the state to stop corruption and fraud, and he stated more than once that it must have the final word on matters of property. Inherent rights of groups are not absolute rights.

We have already discussed the right of self-development which Figgis thought should be secured to groups. What other rights should groups possess? They should be allowed to exercise authority over their members, while they remain members (and the state should make sure that people are free to leave groups when they wish to). Figgis laid considerable emphasis on the right belonging to a family of supervising the upbringing of children. Are we, he demanded, to have a system in which 'there shall be no intermediary between the State and the child', and where 'the claims alike of the religious body and of the family are to be set aside or rather denied?'[29] There is a tendency for the state to recognise only individuals in this matter of education, and to ignore the corporate claims of groups. He objected to an 'undenominationalism' in religious education, which teaches an etherial 'christianity' without reference to its embodiment in religious institutions. It attempts to do away with the church, and to consider only individuals. 'What,' he demanded,

> is the real objection to undenominationalism? ... It means the denial of religion except as an individual luxury or a State boon. ... The only home is the State. The State is to consider individuals only – and in no way to recognise churches for the educational period of the great majority of its citizens.[30]

As Mandell Creighton had pointed out in a previous decade, the church wants nothing more than a guarantee that church parents should have the rights to give their children a church education; and 'The same liberty which we ask for ourselves we ask for all others.'[31]

In addition to these rights a group should be allowed to determine the basis of its membership and to expel those who violate this basis. A free political community does not demand that individuals of whatever opinions should have the right of joining any group which they choose to join. There must be freedom for the group too – freedom to exclude those who violate its rules. 'The hopeless confusion of thought,' Figgis wrote,

> between the right of the individual to choose for himself and his right to remain in a society pledged to one thing while he himself is pledged to the opposite would be incredible were it not so widespread, and would be the death-blow of all the political clubs that ever existed.[32]

Figgis was particularly concerned to establish the right of religious groups to excommunicate or to expel members whose actions or expressed beliefs put them out of sympathy with the purpose for which the group exists. He maintained that the group itself should be the judge of these matters but as a churchman he urged that such powers be used only in the most extreme cases, as we shall see in chapter seven.

III

Laski accepted much of what Figgis wrote on the relationship between the group and the state. Yet there are certain significant differences between them. Instead of seeing the state as a peculiar kind of group – itself composed of societies – Laski seems to have regarded the state as just one among many groups in 'society'. The state, he wrote, 'is only a species of a larger genus.' We must therefore distinguish clearly between state and society; the allegiance of citizens to the state is, he asserted, less important than their allegiance to 'society as a whole'.[33] It is not at all clear, however, what this latter term refers to. What is the nature of this 'society' to which people owe allegiance? What are the interests which bind it together? What are the relationships existing between its members? As we have noted in a previous chapter, Laski maintained that the state has a personality, as any other group has. In the early twenties Laski's individualism forced him to modify these ideas about the personality of groups, and about the 'group will' which they were thought to possess. This will, insisted Laski, is nothing more than a number of individual wills acting in concert to achieve an agreed set of objects. The unity is not in the wills, but in the common object willed. And so there is nothing mysterious about the state; it is simply a group of people acting to realise a common purpose. 'One says America when one means a particular group of persons.'[34] A theory of the state, he maintained, is nothing more than a theory of the governmental act. He thus envisaged this group working together in a close way, accepting common aims and objectives, so that he could still use the concept of personality to apply to it.

What is the nature of this common objective which the state pursues? At times Laski wrote of the state as a 'great public service corporation' having a limited but important welfare function. On other occasions he saw a much more glorious role for the state; ideally it should be concerned with 'the highest life for its members'. In these writings the hands are often the hands of Léon Duguit, but the voice is unmistakably that of T. H. Green. Laski became more and more convinced, however, that whatever the ideal may be, the state as it actually exists in a capitalist society operates in such a way as to secure the interests of a section of the community only. Even in his early writings, he had maintained that the real source of authority in a state is with those who hold economic power, insisting that what confronts us is 'a complex of interests; and between not a few of them ultimate reconciliation is impossible'.[35]

Nevertheless Laski's doctrine of the state, as an ideal, implies a belief in the possibility of a common good, or a general will, representing the interests of the whole society, rather than those of the governmental clique. It has in fact been suggested that Laski's pluralism was partly the result of his belief that power in the liberal capitalist state of his day was in the hands of a small class; pluralism would do something to 'neutralise' the power of the state and thereby of that class.[36] It is clear from this discussion how Laski felt compelled to abandon the pluralist ideas which he had held in his early years, and to embrace a marxist notion of the state. If there is no common interest in a country, the state, conceived of as a body which is concerned with securing the highest life for all its members, can have no purpose, and without a common purpose it cannot exist as a social entity at all. But in fact states do exist, and they do have a common interest binding them together; but it is the interest of the ruling class, whose aim it is to maintain a capitalist society in being, and to guarantee their own position within it. In chapter three I concluded that Laski believed the state to lack the power always to impose its will upon other groups, and that he further believed that it is usually unwise of the state to attempt to do so.

Groups, in Laski's view, possess certain rights which would make it immoral as well as unwise for the state to interfere with their activities, in so far as these do not affect the rights of other groups or individuals. Yet he avoided a detailed discussion of the respective spheres of the state, the group and the individual, arguing that this should be left to 'the test of the event',[37] whatever this may mean. From his discussion of certain legal and political issues, like the *Free Church of Scotland* case, the *Taff Vale* decision, the *Kulturkampf* in Germany and the secularist movement in France, we may gather that he advocated a considerable degree of freedom for the group. With respect to economic life, he envisaged a devolution of industrial power to functional groups, which would have authority to determine matters relevant to their particular industry. This had already happened to a considerable extent in the medical and legal professions. Democracy ought, he held, to be extended from the political to the industrial field. Workers should be given a real voice in the choosing of management. He further believed that there should be set up a federal council of producers to regulate industrial and economic matters, along the lines recommended by some of the guild socialists. Laski nevertheless concluded in his *Grammar of Politics* that adjudication by an assembly based upon universal suffrage and upon geographical representation was 'the best method of making final decisions in the conflict of wills within the community'.[38]

It is necessary to refer briefly to the ideas of G. D. H. Cole, and to try to unravel some of the confusions and contradictions in his theories of the state. The central theme running through Cole's early writings is an insistence that 'the various industries and services ought to be democratically administered by those who work in them'.[39] But the trouble began when Cole tried to put forward some theory about the relationship which should obtain among these groups, and between groups and individual citizens.

The state was seen as being distinct from society, and as but one of the many associations within society; it is no more than the first among equals. The state is the organised machinery of government, and in the democratic countries of his day it rested upon the consent of citizens, secured on the basis of geographical representation. The state had in the past, according to Cole, made claims to exercise three kinds of function: economic, political and co-ordinational. He argued, however, that the state can properly concern itself only with those things which affect all members of the community in an equal way.

With respect to economic functions, there are, he maintained, two aspects: consumption and production. The state can rightly act as a regulator of the former, but not of the latter. It is not at all clear why Cole thought that matters of consumption affect all equally, while questions of production affect them differently. People do not consume the same amount of brandy, and some people abjure its use entirely.[40] By the political function of the state Cole meant the regulation of personal relationships in society, and he appears to have believed that this is a valid function of the state. Finally he denied that the state can properly perform the role of coordination; it cannot justly act as the adjudicator and adjustor of relationships between associations for the simple reason that, being itself an association of consumers, it would often have to act as judge in its own cause. He held a Rousseauite view of the sovereignty of the people, which cannot fully be represented by any association, and certainly not by the state. Nevertheless he did believe that a federal body, in which the state and other functional associations would be represented, would be able 'to speak in the name of our Sovereign',[41] and would act as the coordinator in a guild socialist society. He might just as well have said that the state should have a functional assembly, as well as an assembly based upon geographical representation, and then act as coordinator.

Bertrand Russell agreed with the majority of pluralist writers that the state should act as the coordinator and controller of groups. With Laski and Cole, he believed that the contemporary state acted, in practice, in the interests of a particular class and 'is largely concerned in defending the privileges of the rich'.[42] He argued that the substantive purposes of the state should as far as possible be conducted by independent organisations rather that by the state itself, and that the state should concentrate upon maintaining order:

> There ought to be a constant endeavour to leave the more positive aspects of government in the hands of voluntary organizations, the purpose of the State being merely to exact efficiency and to secure an amicable settlement of disputes, whether within or without its own borders. And with this ought to be combined the greatest possible toleration of exceptions and the least possible insistence upon uniform system.[43]

Russell maintained that the theory of democracy demands more than majority rule; it requires the division of the community into more or less autonomous groups, which should have the right to determine those matters which affect their members only. Actions of groups which are likely to have direct effects upon non-members should be regulated by the state.[44]

IV

The pluralist writings of Maitland, Figgis, Laski, Russell, Lindsay and others certainly amounted to a vigorous attack upon the sovereignty of the state, and on the inordinate claims for the state which were being made in many liberal and socialist circles. Ernest Barker was able to write in 1915 that 'the State has generally been discredited in England'.[45] It is manifestly true that pluralist theories involved an attack upon certain doctrines of the state.

From the preceding discussion it is clearly nonsense to talk of the pluralists' 'studied disregard of the state', as Adam Ulam does.[46] Some pluralists may well be criticised for an incoherent and shifting view of what the state ought to do, but they certainly did not disregard it. Ulam further assumes that pluralism implies the rejection of state regulation of groups. This, as we have seen, is untrue of most of the pluralist writers. Cole alone, of the writers considered in this book, specifically denied that the state ought to regulate and control the groups; yet he invented a federal body to do the job. The other writers thought that the specific function which distinguishes the state from other groups is that of regulation and control. What they denied was that the state is infallible; there may be occasions when groups and individuals ought to resist the commands of the state. It may be said that this opens the gate to anarchy. Laski grasped the nettle finally and admitted that 'at the root of our social system there is a contingent anarchy',[47] for the group and the individual can never properly hand over to the state their rights of resisting unjust laws. Figgis had made the same point:

> The only way to be sure an individual will never become a criminal is to execute him; the only way to secure a State from all danger on the part of its members is to have none. Every State is a synthesis of living wills. Harmony must ever be a matter of balance and adjustment, and this at any moment might be upset, owing to the fact that man is a spiritual being and not a mere automaton.[48]

I have observed in a previous section that many of the idealists were pluralists of a kind. They recognised the importance of social groups in the state. The pluralists, for their part, were not all philosophical pluralists, and even those who were did not accept the kind of ethical pluralism which denies the possibility of any right action by an individual in a given situation, resolving the individual into a number of 'roles'. How then did these pluralist writers differ from the Hegelians? They agreed that in an ideal situation the commands of the state would not conflict with the legitimate purposes of the groups, and that the individual would not be faced with a conflict in loyalties. But the pluralists denied that this total situation could ever be embodied institutionally in a single organ – the state.

Perhaps the most interesting contemporary criticisms of political pluralism came from M. P. Follett in her book *The New State*, published in 1918. She there argued that the pluralists were under the mistaken impression that unity involves absorption, whereas a true unity takes differences into account and transcends them by including them in a higher unity. This ultimate unity is the state, in its idea. The state is composed of individuals, and this ideal state 'demands the whole of me'; 'the home of my soul', she declared, 'is in the state'.[49] In an article published some months after her book, Follett maintained that the pluralists had based their theory on 'a nonexistent individual'.[50] There can never be a situation where the individual has to choose between loyalty to a group and loyalty to the state; anyone who thinks otherwise ignores the time factor, and forgets that community is 'a process'. There is, she insisted, no individual who stands outside and looks at his groups. Whether the person stands outside or not is doubtful, but the pluralist writers were surely correct in believing that a person may on certain occasions be forced to make a choice between his loyalty to his church or trade union, and the demands of the state. This is just the kind of decision which workers have to make if their union calls an illegal strike. It is the kind of decision which churchmen have to make when a government passes laws which they believe to be inconsistent with the rights of their church. Vivid examples of this kind of conflict can be seen in a little book edited by H. Gollwitzer called *Dying We Live*. In this book the case of C. F. Goerdeler, who put the interests of his city above what he regarded as the unjust claims of the state, is particularly relevant.

Follett was clearly wrong when she asserted that a person's loyalty to a particular group can never conflict with demands made by the state. She used as evidence the fact that a man can vote for one thing at a branch meeting of his trade union today, and for a party which opposes this policy tomorrow. This is, of course, true but it is not evidence for the assertion that individuals can never be faced with a moral dilemma of having to choose. A person may in this particular instance be acting irrationally, or may have changed his mind about the merits of the policy in question, or may have voted for the party despite its labour policy, or the situation itself may have changed overnight. But in certain cases of this kind the individual is most assuredly faced with a moral problem, and is obliged to act as far as possible in a rational and consistent manner. In her book, however, Follett seems to have been arguing merely that in the *ideal* situation the individual would not have to make these decisions – that in a 'true federalism' these problems ought not to arise. 'We should not,' she wrote, 'be obliged to choose between our different groups.'[51] With this the pluralists would have had no quarrel.

Adam Ulam makes what appears to be a similar criticism when he states that 'the dichotomy between the state and other social groups is as unreasonable as the one between the individual and the state'.[52] By 'dichotomy' Ulam obviously does not mean classificatory distinction; no one could possibly deny that there is such a useful classificatory distinction between the individual and the state, and most of the pluralists insisted on a classificatory distinction between the state and other groups (though, as we have seen, Laski did not). By 'dichotomy' he must mean antagonism. Some pluralists would have agreed that in an ideal situation there would be no such antagonism, but in the world as we find it, anyone who denies the possibility and indeed the likelihood of such an antagonism frequently manifesting itself is politically illiterate.

A more valid criticism of these pluralist writers would be that they failed to take seriously the challenge to individual freedom which might come from the group itself, and therefore hardly considered the criteria according to which the state might properly intervene in the internal affairs of a group to secure the rights of individual members. In general they believed that so long as the individual was formally free to leave the group, then any discipline to which he submitted was voluntary and not a matter with which the state should interfere. But there may be economic and social pressures which make it practically impossible for the individual to leave the group, and in this situation the only hope for the individual might be some kind of external intervention. An obvious example would be the 'closed shop' situation, where to leave the union would involve losing a job. What is more, if the ultimate purpose of the state is to allow for and encourage the development of human character, may it not be the case that there are certain groups whose ways of life and systems of belief cramp or cripple the characters of their members and which ought therefore to be interfered with by the state? The answer of pluralists to this is that as a general rule interference causes more harm than good, and therefore ought not to be encouraged. J. S. Mill had insisted that the state should never interfere with an adult civilised person for his own good. The pluralists adapted this dogma and applied it to the group: the state should not, as a general rule, interfere with the life of a group for the good of the group itself (nor for the good of its individual members). Ultimately the bad consequences of this kind of interference will outweigh the advantages.

A further criticism must be considered. It may not always be true that powerful groups are successful bulwarks against tyranny. By making an alliance with the leaders of the most powerful groups in the state the potential tyrant might be able to exercise a degree of social control which otherwise would be difficult to achieve. The machinery for such control is ready-made, and needs simply to be taken over by the aspiring tyrant. If he is able to enlist the support of the leaders of well-organised groups he might be saved the bother of exercising direct control over large numbers of citizens, much of which might be done for him by the group leaders. Yet these leaders will represent a continual threat to the tyrant's position unless he is able swiftly to replace them with persons selected by himself. Tightly controlled, hierarchically organised, well-disciplined groups may be a more formidable bulwark against the pretensions of a tyrant whose policies they reject than are loosely organised and less disciplined groups, but the former are potentially of more use to the tyrant once he is able to secure control of them. Opposition from the Roman Catholic Church may have been one of the principal factors in eventually destroying the Perón government in Argentina and the Trujillo regime in the Dominican Republic, but in Franco's Spain, Mussolini's Italy and Salazar's Portugal the church was a bastion of tyrannical regimes, and one of their principal instruments of social control. In the early years of the Duvalier regime, the church in Haiti was one of the most important centres of opposition to the claims and aims of the government. Once its hierarchy was changed in accordance with the wishes of the president, the church became a more or less docile instrument in the hands of the government.[53]

V

British political pluralism, it might be said, evolved in a situation where people normally belonged to a number of different groups and where group membership was 'cross-cutting'. The different loyalties of individuals tended not to reinforce one another, so that christians and non-christians might belong to the same trade union and people of different classes might belong to the same church. Yet some divisions did reinforce each other. Golf clubs in most parts of the country were restricted to members of particular social classes, and certain geographical districts were exclusively occupied by one class or another. The pattern of church membership was also characterised by a degree of reinforcement. If one compares the situation with that found in certain colonial and post colonial territories, however, there was not a high degree of segmentation.

Theories of social and cultural pluralism must clearly be distinguished from the political pluralism with which this book is principally concerned. J. S. Furnivall employed the term 'plural society' to describe a situation resulting from the European colonisation of tropical lands. A plural society, according to Furnivall, exists when there are a number of distinct groups living side by side, but separately; they meet only in the market-place. Religious, cultural, racial and linguistic divisions reinforce one another so that the groups form quite distinct segments. The political entity is held together, not by shared values or by common institutions, but by force, which is exercised by an elite of colonial administrators and their local collaborators who form a small but coherent minority. Furnivall also claimed that these segments into which plural societies are divided are not natural, organic associations, but are aggregates of individuals – crowds and not communities. The capitalist economic system which has been the invariable companion of modern imperial expansion led to the break-up of village life and of traditional ties.[54]

These ideas have been modified and developed by M. G. Smith, L. Kuper, P. L. van den Berghe and others, who apply the concept of social and cultural pluralism to the post-colonial nations of Africa and the Caribbean.[55] Curiously, Ralph Dahrendorf uses the term 'pluralism' in a completely opposite sense, and differentiates pluralism from what he calls 'superimposition', as ideal types of society. The latter type exists when all divisions among the population reinforce one another: political class conflict, industrial class conflict, regional conflicts, conflicts between town and country, possibly racial and religious conflicts all are superimposed so as to form a single and all-embracing antagonism.[56] In what he calls pluralist society, conflicts are dissociated and exclusion from the dominant or majority group in one sphere does not necessarily imply exclusion in other spheres. There is what another sociologist called a *web* of group affili-ations.[57] Thus a plural society, as understood by Furnivall and Smith, is practically equivalent to Dahrendorf's superimposed society, and is therefore opposed to his notion of a pluralist society.

How does the political pluralism of Figgis and his contemporaries relate to the social and cultural pluralism of Furnivall (or to the superimposed society of Dahrendorf)? As we have seen, when the British pluralists talked about groups in a state, they more or less assumed that most people would belong to a number of different groups which were not coterminous in their membership. They were looking principally at the situation in Britain, which was a relatively non-segmented country, rather than at plural soci-eties (in Furnivall's sense). Their theory was essentially normative (though, as we have seen in chapter four, it was to some extent based upon their assessment of social facts), while the theory of Furnivall and Smith is purely descriptive. Nevertheless it would be possible to apply the theory of political pluralism to those nations where group divisions are superimposed.

The likelihood of serious and violent conflict occurring in situations where divisions are superimposed might seem greater than it is in states where group affiliations overlap. Some may think it wise, in such countries, for the government to adopt a dynamic policy of national integration, using all the means in its power to inculcate a national culture and impose a uni-form system of values upon the population. According to this view, the political pluralism of Figgis could not safely be pursued in Furnivall's plural societies for it would exacerbate divisions. This argument appears to be one which is accepted, implicitly or explicitly, by a large number of the leaders of the new nations, who have been egged on by an almost endless procession of 'nation-building' political scientists, and 'missions' com-posed of international 'experts'. Now this is a false view of the situation, as some governments are beginning to discover. The attempt, made by a gov-ernment, to achieve national unity is often seen by minority groups as con-stituting a threat to their way of life or to their very existence. Thus by following a dynamic policy of national unification, a state may well bring upon itself that very disintegration which it was the purpose of the policy to avoid. The government will in any event find the task of maintaining order a difficult one; eventually the state may split into two or more parts. In some circumstances there may be no way of avoiding this. But so far as distinct segments exist within a single political entity, it behoves the gov-ernment to recognise their existence and allow these segments as much freedom to arrange their own affairs as is compatible with peace and order.

It is, however, by no means certain that segmented states (where group affiliations are superimposed) are more prone to violent conflict than those where there is a measure of cross-cutting in group affiliation. The most volatile situation may indeed exist where segmentation is breaking down and ethnic groups, for example, are beginning to move into jobs previously monopolised by other ethnic groups. The likelihood of conflict in these states needs to be assessed dynamically rather than statically.

Trinidad is sometimes referred to by anthropologists as a country which manifests a high level of social and cultural pluralism, and which therefore approaches the ideal type of a plural society, but there is in fact a considerable degree of overlap in group affiliations. Indian businessmen join with French Creoles, Syrians and Chinese in chambers of commerce; Portuguese, Chinese and Negroes are fellow Roman Catholics; there are rich hindus and poor hindus; urban muslims may join one political party while their rural co-religionists may support a rival party. No doubt, racial loyalties are often stronger than any others, though the Black Power movement of 1970 would seem to indicate that divisions among Afro-Trinidadians can at times be as significant as division along racial lines.[58]

The pluralist theories of Figgis and his contemporaries could certainly apply to a country like Trinidad. Racial, religious, cultural and economic groups must be recognised by the state and should be left to pursue those ends which they set for themselves, within a framework of order. Pluralists would encourage the groups themselves to be more active and creative, and not to spend all their energy persuading the government to do those things which they could perfectly well do for themselves. Cultural associations like the Chinese Association, the Himalaya Club and the Portuguese Association could play a much more constructive role in the country than they do. Why, until recently, has there been little support for forming an African Association? These cultural groups should not be regarded with suspicion by the state, nor should their exclusivism necessarily be condemned. Any rigorous efforts by the government to impose upon the population a single 'Creole' culture would be interpreted by minority groups as an attack upon their legitimate interests and distinct identity.

In recent decades ethnic minorities in Britain and other parts of western Europe have become increasingly self-conscious and ethnic questions have become salient. The children and grandchildren of early migrants, born in Britain, have experienced discrimination and have in many cases demanded a recognition of their distinctive interests. In particular muslims have asserted a right to run their own schools and to receive the same state aid as controlled and aided christian schools receive. These requests have been turned down on the stated ground that the schools do not reach the required educational standard. Muslim leaders have claimed, however, that the true reason for the refusal is ideological and religious. Some people have indeed opposed state recognition and assistance to such schools because they would be socially divisive, as sectarian schools have been in Northern Ireland. Other opponents argue that this is a christian country and that such recognition would subvert its character. Others again, more plausibly, maintain that Britain is effectively a secular state and that muslims are explicitly committed to undermining pluralism by the establishment of an islamic state, where ever this is possible.

In reply a pluralist would argue in the first place that separate schools would not necessarily reinforce hostility between muslims and others. Such recognition would in fact reassure muslims that their religion and culture is protected. The Northern Ireland parallel is misplaced, owing to the fact that there has never been any genuine attempt by the protestant majority in the province to establish a genuinely secular or pluralist state, giving equal rights to all citizens. The power-sharing experiment was never accepted by the majority of protestants. Separate schools in the province are just part of a system of domination, where the state is seen not as a structure enabling the different groups to live their own lives and pursue ends which they choose for themselves, but as a 'pork-barrel', providing jobs, contracts and other forms of patronage to a particular section of the population to the virtual exclusion of others. Some of these issues will be taken up in the next chapter.

Secondly the argument against state aid for muslim schools, based on the idea of a christian society, fails to recognise that the state today is effectively secular, and that the christian influence is largely historical. Also the supposed christian values that remain a part of public life are generally values that muslims can also endorse. The final point, that muslims are committed to the idea of an islamic state, refusing to give ideological backing to pluralism, is misconceived. In the first place the establishment of an islamic state in Britain is, as all parties recognise, inconceivable. Secondly, muslims are perfectly prepared to give practical backing in Britain today to a secular pluralist state, which treats all religious groups equally; to demand anything more than this is, as I shall argue in the next chapter, unreasonable. This leads on to the question, what are the ideological and practical conditions necessary for the establishment and preservation of a secular state?

6 The Ideological Foundations of a Secular State

One of the consequences of political pluralism, in the form advocated by J. N. Figgis, was an acceptance of the idea of a secular state. A particular church is seen, socially and politically, as merely one among many religious, non-religious and anti-religious groups in the state and, as such, it can claim no special privileges. With respect to religion, the secular state adopts a self-consciously neutral stance. A secular state of this kind should be distinguished from a *secularist* state, and from a 'secularised society'. The latter refers to a situation allegedly found in the modern western world, where the population has generally abandoned the practice of religion and belief in the supernatural, seeking for 'scientific' or natural explanations for what occurs.[1] Some modern theologians and publicists have attempted to translate the christian gospel into secular language and concepts, attempting to address a situation summarised in 1922 by G. K. Chesterton, 'the modern world has really come of age'.[2] Other sociologists reject the idea of modern secularisation.[3]

A secularist state, like that in France in the early years of the present century or in the countries of Eastern Europe under communism, is militantly anti-religious, and aims to suppress or inhibit religious groups, thereby seeking to hasten the process of secularisation. Sometimes such a secularist state may evolve into a secular state – as in France itself, or in Mexico – when governments lose their anti-clerical impetus and accept religious groups as legitimate, without giving any of them special privileges. Again a secular or even a secularist state may exist when the population is very far from being 'secularised', as in Poland before the fall of communism. In such a state adherence to religious movements and profession of beliefs may be relatively high, as in India and possibly the United States. A state positively committed to a particular religion or church might be called a confessional state. In this chapter I shall consider the idea of a secular state and look at the supposed need for some kind of common values, political culture, public philosophy or civil religion to support the existence of a secular, pluralist state.

96

I

In medieval Christendom there was very little conception of two distinct societies, the church and the state. Church and state were two aspects of a single christian commonwealth. The dichotomy was not between two distinct bodies, but between two sets of officials, two rival hierarchies, representing *regnum* and *sacerdotium*. This assumption was made by all medieval thinkers, even by anti-clerical writers like Marsilius, whose distinctive position was simply that, within the single commonwealth, lay people, and particularly the king, should have increased power. The same would hold with respect to Erastus.[4] This notion of a single society was perpetuated in the post-reformation period, particularly among Anglicans and Lutherans. 'With this view,' Figgis asserted, 'either an ecclesiastical or a civil tyranny is almost inevitable.'[5]

Figgis traced a new view to the Presbyterian and Jesuit writers of the sixteenth and seventeenth centuries, who, when in a minority, developed the idea of a church as one group in a secular state, in order to secure toleration for themselves.[6] Among Anglican writers, from Thorndike through Stillingfleet to Warburton, he saw a growing awareness of the church as a distinct society. The Oxford Movement had essentially involved the demand for spiritual independence for the church, as a distinct body from the state and part of a catholic and apostolic church, spatially universal and stretching back to the time of the apostles. As Laski observed, 'Tractarianism is essentially the plea of the corporate body which is distinct from the State to a separate and free existence'. He saw Figgis's theory as 'the lineal successor to Pusey's tract on the royal supremacy'.[7] This is only partially so, as most Tractarians would have rejected Figgis's championing of a secular state. He insisted that all talk about a national religion was, by the beginning of the twentieth century, misleading and dangerous. The Church of England was no longer co-extensive with the nation. Toleration which, as we have already noted, was achieved largely through the demands made by intransigent religious minorities, had itself led to the multiplication of sects. 'So far as numbers go,' declared Figgis,

> the Christian Church is not more than a section of the modern world. ... People dislike calling it a sect or a denomination, but it can be nothing else, so long as there are large numbers who repudiate all part or lot in it, and in many cases detest its ideals.[8]

The only way to achieve a national religion would be on the basis of a highest common factor of the religious beliefs of the people. It would be a religion of disembodied ideas, shorn of the supernatural, and would end with 'the establishment and endowment of the Pleasant Sunday Afternoon'.[9]

The nation was, then, no longer christian in any significant sense; this was the fact. But Figgis went on to argue that a tolerant secular state, which admits the possibility of competing religious groups within it, is the best kind of state which can be hoped for in this fallen world. The state should allow religious groups to exist and to order their own affairs without interfering. These religious groups should in turn be able to prescribe their creeds and must have the right to determine the limits of their membership. But they must not try to force upon the whole nation religious practices or moral prohibitions which stem from their peculiar beliefs. 'We cannot eat our cake and have it,' he wrote,

> We cannot claim liberty for ourselves, while at the same time proposing to deny it to others. If we are to cry 'hands off' to the civil power in regard to such matters as marriage, doctrine, ritual, or the conditions of communion inside the Church – and it is the necessary condition of a free religious society that it should regulate these matters – then we must give up attempting to dictate the policy of the State in regard to the whole mass of its citizens.[10]

When judging political questions we should do so as citizens, and not as churchpeople, remembering that many fellow citizens are not even christians, let alone members of the Church of England. As citizens, he maintained, christians have no right to appeal to motives or ideals which are distinctively christian. It would be quite wrong for the church to advocate a policy which is specifically christian in a community which is heterogeneous in religion.[11] Figgis insisted that as clear a distinction between sin and crime, between private morality and law, should be drawn as is possible. It would, for example, be a mistake for the church to attempt to impose upon the nation its own view of marriage, though if it chooses to forbid its members to remarry after divorce that is no business of the state. 'Primarily,' Figgis wrote, 'the business of Christians is with the moral standard of their own society and with themselves as its members. The raising of that will gradually bring about the elevation of the great mass of those who do not belong to it.' In the modern secular state no policy can properly be recommended on christian grounds alone.[12]

In recent years some American moral theologians have addressed this issue. A radical view on the matter has been stated by John Howard Yoder in a number of his works. Christian morals have evolved within the context of a christian community and can apply only to christians. It is not the duty of christians to improve the world or to impose their ideas about right and wrong on unbelievers. Stanley Hauerwas has developed these ideas, challenging the notion that christian social ethics is primarily an attempt to make the world more peaceable or just, 'the first social ethical task of the church is to be the church – the servant community'.[13] He has been criticised widely for encouraging christians to withdraw from public life, or insisting that if they do engage in politics they should do so on purely secular assumptions; he argues that it is the role of christians to help the world to see itself as God's creation, but not to impose its values on a secularised population. Christian morals, these 'post-liberal' thinkers argue, can apply only to christian churches and cannot, in a secular state, validly been appealed to in debates about public policy.[14]

Christians, Figgis argued, must emphasise the distinctiveness of the gospel and he denounced those who wish to cut and trim the christian story to fit in with the latest secular trends, removing the supernatural and other-worldly elements. His principal criticism of George Tyrrell's *Christianity at the Crossroads* was its assumption that 'wherever Christianity conflicts with our modern scheme it must be trimmed to make the two square. This view,' he went on, 'seems to be quite without ground'; why should we believe in the 'infallibility of the modern Western mind'?[15] In a recent and important essay George Lindbeck has criticised churchpeople for an often heedless attempt to translate the christian gospel into the language and concepts of the latest secular trend, both at the level of theology and of more popular apologetics. As some of the Oxford Movement thinkers argued, there should be 'reserve' in communicating the gospel.[16] 'The post-liberal method of dealing with this problem,' writes Lindbeck,

> is bound to be unpopular among those chiefly concerned to maintain or increase the membership and influence of the church. This method resembles ancient catechesis more than modern translation. Instead of redescribing the faith in new concepts, it seeks to teach the language and practices of the religion to potential adherents. ... Pagan converts to the catholic mainstream did not, for the most part, first understand the faith and then decide to become Christians; rather the process was reversed: they first decided and then understood.[17]

How do these 'sectarian' tendencies affect the prospects of a pluralist and secular state? Figgis did not advocate that christians should withdraw from politics, and it would seem that his views would require the possibility of a secular morality being adopted by the state – based, perhaps, on natural law and distinct from specifically christian morality. The law should not necessarily forbid divorce, but it should certainly condemn murder. He believed that citizens can unite upon matters of political ethics with those who differ widely in their theology or in their metaphysics, and argued that the notion of a secular or pluralist state is one which, though demanded by christian ethics, could also be accepted by non-christians. But what is the nature of this secular morality which governs the actions of the state? Unfortunately, Figgis was not sufficiently explicit on this matter. One possible answer would be that there is a natural law which is conceptually distinct from the revealed law (though partially overlapping in content). It is a law that applies to all people because of their shared humanity, being discoverable by reason, which is our common possession. Natural law according to this view provides the basis of that common good which it is the duty of the state to realise. But Figgis did not believe that it was the function of the state to achieve some substantive common good for its members; this was to be achieved by those smaller associations and groups to which all citizens belong. The state should simply seek to maintain in existence a situation where there is as much freedom as possible for groups and individuals to pursue ends which they choose. This would imply taking steps to defend itself from enemies without and within. In addition to settling disputes between its constituent groups and protecting citizens against tyrannical groups, the responsibilities of the state must include a common foreign and defence policy.

II

A more fundamental problem, however, concerns the ethical basis of this very theory of the state. By what kind of arguments can pluralists defend the pluralist state? The basis must be wide (though not absolutely unlimited), the pluralist state may well be compatible with many ethical theories, but it is surely the case also that it is incompatible with some.

Natural law may indeed provide a basis for that mutual respect for one another and a justification of the conviction that people best develop their characters by making free decisions about the style of life they will lead and what associations they will join. These beliefs provide a rationale of a pluralist state. Perhaps the existence of objective moral principles provide the only long-term and solid rationale for such a state. But there may be numerous other reasons for groups to defend such a structure. Some may just enjoy the freedom it provides and be indifferent about truth. Others would perchance wish to impose their own way if they were strong enough, but seeing no prospects for becoming a majority are prepared to settle for a pluralist state as a second best. This latter position is similar to the so-called 'thesis-hypothesis' position adopted by many conservative catholics

and some contemporary muslims. It is important for those who are pluralists by conviction to make a pragmatic alliance with these others in order to
protect the pluralist structure of the state. But is this a firm enough basis for
pluralism? Must there not be certain widely shared or common values
among the people in such a state, and must not the state itself be committed
to certain ideas of the good life, or at least certain moral beliefs about what
is right or wrong?

These issues have been aired in recent years in the debate between so-
called 'communitarians' and liberals. The former have criticised liberals
for trying to establish a neutral state, with no commitment to any substantive idea about what is good or bad, apart from acceptance of a certain
formal notion of justice, as classically set forth by John Rawls.[18] Communitarians, like Charles Taylor and Michael Sandel, defend the idea of a
substantive common good which the state must be concerned to promote.[19]
Pluralists would clearly renounce the communitarian vision. Though agreeing with some communitarian criticisms of liberal individualism, they
would firmly reject the assumption that the modern state can be or should
become a 'community' pursuing a concrete and substantive idea of the
good life. Attempts to realise this kind of polity in the modern world will
inevitably tend towards totalitarianism.

Pluralists would accept the liberal claim that a neutral state is a desirable
goal, with groups pursuing their own ideas of the good life within a framework of order and mutual toleration. Some would, as we have seen, insist
that this ideal is itself based upon certain moral values (such as respect for
the development of human personality) and that these values might on
occasion influence the process of adjudication between the rival claims
being made by groups in the state. Liberals insist that a formal principle of
justice (involving equal consideration to all persons) enables the state to
arbitrate without contravening the canons of moral neutrality, but in such
complex problems as abortion, there is disagreement on what constitutes a
human person. Are unborn children persons or potential persons and do
they merit equal consideration? It is not possible to say that those groups
which choose to practise abortion can be permitted to do so, while those
opposed to it may refrain. Those opposed are opposed to anyone practising
it, as most people are in the case of murder. Pluralists are inclined to admit
the need for certain moral values, beyond the formal principle of equal consideration, to influence the adjudications of the state, on certain occasions.
A group devoted to child molesting, for example, would be outlawed, for
children must surely be protected but it is difficult to see how such outlaw-
ing would be justified on the liberal principle of moral neutrality. We don't
'protect' children from things which are good for them. The state must

adopt some idea of good and evil in order for the notion of 'protection' to be meaningful.

III

Figgis's theory of a secular state appears to assume that christians and non-christians can agree on a broad political ethic, while disagreeing in their theological or metaphysical pictures of the world. The kind of politics we pursue or advocate certainly depends, in some degree, on the moral beliefs to which we subscribe, and our moral beliefs are often closely connected to our religious beliefs. Political ends are not self-evident, and politics is not an autonomous activity. It depends upon moral ideas.[20] But is it possible to arrive at generally agreed moral ideas – a social ethic – which is unrelated to theological or metaphysical beliefs? J. F. Stephen denied that you can reconcile the morals of Jesus Christ with the theology of Julius Caesar, and Figgis seems to have agreed with him. He praised Nietzsche for seeing 'that it was hopeless to maintain the Christian standards apart from the Christian faith'.[21] Discussing the period when Matthew Arnold thought that christian morals could be retained while dispensing with dogma, he wrote,

> Differences of creed have at length revealed a yawning chasm between our moral ideals. Apologists of those days were scorned as narrow-minded for venturing the view that Christian ethics were bound up with Christian dogma, and that with the decay of the one the other could not long maintain its hold. What they said, however, has come true.[22]

Might it not be the case that, when he denied the likelihood of retaining a christian morality after the theological foundation has been removed, Figgis was referring solely to individual morality? This cannot be so; for one thing it is difficult to separate personal from social morality in this way, and he explicitly stated that christian ethics 'form the only enduring basis of a noble social life'.[23]

If then our ethical ideals depend intimately on our theological beliefs, if scepticism in the one will lead to corruption of the other, then the prospects of a secular state can hardly be said to be hopeful. If indeed there is no possibility of christians and non-christians agreeing on the moral and political principles which lie at the basis of our social life, how are we to ensure the future of that idea of the state which we have called pluralist? If this pluralism does rest upon a christian ethic, which in turn relies upon christian dogma, what will happen to the state when the dogma is no longer believed? Might it not be that if Figgis's theory of the dependence of ethics on theology be true, then the worst possible step for the church to take is the very one he appears to have advocated, namely accepting the position of a mere sect and ceasing to prescribe rules for those outside its borders? If our social ethics depend upon belief in God, should not the church continue to impose (as far as it can) its dogma upon the nation as a whole. Should it not maintain and increase its control of education, ensure that the legal system favours religion and attack the growth of secular thought with all the weapons in its power? If Figgis really believed with Mandell Creighton that it is a fallacy to hold 'that Christian ethics could stand by themselves apart from Christian doctrine',[24] should he not have accepted the 'christian nation' theory which Creighton himself held, rejecting the secular state as disastrous?

Alternatively, if he wished to accept the secular state, would it not have been more consistent to have adopted Lord Acton's optimism about the possibility of a basically christian social ethic divorced from christian theology? If we deny God, Acton held, whole branches of deeper morality lose their sanction, yet an adequate system of social ethics can be maintained without recourse to theology. Acton's admiration for George Eliot was enormous, and the reason was quite as much moral as literary. She was for him the perfect atheist, and her writings demonstrate how it is possible to have morals without religion. For Acton, ethical theory was basic, and religious doctrines were to be judged mainly in terms of their moral content. Religious differences do not necessarily imply a diversity of moral principles. With these ideas it is, of course, quite possible and legitimate to advocate a secular theory of the state, in which this non-theological morality could be assumed as the basis of a liberal politics. It therefore looks as though Figgis must sacrifice one of his masters, and it is most likely that he would have given up Creighton's idea rather than the concept of a secular state, and have argued for a minimum of ethical autonomy.

It might, however, be said that, so far from good social ethics being the invariable companion of christian theology, immoral social practices like persecution and all sorts of bigotry have not only been held by christians to be a right but a duty, imposed upon them by their faith. When the church has been politically influential and strong it has often been morally corrupt, accommodating itself to the standards of the world around it. It may be the case that not only can christian morality be held apart from the public profession of christian dogma, but that it flourishes best when the church has to struggle to maintain its faith. Indeed, Figgis himself recognised this in some of his writings. He thought that the effect on the church of the gradual dechristianising of social life is by no means wholly bad. The church has lost in extension, but it has gained in intensity. 'I always feel more inclined to regret that the Church is so big,' he declared, 'than to be sorry that so many have frankly given up a profession which is at variance with the whole structure of their lives.'[25] Although the church is no mere sect of devout persons, much harm is done by making christianity so wide that all are included whatever their beliefs. We cannot expect the church to contain everyone. It is leaven not the whole lump. The best we can hope for is a religion which makes a universal appeal. 'There will be fewer', he told a Cambridge congregation,

> that comes of liberty. For two hundred years religious freedom has been developing. With this, the proportion of any one religious body to the whole must be smaller.[26]

Figgis's position may then be summarised thus:

- a secular, pluralist state can subsist in a situation where there are *different* moral beliefs and practices
- the most *solid* basis for such a state is a widespread commitment to the importance of freedom, of conscience and the development of human character;
- this moral position is one which has developed *historically* within a christian context and on the basis of christian dogma;
- it is therefore important for christian faith to continue to be a powerful influence in the state;
- this is best achieved by 'a free church in a free state';
- establishment, in contrast, weakens the distinctive witness of the church; and the political power or influence implied by such a formal involvement with the state leads the church away from its belief in those values which form the basis of a secular, pluralist state;
- though christianity may be the most satisfactory and solid basis on which to maintain a pluralist state, it is important for christians, on pragmatic grounds, to join those of different or even conflicting religious and moral beliefs to defend the structure of a secular, pluralist state, which they all find congenial for a variety of different reasons.

The mass of people have become dechristianised despite the church's clinging on to the old notion of a christian commonwealth. The church must acknowledge the secular state and do the best it can in the situation. Christian theology has a better chance of surviving when a vigorous church lives in a secular state than when a flabby church exists as part of a nominally christian commonwealth. Figgis had little faith in 'diffused christianity'. Yet he firmly rejected the assertion that the world of his day had become secularised and had rejected religion *tout court*. People were turning to all sorts of bizarre religion and superstitious practice.

IV

The theory of a secular state has continued to be a matter of acute controversy in many countries. In the United States, for example, there have been wide disagreements about the interpretation of the constitutional provision, forbidding the establishment of religion. Symbolic issues like prayers in state schools and the official use of the phrase 'In God we trust' have revealed important theoretical disagreements about the notion of a pluralist or secular state. While a few have demanded the frank adoption of christianity by the state, others, accepting the basically secular nature of the state, have called for some kind of 'public philosophy', or even 'civil religion' to supply and propagate an ideological and quasi-religious basis to the liberal pluralist state, sustaining that value consensus which is the allegedly necessary condition for the existence of pluralism.

There is an ascending hierarchy of supposed necessary conditions for the existence of a secular pluralist state. Some people simply assert that *common values* are necessary; others claim that such values must necessarily find their roots in a *public philosophy*; others again insist that such a public philosophy must, if it is not to be a mere system of abstract ideas, involve some kind of *civil religion*, providing symbols and pieties which engage, not merely the intellect but the imagination and the emotions of citizens. Finally there are those who point out that an effective religion must be embodied in an institution, however loosely organised, and this requires the existence of a *national church*. This entails something of a paradox: in order to maintain a secular state in existence it is necessary to have in place a national church which is itself precluded by the very notion of a secular state.

If by value consensus we mean agreement on the more profound issues about the meaning and substantive content of the good life, then it is unlikely that, if this situation obtains, the state will be pluralist at all, for pluralism implies likely disagreement about these ultimate values. If by value consensus we mean simply an agreement to accept a structure within which diverse groups may each pursue a distinctive way of life, and common procedures for settling disputes and drawing boundaries, then it is not at all clear why such an agreement must be rooted in a public philosophy or a civil religion. Members of a 'society' (like the Society for the Protection of Wild Birds) must indeed share substantive values, possibly implying the acceptance of a common philosophy, but there is no reason to think that the modern state is or can become such a society, nor that it requires anything more than the very restricted notion of common values outlined above in order to subsist. I shall return to this issue in due course.

John Dewey and Walter Lippmann were among the most vociferous American writers maintaining the need for a public philosophy. Only such an ideology of humanism and moderation is able to sustain the common values thought to be necessary for the existence of a pluralist state. Dewey in *A Common Faith*, envisaged a quasi religion which would be taught in schools and generally promoted by the organs of public culture. Like Lippmann's idea of a public philosophy it assumes agreement on basic moral values in the face of widespread disagreements about religion. Lippmann's appeal was to a higher law, which has close affinities with the classical idea of natural law. It involves a tradition of 'civility' which excludes the possibility of arbitrary action by those in power.[27] Lippmann believed that this public philosophy had disappeared from the USA, leaving 'a great vacuum in the public mind, yawning to be filled'.[28] His concept of a public philosophy, however, would appear to undermine a pluralist state, in any radical sense of this term. It might allow for a plurality of groups and associations, but not a plurality of values and beliefs. In an attempt to undermine this criticism, Richard John Neuhaus argues that a public philosophy should incorporate the notion of pluralism:

> A public philosophy will not be embarrassed by, nor will try to override, the fact that we are a society of many societies, a community of many communities. ... Such a public philosophy will not speak of *the people* in the singular but of people in their astonishingly diverse particularities; it will speak less of *the public* than of the myriad publics which it is the obligation of the state to respect and to serve.[29]

Critics would, however, demand how such a single public philosophy is possible in the context of so many publics. If we define pluralism as involving the coexistence within the state 'of groups holding divergent and possibly conflicting views on ultimate issues of human destiny',[30] is there any likelihood or even possibility of such a philosophy emerging or surviving?[31]

The sociologist Robert Bellah has been among the leading proponents of a civil religion, combining prescription and description in his discussion of the concept. He points to certain customs and practices in the United States which suggest that something like a civil religion is already in place. His apparent wish is to indicate its existence and also to defend it. One of Bellah's disciples writes 'a pluralistic, democratic society cannot exist without such a binding ingredient as civil religion provides'.[32] Rousseau and Robespierre had already insisted that a public religion is a necessary foundation for the state. But the kind of state they wished to promote was very far from pluralism. Proponents of civil religion realise that the prospects for a public philosophy as a collection of intellectual principles are not bright. This was a problem humanists like T. H. Huxley had to face in the late nineteenth century. The rational element in human nature is only one of the forces, and not usually the most powerful, affecting human behaviour. It was for this reason many humanists set up ethical 'churches', with all the paraphernalia of a religious cult.

The attempt to promote a civil religion giving supernatural legitimation to the state has been denounced as idolatrous or henotheistic, crediting the state with an ultimacy which can only properly be ascribed to God. Such a tendency, characteristic of many 'primitive' communities was evident in the National Socialist and Fascist regimes of the 1930s. It may also take a 'democratic' form, as in such movements as 'Americanism'; Thomas Davidson, for example, proclaimed that in 'teaching children to lead the life of true Americans, we shall be leading them in the paths of eternal life'.[33]

Finally there are those who, recognising that disembodied religious and philosophical beliefs are largely powerless, argue in favour of a national church establishment. S. T. Coleridge in the nineteenth century and T. S. Eliot in the twentieth defended such an institution. For Coleridge the national church (which he distinguished from the christian church, though he believed that in England by a happy accident they were effectively the same) was manifested in a clerisy of intellectuals, teachers and clergy whose job it was to maintain and develop the national culture.[34] Eliot told the Malvern Conference of 1941 that it is 'the task of the Church to christianize the State and society'.[35] But neither of these poets was defending a pluralist state, as we understand the term.[36]

In a recently published work, the political philosopher John Rawls has (belatedly) recognised the 'pluralist' nature of the modern state and has adapted the theory – which he originally put forward in his classical work on *A Theory of Justice* – taking this into account. The modern state is characterised by an ineradicable plurality of 'incompatible yet reasonable comprehensive doctrines'. The kind of moral consensus generally assumed in his earlier work is seen to be unrealistic. The Harvard philosopher envisages the state as composed of citizens, 'reasonable and rational, as well as free and equal', but who hold a 'diversity of reasonable religious, philosophical, and moral doctrines'. Though they differ in fundamental world views, they may each find a place in their system for a belief in toleration and for the legitimacy of a set of democratic institutions designed to adjudicate conflicting claims. Rawls believes that in order to achieve stability there must be not merely the acceptance of a constitution as a *modus vivendi*, but a constitutional consensus. This requires that over time 'the initial acquiescence in a constitution satisfying these liberal principles of justice develops into a constitutional consensus in which those principles themselves are affirmed'. From here he suggest the possibility of what he calls an 'overlapping consensus', whereby the different comprehensive doctrines endorse, each from its own point of view, the idea of justice as fairness which underlies a liberal constitution.[37]

V

Perhaps the most striking aspect of this Rawlsian pluralism is its idealist character. It is essentially a pluralism of ideas or doctrines or beliefs. In fact the pluralism which politicians have to face in the real world is a pluralism of groups, associations, churches and other religious communities, ethnic and cultural clubs and organisations. The pluralism in Northern Ireland, for example, is not a pluralism of doctrines and ideas, but of Orange lodges and Catholic clubs, of school and neighbourhood communities. Some of these groups indeed adhere to a particular set of doctrines, but this is hardly what binds them together. Their solidarity is based rather on symbols, flags, historical myths and other non-rational factors. So long as we view the state as made up of rational and reasonable, free and equal individuals holding a plurality of doctrines we shall misconceive the nature of politics. The best that can be hoped for in a situation like this, and we might add in other parts of the United Kingdom, is a *modus vivendi*, according to which these groups are willing, for different reasons, to acquiesce in a constitutional and legal system which enables disputes to be settled in some kind of orderly way. Pluralism does not require consensus.

This point is forcefully argued by Nicholas Rescher in a recent monograph. Again, however, he is thinking of a pluralism of ideas and beliefs, rather than groups and associations and in a typically academic manner believes that methodological pluralism is more important than a pluralism of substantive positions. He argues that to accept a pluralism of cognitive and normative doctrines, and even to recognise the rationality of those positions which differ from one's own, implies neither scepticism nor a relativistic indifferentism about the truth of such doctrines. He stresses for example that a person who has had different experiences from me will *rationally* hold moral or cognitive positions different from mine. 'Evaluative disagreement,' he writes, is not only pervasive but is in fact rationally inevitable because rational people's values are bound to reflect their circumstantially conditioned experiences, and circumstances differ. Accordingly, the impersonal universality of the principles of reason does not mean that an evaluative consensus can be expected – or demanded.[38]

He wishes, nevertheless, to say that a person's own perspective must be seen by him- or herself as 'rationally superior to others'.[39]

Rescher's critique of consensus as a criterion of truth or rationality is convincing. He also echoes J. S. Mill in arguing that 'dissensus and variety of opinion and valuation provides for enhancement rather than impoverishment of intellectual culture' and that a state that can come to terms with diversity 'is enriched by it'.[40] If this is indeed so, it is not clear why he concedes a few pages earlier that consensus is 'inherently preferable to acquiescence when other things are equal'. At all events he believes that consensus is not necessary for a stable political order, believing that a practical acquiescence in the constitutional and legal machinery for settling disputes is quite sufficient. A willingness to 'live and let live' is as much as we can want. Unfortunately Rescher fails to distinguish the particular role of the state from that of the groups within it, nor does he see that the kind of *modus vivendi* of which he speaks is possible only in a state where substantive goods are pursued by the groups and associations within it, rather than the state itself attempting to impose its own conceptions of a substantive common good on its citizens. The more the state attempts to do, the less chance there is of maintaining the kind of acquiescence which he rightly defends.

VI

Although Figgis's theories had no spectacular results, there are indications of a gradual adoption of his notion of a secular state. 'All students of the subject,' wrote a later author on church and state, 'must be consciously or unconsciously influenced in what they write by the many-sided contributions of the late Dr Figgis.'[41] His ideas were to some extent put into practice by William Temple and the *Life and Liberty Movement*, which demanded more self-government for the church. It was to a considerable degree due to the agitation of such men as Temple and Sheppard in this movement that the *Enabling Act* of 1919 was passed, allowing the Church Assembly to present to Parliament legislation on church affairs which must either be accepted or rejected *in toto*, no amendments being allowed. In 1921 the *Scottish Church Act* used language which is reminiscent of that which Figgis had used in this context. In particular, article five spoke of the 'inherent right' of the church to live its own life, free from state interference.

In England the Church Assembly made use of its powers in presenting to Parliament a revised Prayer Book in 1927, which was rejected by the latter body. A further effort was made in 1928 with a slightly different book, but this too was turned down. The action of Parliament led to renewed demands for disestablishment and freedom for the church. Bishop Charles Gore pleaded that Figgis's theory of the place of groups in the state should be accepted by the 1935 Commission on church and state. The state has, argued Gore, been disloyal to the church; in the army, in prisons and in schools the established church is treated as just another religious group. 'We are,' he pointed out, 'finding ourselves disestablished almost everywhere except in the lunatic asylums.'[42] The Commission decided not to recommend disestablishment, but an increased freedom within the establishment, though the details need not detain us here. Later commissions on church and state have recommended more independence for the church in such matters as the appointment of bishops, and the control of liturgy and doctrinal formularies. A later commission was clearly divided on some of the most important theoretical issues at stake. One section of the commission stated categorically that 'the State is a secular state', and that bishops of the Church of England should no longer be selected by the Queen on the advice of the Prime Minister.[43]

What I am here maintaining is that a pluralist state can exist very well without an established church, a civil religion or a public philosophy, and that if a value consensus is necessary, it is only in the most restricted sense of that term – viz.: the acceptance of that peculiar concept of the state as regulator, pursuing no substantive purposes of its own, which is inherent to the very idea of pluralism. People may join together in defending such a state for many different (and even conflicting) reasons. It is, nevertheless, important that there are some individuals and groups who are prepared to defend a pluralist state on moral or on religious grounds. Groups likely to do this are those which are spiritually vigorous and ecclesiastically autonomous, often called 'sects' by defenders of religious establishments. Nevertheless Figgis rightly argued that in Britain 'disestablishment' was a peripheral issue, a fact well illustrated in the *Free Church of Scotland* Case, where a non-established church received from the courts scant recognition of its status as a living body. The real issue is not establishment or disestablishment, but an acceptance of the inherent rights of religious (and other) groups to live their own lives and pursue purposes chosen by their members, without hindrance from the state.

7 Authority in the Church

The structure of authority within associations and groups is a question distinct from that of authority in the state, of which they are a part. It is perfectly possible to envisage a pluralist state composed largely of groups whose organisation is centralised and hierarchical, with little place for participation of their members in the policy and management of the group. Although a pluralist state would not attempt to impose a particular form of government on its constituent associations, its advocates would perceive a danger in the authoritarian mentality which such hierarchically organised groups might engender – a mentality which could ultimately undermine the necessary conditions of the pluralist state itself. In the first place, Figgis and the other writers with whom we are principally concerned in this book, argued that the pluralist state is justified ultimately by the likelihood that it will maximise individual freedom and thereby allow persons to develop their characters; they cannot therefore totally ignore the possible threat to this freedom which might emanate from the groups which compose such a state. Pluralists might otherwise justifiably be accused of handing over the individual from one tyranny to another. Secondly, it is likely that many of the arguments which the pluralists used against a concentration of power in the state will apply to the large associations which are found within the state.

An American writer has distinguished between the 'pluralist' – 'arguing for the autonomy of the private association from the absolutism of the state' – and the 'liberal pluralist' – who insists also on 'the independence of the individual from the absolutism of the group'.[1] Other contemporary American writers generally sympathetic to the pluralist position have warned against the danger of group tyranny. Philip Selznick observes that 'the private organisation can be more oppressive than the state',[2] and goes on to consider ways in which legal ideals can be applied to the group life of the modern state. Small voluntary groups are able to evolve a democratic and participatory form of internal government, but once groups acquire a sizable administrative staff, and develop what Selznick calls 'a dependent constituency', the situation is likely to change. The bureaucrats become the central feature of the organisation and the members become mere clients. The voluntary nature of the association is eroded as systems of private taxation and various types of sanction are introduced and 'as the effective enterprise, carried forward by the administrative organization, gains the capacity to perpetuate its existence'.[3] It is therefore not out of place in the present volume to take the problem of authority and power in the church, as viewed by one of the leading pluralist writers, as a case study in the more general problem of the internal government of groups in a pluralist state.

I

Like Joseph de Maistre in the previous century, Figgis saw the problem of authority in the church as analogous to that of authority in the state, though in their evaluation of the situation these men were totally opposed to each other. '*Infallibility* in the spiritual order, and *sovereignty* in the temporal order,' declared the Savoyard ultramontane,

> are two words perfectly synonymous. Each expresses that high power which dominates all others, from which all others derive, which governs and is not governed, which judges and is not judged ... because all government is absolute.[4]

Figgis saw ultramontanism in the church as 'a theory analogous to that which we have been combating in the State,' and quoted Hobbes's discription of the Papacy as 'The ghost of the Roman Empire sitting crowned on its grave'.[5] He insisted that ideas of state sovereignty are closely linked to false views about authority in the church, describing how the 'civilian' doctrine of the emperor as the source of all law had been applied in the church. 'That notion of authority', he wrote,

> which reaches its limit in Ultramontanism is, at bottom, a false legalism, accepted from the antique city state, to which the individual was only a means, developed in the jurists' theory of the Roman law, and transferred during the course of the Middle Ages from the civil power to the ecclesiastical.[6]

It was this ultramontane theory, rather than the idea of the papacy in itself, to which Figgis objected. The ultramontane's idea of authority is absolute and oracular, and the church is seen as a monolithic unit 'with all power centred in the pope or derived from him, and no jurisdiction nor any rights existing except expressly or tacitly by his delegation'.[7] This theory holds that all authority is derived from the centre in precisely the same way that the theory of sovereignty derives all civil rights of groups and of individuals from the state. As a result, episcopal authority is unduly depressed, as the jurisdiction of each bishop is held to emanate from Rome; bishops and priests become mere delegates of the pope.[8] Figgis agreed with George Tyrrell that the ultramontane idea of authority was as individualistic as that of the protestant sectarian. 'They have many Popes,' remarked Tyrrell, 'we but one.'[9]

The church must be seen rather as a living organic community, not an organisation handing on a set of writings or dogmas formulated at a particular date in history. Figgis was therefore critical of fundamentalists who treat scripture as the sole authority, and of those Anglicans who were imprisoned in the era of the first four general councils. Both denied the living, developing life of the catholic church. At least, he pointed out, Roman Catholics are delivered in a curious way from such enslavement to the past by the doctrine of papal infallibility.[10]

Figgis was firmly committed to the notion of the development of doctrine, as proposed by Newman in his classical *Essay.* 'Each age does not merely carry on; it transcends all ages before it.'[11] In the process of development there is a continuity of tradition. The authority which determines the validity of such developments is to be sought in the life of the whole church rather than in some centralised bureaucracy at Rome. In his admiration for Newman, Figgis failed to see those aspects of the cardinal's thought which were radically individualist and resolutely authoritarian, undermining the very idea of the church as an organic, federal and participatory community for which the Anglican monk argued. He was misled by Newman's rhetoric, thinking he believed in a truly positive and constructive role for the laity. In his preface to the third edition of the *Via Media,* Newman distinguished three offices of the church, the prophetic, the priestly and the regal. In his discussion of the latter his controlling model of the church is that of a collection of pious individuals bound together into a collectivity by subordination to a centralised authoritarian government. The image is political. The church is 'an imperial power', 'a sovereign state', exercising over its members 'an absolute and almost despotic rule'.[12] These images are quite alien to Figgis's outlook, but he was neither the first nor the last to fall under the spell of Newman's rhetoric. Church like state, in this view of political authority, is divided into a minority who exercise authority, by issuing commands to a majority; there is a teaching church and a taught church – *ecclesia docens* and *ecclesia discens.*

Theories of absolute state sovereignty and ultramontane interpretations of papal jurisdiction are thus related and are furthermore connected to a particular notion of God as an absolute and arbitrary ruler. 'Earthly rule,' Figgis observed, discussing absolutist theories,

> must be a copy of the heavenly; God is a single individual ruling as an autocrat; so must be the Pope. It is noteworthy that this doctrine of

sovereignty leads in the long run to false views about God, no less than
the State.[13]

I I

Authority is a phenomenon which is manifested in all established groups
and is, according to Figgis, an expression of the social nature of humans.[14]
In his remarkable series of lectures on the nature of the church, *The Fellowship of the Mystery*, he outlined his belief in a federal, participatory church.
He insisted that, as in secular matters so in religion, there is no such thing
as the isolated individual. It is through their membership in religious
associations that people come to a knowledge of God. All relationship
between Christ and the believer must be mediated through scripture,
through tradition and through the life of the christian community. Within
the church, authority ought not to be seen in terms of a set of officials
giving orders to the rank and file members, and it is quite wrong to think of
lay people as basins into which the truth is to be poured.[15] He attacked
clericalism, and insisted that lay people share in the authority of the church.
He used the analogy of a school, where the new pupil sees the ethos and
traditions of the school as something alien, but soon begins to contribute in
a small way to its life. Authority is then not merely external but is something in which each member participates. 'All alike share it,' he wrote, 'all
in some way submit to it; and all contribute to it.'[16] An individual can
recognise the authority of a body to which he belongs and generally agree
to abide by its rules without seeing it as alien and entirely external to
himself, nor need he regard this authority as infallible.

Thus Figgis rejected the model of the church which assumes a *magisterium*
set over against the mass of church members. For practical purposes there
is a teaching office of the church represented by the bishops singly and in
council. Their formal declarations constitute authoritative declarations for
the guidance of church members, but they can properly be questioned, and
only become binding when received by a general consensus. This indeed
was a position which was asserted by Newman, in his discussion of the role
of the laity and in his consideration of the issues raised by the definition of
papal infallibility.

There are, Figgis suggested, two principal bulwarks against ecclesiastical
tyranny: the devolution of power and of decision-making to small
groups within the church, and the ultimate supremacy of conscience.
'Within the Catholic society let there be groups as many as you will,'
he declared.

We need more, not less, of the guild principle. So long as human life exists there will be temperaments in which the personal side of religion is uppermost; others which emphasise the critical; others the sacramental and institutional.[17]

These permanent and semi-permanent groups within the church have an inherent life which is not derived from the centre.[18]

Figgis saw the conciliar movement of the fifteenth century as a great and noble endeavour to achieve the ideal of a federal catholicism. The aim of Gerson, D'Ailly, Zabarella and others had been to reintroduce federal democracy into the church, to recognise the limited autonomy of national and provincial churches, and to regard final authority as belonging to the whole body rather that to a small group of officials headed by the pope; this final authority manifests itself in the form of a general council.[19] The conciliar movement represents 'a definite assertion within the Church of the needs of a balanced constitution, of what men in a later age were to call a mixed or limited monarchy'.[20] Figgis saw the failure of the conciliar movement as a tragedy for the western church, making reformation in a more drastic form almost inevitable. A later writer has remarked on the fact that most twentieth-century catholics would regard the existence of national churches as incompatible with the fact of a universal church. 'Yet the truth is,' he went on, 'that the very same notion that sounds so shocking to many good Christians of our day had no terror for the early Christians.'[21] It was this general interest in the question of national churches that led Figgis to a study of Bossuet and Gallicanism.[22] Bossuet had opposed extreme papalist claims and had argued in favour of a limited autonomy for national churches. Febronianism can be seen as another example of this claim for limited national autonomy within the catholic church. Figgis noted other movements which had made similar claims.[23]

It was in this general context of federalism within the church that Figgis viewed the position of the Church of England. 'We are standing up in England,' he wrote of the Anglican position,

> not only for individual freedom so much as for the reality of the group-life within the Church, for a conception of the religious society which is organic and federalised, as against one which is merely unitary and absolutist.[24]

Figgis emphasised the debt which the Anglican churches owe to Rome, and saw no reason why Anglicans should not be willing to accept the idea of papal primacy in a unified church.[25] He even suggested that the doctrine of papal infallibility was susceptible of an interpretation which Anglicans might accept, 'just as the legal doctrine "the king can do no wrong" can be interpreted in a way favourable to freedom'.[26] While he defended the distinctiveness of the English church he insisted that it must be seen as part of a larger whole. 'The notion of absolute, independent entities must go,' he insisted, 'the national group is real, with its own real life, but it is a group, a part.'[27]

The second bulwark against ecclesiastical tyranny is the ultimate duty of each person to follow his or her conscience, to do what he or she believes to be right, after having considered the evidence, giving due weight to the appropriate authorities. Figgis agreed with Newman in wishing to drink 'to Conscience first, and to the Pope afterwards'.[28] Yet he denied that individual conscience is to be seen as an authority in religion; it is rather the faculty for discriminating between authorities and for sifting the evidence. The Quaker idea of the 'inner light' as source or an authority in religion is not, Figgis argued, a christian one at all.[29] Nevertheless the christian faith should be preached in such a way as to find a genuine response in the individual conscience; it is not a list of propositions to be accepted on the basis of some external authority. 'Wherever blind obedience is preached,' he declared, 'there is danger of moral corruption.'[30]

III

While each person ought ultimately to do what he believes to be right, a church must have the power to draw the line at some point and be able to expel those who transgress that line. We have already noted, in a previous chapter, the pluralist insistence that this power of exclusion be accorded to the group, otherwise it would be unable to perpetuate itself as a distinct entity. The power of excommunication is, in pluralist theory, a necessary condition for the existence of groups. Nevertheless Figgis was particularly concerned that this right should be exercised by church officials only when absolutely necessary, only, that is, when the gospel was being endangered or when the very life of the church was at stake. At the time Figgis was writing the Roman Catholic Church was going through the modernist crisis, and in the Anglican churches liberal protestantism was becoming influential. This raised problems of church discipline. When are the bishops justified in attempting to suppress unorthodox opinions? Under what conditions can people legitimately subscribe to articles and credal statements when they believed them, if at all, in a non-literal sense? Henry Sidgwick had advocated a strict interpretation, arguing that any subscription which is not based on a lit-

eral and total acceptance implies dishonesty. He had himself resigned
his Cambridge fellowship rather than subscribing to beliefs which he
could not accept.[31] A considerable debate ensued on this question, with
bishops like Mandell Creighton and Charles Gore accepting the strict
interpretation of Sidgwick, and theologians like Rashdall, Bethune-
Baker, Gwatkin and Sanday arguing for a more liberal construction of
subscription.[32]

In the Roman Catholic Church writers like Acton, Tyrrell and many
of the modernists had to face a similar problem. Tyrrell himself argued
that as long as liberal catholics believe themselves to be in communion
with the spirit of the whole church, they need not trouble themselves
about the views of its officers for the time being, unless obedience to
them on some particular matter would put them in a false position. Lord
Acton's predicament was somewhat the same.[33] It is only if you assume
that official absolutism is of the essence of the church that liberal catholics can be condemned in their attitude to the question of conformity,
and it is this very idea which they disputed. It was, Tyrrell argued, only
by remaining where they were that the liberals can hope to break the
grip of officialism.[34]

Although Figgis disagreed with Tyrrell on a number of substantive
theological issues, adopting a generally more conservative position, he
strongly sided with the liberals on this matter. So long as a person believed
that the church is the society for promoting the will of God and was prepared to accept the obligation to recite the creed as a minister in that
society, it would be wrong to accuse him of dishonesty or disloyalty if his
interpretation of the articles of the creed were not exactly that which was
accepted by the government of the church. The hierarchy should not be
confused with the church, nor should the catholic faith be equated with the
current theological opinions accepted by this set of officials. A person does
not cease to be British as soon as he criticises the government of the day,
and 'cases there are like that of Athanasius, when the individual by his
courage to stand alone, has saved the church'.[35] Figgis summed up his
position on the question of loyalty and the ethics of subscription in the
following words:

> Loyalty to the idea of the Church, to its living Lord, to its earthly mem-
> bership, to its multitudinous life, to the many-coloured richness of its
> sanctity, to the romance of its origin, to the treasures of its present inher-
> itance, but above all loyalty to the splendour of its future glory; – that is
> the root of the matter. When a man feels that he has that, who are we that
> we should lightly charge him with dishonour, merely because he applies

in one place methods of exegesis which each one of us applies elsewhere?[36]

With respect to the freedom of the church, he reminded his readers that creeds are formally known as 'symbols'. This is not the place to examine in general the theological position adopted by Figgis, but he shows that it is quite possible to be theologically conservative and ecclesiastically liberal, just as the late bishop E. W. Barnes, of Birmingham, demonstrated the possibility of the reverse combination.

As we have seen, Figgis had come to the conclusion that churches in the England of his day must accept their position as voluntary groups in a secular state, nevertheless he was a fervent critic of 'sectarianism', in the theological sense of that term. He attacked puritanism for attempting to turn the church into a sect of like-minded people. Intellectualism in religion also tends to be oligarchic, while certain forms of mysticism, such as that of Fénélon, have an aristocratic tendency which is contrary to the catholic idea of the church.[37] The catholic position, on the other hand, allows for different types and levels of spirituality. 'The Church,' he insisted, 'is not meant to consist only of spiritual athletes, still less is it meant to consist of spiritual dilettanti.'[38] Although the Church of England should cease imagining that it is the religious side of the nation, it should continue to make an appeal to 'all sorts and conditions of men', and avoid turning itself into a clique of respectable people concerned with cultivating their own souls. Some of the consequences of Figgis's attempt to combine sociological sectarianism with theological anti-sectarianism, thus challenging a basic thesis of Troeltsch,[39] have already been considered.

IV

The question of the structure of authority within the church has continued to be a vexed one, and it was a principal concern of the Second Vatican Council. There have been significant developments in the Roman Catholic Church in recent years away from centralisation towards a more federal conception of the church. 'Why,' demands one writer in the journal *Concilium*, 'did a Church which began as a loose assemblage of quasi-autonomous communities become a massive bureaucratic organisation with power and authority concentrated in the pope?' He states that the principal causes of this centralising tendency have been 'defensive responses aimed at dealing with uncertainty and threat'.[40] In recent years national and regional churches in the Roman communion have acquired new powers and fresh initiative, and it has been suggested that institutions like the patriarchate might be revived as part of a move to decentralise.[41] Regional councils of bishops, especially in North and South America, have played an important role in recent years, especially in the field of social thought and action.

Karl Rahner has argued that, in addition to a geographical pluralism, there is to be found in the post-Vatican II church a theological pluralism of a quite new kind. 'The quantitative increase in theological pluralism over the centuries,' he writes, 'has produced, as it were, a qualitative mutation.'[42] In the past, he maintained, there were disagreements, but theologians either 'shared the same terminology, philosophical presuppositions, speech world and outlook on life', or they did not explicitly recognise theological disagreements.[43] A consequence of the present lack of agreement on philosophical presuppositions, with its accompanying theological pluralism, is that the *magisterium* of the church will not in the future 'be able to formulate new emphatic doctrinal pronouncements'. This is because such dogmas must be defined in the language of some theology, and there is today no such generally accepted language. The *magisterium* might then be restricted to setting limits to theological speculation from time to time, and to making occasional pastoral directives. When it does so, it will really be saying: 'You cannot talk like this in the Church without endangering your own faith or the faith of others and doing injustice to the doctrine involved.'[44]

Professor Maurice Wiles has attempted to develop these ideas of Rahner. He argues that 'the newer approach' regards theology as 'inductive and empirical' and consequently as 'inadequate and provisional'.[45] There are no 'fixed criteria' for the determination of theological truth. Wiles therefore suggests that the church should be willing to tolerate 'a considerable measure' of what appears to be error, and to allow 'a wide range' of theological differences within her borders. With most of this Rahner could agree. But Wiles goes on to speak of the truth which is made known in Jesus Christ as 'something for which we have continuously to search', and criticises attempts to tie down speculation by ecclesiastical pronouncements. We need rather to be prepared to trust one another and to be ready to be at one with all those who are ready to be at one with us in the name of Christ. Although Wiles manifestly believes that there must be some limit to theological speculation (as it is only a *considerable measure* and a *wide range* of disagreement which should be permitted) he gives no indication of the criteria for determining such limits. Rahner's position is quite different from that of Wiles. He clearly distinguished the 'givenness' of the christian faith from the words in which it is expressed, seeing these as

signposts which point to realities. 'These realities,' he insisted, 'are mediated to us by words, but they are experienced as being present not absent.'
The christian faith is 'a given datum totally independent of the problem
posed by contemporary theological pluralism'. We have already noted
Rahner's belief that the church can properly set limits to theological
speculation, and he explicitly denied that theological pluralism legitimates
soft tolerance for everything and anything.[46]

The position Rahner maintained is similar to that for which Figgis had
argued. The question of authority and power within groups and associations is one which must concern the pluralist who bases his political
theory upon the importance of liberty. He will argue that a decentralised
system of power, and a diffusion of authority throughout the group, are
valuable, and that a concentration of power at one point is likely to lead to
corruption, and constitute a threat to the liberty of individual members of
the group. Nevertheless this recognition by no means implies that the state
should, as a general rule, intervene to secure this structure within groups.
Such state action may well fail to achieve what is intended, and may have a
number of unfortunate consequences. As Grant McConnell has pointed out,
with respect to trade unions:

> If a strong external system of limitations is imposed on union power, the
> unions may lose much of their usefulness within the social system or
> their sense of grievance may be whetted to a dangerous edge. If
> extensive regulation of internal union affairs is legislated, the unions
> may become so debilitated that their subsequent survival will be a
> matter of indifference.[47]

Recent steps by the British Conservative government to impose a particular form of election upon the unions by statute are open to this sort of
criticism. An attempt by the state to inflict such a democratic system upon
hierarchically organised religious groups might be the sequel, and this
would meet with considerable resistance.

V

In discussions of authority in the church it is perhaps inevitable that political models will be used. The idea of political authority assumed is often
that of a person or body of persons issuing commands or instructions to a
mass of people, such that these commands constitute for the latter a conclusive reason for their complying. People might have other reasons for
following the prescribed course of action, and indeed may have reasons for

not doing so, but the authoritative command supersedes these other reasons. Even with this view of authority, certain conditions needs to be fulfilled before the command issued is authoritative. Some ministerial orders, issued under delegated legislation, might, for example, require prior consultation or the holding of a public inquiry. In a similar manner most theologians (even ultramontanes) would argue that the pope, to speak infallibly, must be speaking *ex cathedra* and that this requires that he is responding to and making explicit the faith of the church. Pluralists would, however, contend that even if the procedures are followed, the commands of political and ecclesiastical 'authorities' are dependent for their validity on being consistent with the provisions of a higher law of justice and right. As we have seen in our discussion of moral sovereignty in chapter three, pluralists denied that there is in the state any person or body of persons whose commands are binding whatever their content. The government of the day may have authority on certain matters and the fact that it has issued an order may provide *some* additional reason why citizens should obey, but not a reason which supersedes all others. No government can remain in power for long which attempts to ride rough shod over the convictions of its citizens.

Two kinds of authority might be distinguished in the church. In the first place there is the need for some body to settle disputes and to deal with behaviour which is thought to be unacceptable. This is similar to political authority and is concerned with actions (including speaking and writing) and not with beliefs. In small associations these matters can be settled by the whole group, in large organisations there is often need for some person or body to act on behalf of the whole. In most churches a judicial or quasi-judicial system has been developed for this purpose.

In the church, however, there is another type of authority, which is concerned with maintaining or defining the truth. Members of the church believe the faith mainly on grounds of authority: the authority of their parents (in the first instance), of scripture, of tradition, of the *consensus fidelium* or of the *magisterium*. As they live their lives they find that these beliefs are confirmed (or perhaps falsified) by experience. Each member may contribute in a small way to a deeper understanding of the beliefs which they have originally accepted on authority. Some may challenge these beliefs, in their current interpretation, or encourage their fellow christians to see things in a new light or from a different perspective.[48] Any adequate notion of authority would see the teaching of the church as responding to new insights and incorporating them into the tradition. So lay christians make a positive contribution to the understanding of christian belief and to the authority of the church.

If the authority of the state must involve listening as well as speaking, even more is it true of authority in the church. The state is interested in external compliance to commands, the church is concerned with beliefs as well as actions, with conviction *in foro interno*, not merely with conformity *in foro externo*. Some types of ecclesiastical instructions are merely intended to silence the unorthodox rather than to convince them, the profounder meaning of authority in the church would see it as influencing the beliefs of its members.

An interesting contrast in the operation of the first type of authority, with respect to some questions of personal morality, may be evident by looking at two different christian traditions. On the one hand we might take the question of birth control in the Roman Catholic Church. The official teaching of the *magisterium* reiterated on many occasions is that the use of artificial methods of contraception is sinful. While most theologians would deny that this teaching, despite being solemnly proclaimed by the pope as head of the Roman Catholic Church, is infallible,[49] they would all agree that this is the official authoritative teaching of the church. Not only is it widely ignored by lay people but is ignored with the connivance of huge numbers of the clergy. Another example might be the celibacy of the clergy, where despite the laws of the church up to forty per cent of Brazilian priests are said to be living in common law or in legally recognised marriage.

A contrasting case would be the situation in the Church of England on the matter of remarriage after divorce. Despite the legal right which clergy have had to conduct second marriages while the former partner still lives, the House of Bishops decided in the 1930s that clergy should not conduct such marriages. Owing to the 'established' status of the church the bishops were unable to apply any sanctions, yet only a tiny number of clergy conducted such marriages. The situation changed in recent years when the episcopal consensus has been fractured. For many years clergy, who may themselves have favoured remarriages, refused to conduct them in compliance with the bishops' rule, despite the fact that no disciplinary measures could have been taken against them.

In the first cases we see authority operating as an authoritarian decree handed down from above, paying scant attention to the beliefs and the experience of lay catholics and of parish clergy. In the second case there was a general consensus (at least among clergy) which was made concrete in the decision of the bishops and generally accepted as authoritative by the parish clergy.

Edmund Hill, a Dominican friar, has distinguished two notions of authority in the Roman Catholic Church: the *magisterial papalist* view and

the *ministerial collegialist* view. Both, he claims, are to be found among
catholics, but the former is the view held by the current government of the
church. Not only does he vigorously defend the ministerial collegialist
view as legitimate, but maintains it is more in line with scripture, and with
certain trends at the Second Vatican Council. His analysis of the former
model of authority is remarkably similar to Figgis's discussion of ultramontanism. It is a purely descending view of authority, in which ultimately
even the bishops become mere delegates of the pope, who

> is indeed an absolute monarch – and one can see that the papacy has for
> centuries been taking on the trappings of absolute monarchy, derived in
> the first place from the archetype of European absolute monarchies, the
> late Roman or Byzantine Empire.[50]

Hill demonstrates how misconceptions about 'priesthood' and 'hierarchy' have led to deformations in the structure and government of the
church. He regrets the tendency to emphasise unity and uniformity at
the expense of catholicity and diversity. 'We think there should be
much less talk about the Catholic Church, and much more talk about the
Catholic Churches.'[51] The New Testament provides clear evidence for
the existence and, at the institutional level, priority of local churches.
While he maintains that the Vatican II decree on the church, *Lumen
gentium*, allows for such an interpretation, this does not reflect its basic
stance which is still essentially centralist, authoritarian and papalist.
Nevertheless the Council did mark a turn of the tide and an openness to
a more decentralised and participatory church. He notes, for example,
the change made in the final draft of chapter four, where *pro* is substi-
tuted for *super*, in the passage dealing with the various ministries in the
church; by the will of Christ, 'some are appointed ... pastors *over*
others' was changed to 'pastors *for the sake (or on behalf) of* others'.[52]
The tide was turning, though since the Council the ministerial papalists
have reasserted their influence. While the Council fathers decided on
general principles about such matters as regional episcopal con-
ferences, they failed to make institutional arrangements to put these
into effect, leaving it to a Curia which was generally opposed to the
whole idea.

The position maintained by Edmund Hill is akin to that for which Figgis
had contended. In attacking the ultramontane theory they both insist that
another conception of authority is tenable within the Roman Catholic
church, and that the future relations with the Anglican church depend on a
shift towards the ministerial collegialist position. Defections from the
Church of England in the wake of the decision to ordain women to the

priesthood will give some temporary boost to authoritarian papalists, but this will do nothing to halt the continuing decline in the active membership of the Roman Catholic church in this country, and more disastrously in Southern Europe and Latin America.

A recent issue which has raised the question of the authority of local churches is the decision in November 1992 by the General Synod of the Church of England to permit the ordination of women to the priesthood. It was argued by many opponents that a local church does not have the right to make major changes to the christian faith or to the structure of the historic ministry. Supporters of the move, while accepting this general limitation, denied that any essential change was being made (from a theological standpoint) arguing that local churches have the authority to make such administrative and organisational changes without the necessity of agreement from the wider church. Ironically some opponents of the ordination of women have announced their intention of joining the Roman Catholic Church, a body which has unilaterally made much more significant changes in christian faith and practice, from the addition of the *filioque* clause to the Marian dogmas of more recent times. The definition of papal infallibility was made by a council at which about half the baptised christians in the world were unrepresented.

A view of authority more in line with pluralist thinking is reflected in the *Final Report of the Anglican-Roman Catholic International Commission.* The ultimate authority in heaven and earth is Christ, he is the head of the church, in which, aided by the Holy Spirit, 'a shared commitment and belief create a common mind'. Authority is to be found at different levels, in the local church but also in that church's communion with other churches in a universal fellowship. The *Report* thus recognises the importance of the local church and also of the ecumenical council. Yet even these councils' decisions are authoritative only when 'they express the common faith and mind of the church'.[53] The view is expressed that in making decisions about fundamental matters of faith an ecumenical council is protected from error. There is a certain ambiguity on the nature of the 'reception' of a conciliar decision which is sometimes said to be necessary. 'Reception,' they write, 'does not create truth nor legitimize the decision: it is the final indication that such a decision has fulfilled the necessary conditions for it to be a true expression of the faith.'[54]

The members of the Commission were agreed that a certain primacy can properly be ascribed to the pope, though 'his intervention in the affairs of a local church should not be made in such a way as to usurp the responsibility of its bishop'.[55] The notion of universal jurisdiction and the exact nature of the alleged infallibility of the Pope were, however, matters on which full agreement was lacking. The report was severely criticised by the Vatican at several points and it is clear that it represents a view of authority which is at odds with the prevailing teaching and practice of the current occupant of the See of Peter. Recent examples of the way Rome intervenes in the affairs of local churches paying scant respect to local opinion is in the appointment of a number of bishops in Germany and Holland. The government of the Roman Catholic church remains a highly centralised autocracy, and this is the principal objection which Anglicans have to reunion. But this is a matter of church government rather than of basic faith, and is therefore one which capable of being surmounted.

8 Conclusion

In this final chapter I wish to look at certain institutional consequences of political pluralism and also to distinguish between the British pluralists and a school of United States political scientists who are referred to by the same name. The former have received relatively little attention in the last half century; so much so that at a recent conference on political thought a paper was given on 'Pluralism', which not only made no reference to the British pluralists, but whose author (a professor of politics in a London university) admitted to never having heard of them! The article on 'Pluralism' in a recent *Dictionary of Political Thought* makes no mention of the British political pluralists.[1]

I

In the second edition of the *Divine Right of Kings*, published in 1914, J. N. Figgis pointed to 'a whole complex of converging forces, economic, social and political and moral', that was making the question of the role of groups with respect to the state an urgent one. For perspectives on some of the concrete issues he recommended a study of the guild socialist and syndicalist movements.[2] He manifestly saw these as legitimate embodiments of the political pluralism for which he battled. Laski, Cole and Russell also saw a clear link between their political theories and the guild socialist movement. The anarcho-syndicalists, however, advocated the abolition of the political state, believing that social life could proceed under the direction of producer co-operatives, trade guilds and other voluntary associations, with no co-ordinating body having power to regulate the groups and eventually impose an adjudication in case of conflict. Many trade unions, particularly in France, turned increasingly to direct action and derived inspiration from Emile Durkheim's essay on the division of labour, though the sociologist himself would by no means have endorsed the whole syndicalist programme.[3]

In the latter part of the nineteenth century there had been a significant anarchist tendency in the French labour movement which, combined with a growing cynicism about parliamentary methods, led to the birth of syndicalism. The term, in French, simply means trade unionism, but acquired a more specific connotation. Revolutionary syndicalists found an eloquent advocate in Georges Sorel. He believed that the marxist notion of a class struggle culminating in a proletarian revolution needed 'demythologising'.

126

The general strike must be preached as a myth, rather than seen as an inevitable outcome. Its function was to inspire the working class to unite and bring down the capitalist state. Sorel preached an anti-intellectualist message, appealing to such writers as Henri Bergson and William James, echoing the cry of John Henry Newman that 'life is for action'.[4] One writer, indeed, blamed Bergson for encouraging blind irrational action, which is 'precisely what syndicalism needs, to justify its policy'.[5] Sorel's writings were later to inspire Benito Mussolini's fascist ideology of commitment and action. Fascism also, as we shall see, claimed to put into practice a corporatism which purported to recognise the significance of social and industrial groups and allow for some kind of functional representation in the state legislature.

Despite publicity achieved by the exotic writings of Sorel, the main significance of syndicalism was its role in the policies pursued by the labour movement, particularly in France. The Confédération Générale du Travail was founded in 1895 and strengthened in 1902 by amalgamation with the Fédération des Bourses de Travail. Workers had become cynical about political democracy and particularly about politicians. They had seen the socialist Millerand joining the government of Waldeck-Rousseau in 1899 and soon abandoning any claim to be a socialist. In consequence the labour movement turned away from political towards industrial action, in the form of strikes, working to rule, boycotts and industrial sabotage. Syndicalists were critical of marxism and of collectivist socialism, for aiming to replace private ownership with state ownership. 'The Syndicalists,' according to an article in the *Syndicalist Railwayman*, 'hold that the State is the great enemy and that the Socialists' ideal of State or Collectivist Ownership would make the lot of the Workers much worse than it is now under private employers'.[6]

The guild socialists modified syndicalist ideas to allow a place for the state, either as co-ordinator and controller of the groups, or as the representative of the consumer.[7] There was in the British labour movement a prolonged struggle between this modified version of syndicalism and what *Punch* called 'sydneywebbicalism', or collectivist state socialism. It was the latter doctrine which carried the day in the Fabian Society, in the trade union movement and in the Labour Party. Nevertheless small groups within the labour movement have continued to reject nationalisation as the ultimate answer to industrial problems, and have advocated various forms of worker control as the only satisfactory basis for a socialist society. In the 1970s there was a revival of this tendency in the labour movement associated with the so-called 'new left' and the resurgence of anarchist theories.[8] More recently these have been joined by disillusioned marxists and repentant Fabians.

Another doctrine which employed the concept of groups, embracing the challenge to state sovereignty made by Figgis and the pluralists, was distributism. This was a variation on the guild socialist theme. With the pluralists they attacked the centralised omnicompetent state. 'The organised movement of our age,' wrote J. E. Gleeson, 'has been in the direction of Centralisation and Concentration. The word Distributism is employed to denote the exact contrary.'[9] Accepting the notion of the guild organisation of production, distributists insisted on a diffusion of ownership in general and of guild property in particular, which the guild socialists were not always willing to allow. Accepting the model of the peasant and craftsman as the ideal they were hostile to large industry and preached the message that 'small is beautiful', later associated with the name of E. F. Schumacher.[10] Distributism was an attempt to restore the system which its supporters believed to have existed in the middle ages, when the ownership of property was spread out among the citizens of the country.[11] To be free, a citizen must own property, and the associative or distributist state would maintain such a situation in being. They attacked the capitalist economy, the wage system and party government, advocating forms of functional representation.[12] Distributism was particularly popular among radical Roman Catholics, who appealed to the social encyclicals of Leo XIII and Pius XI, which attacked communism and socialism, but which were equally critical of unrestrained capitalism and defended the right of workers to form trade unions. The Dominican, Father Vincent McNabb, was particularly outspoken in his defence of distributism as an alternative to socialism.[13]

We have already alluded to corporatism. A theory of corporations was outlined by Hegel in his *Philosophy of Right* and the history of the role of guilds and corporations was exhaustively expounded by Otto von Gierke.[14] Durkheim too, whose ideas on group personality I have referred to in Chapter 4, developed a corporative theory, stemming from the division of labour characteristic of the modern world. This division had led to the development of professional organisations and associations based on particular industries, which allowed for increased solidarity and helped to mitigate the atomising tendency of capitalist social organisation.[15] The constitution established after the First World War by Gabriel d'Annunzio in Fiume included provision for corporations based on function, while the second chamber, the Council of Provvisori, was functionally based. Mussolini and the fascists followed d'Annunzio in some respects, forming a functional assembly and also maintaining a system of syndicates and corporations. Sir Ernest Barker suggested that the corporative state of fascism was an attempt to put into practice the Althusian-Gierkian conception of the state as a *communitas communitatum*, but the corporations were firmly under the umbrella of the totalitarian state.[16] Many of the guild socialists and their sympathisers, such as A. J. Penty, Ezra Pound, Odon Por and Ramiro de Maeztu became followers, to a greater or lesser extent, of fascism. They saw in fascism a theoretical similarity to their own ideas. Others, however, were not misled by the theoretical façade and saw the hard features of totalitarian autocracy through the smokescreen of corporatist propaganda. Lip service to corporatism was also paid by Nazi Germany, but the actual organisation of the state had little in common with corporatist principles.[17]

In the mid-1970s there was something of a revival of corporatism, though less as a political policy than as a tool of analysis in political science.[18] Struck by the inadequacy of American group theories of politics, associated with the names of A. F. Bentley, David Truman and Earl Latham (which we shall discuss in due course), a number of academics argued that in certain Western liberal democracies there had developed a peculiar, 'corporatist' relationship between powerful groups and the state. Rather than seeing the state as a referee that merely ratifies and records the compromises in which the power struggle between rival groups results, the state plays a much more active role. It co-ordinates and collaborates with the large corporations, including trade unions, in elaborating a joint strategy for the management of the economy. Corporatism was said to be distinguished from pluralism (American variety) by the co-operation, particularly on economic policy, taking place between groups, orchestrated largely by the government. An important feature was the responsibility taken by the corporate leaders to ensure that their members act in accordance with agreed policies – 'an organized group's enforcement of government policy in relation to its own members', in the words of one critic.[19] Some writers trace the phenomenon back to the First World War, others to the Second World War.[20] The 'social contract' of the mid-1970s is sometimes referred to in the context of corporatism, though it was the result of agreement only between government and trade unions.

Another political arrangement which sometimes grows out of pluralist theories is functionalism, which seeks to replace or supplement geographical representation by functional representation. It was advocated, as we have already seen, by the guild socialists and was put into practice in Fascist Italy, in Weimar Germany and in the post-war West German state of Bavaria, among other places. In post-war France the MRP was eager for a functional assembly, but being opposed by the socialists, they had to be content with an Economic Council. In England there have been various suggestions in this direction from thinkers as diverse as the guild socialists, Winston Churchill and Leo Amery. Criticisms have come from several

quarters. Yet there is no necessary connection between pluralism and functionalism; it is quite possible to imagine a state which is monolithic,
centralised and functional.

The proliferation of interest groups of various kinds in the modern state,
and a growing acceptance of these groups as a legitimate feature of liberal
politics and subject of respectable academic research is also remotely related
to the emphasis placed on group life by the pluralists. In a later section I shall
consider in a little more detail the ideology of pressure group liberalism
which is put forward by a number of contemporary American political scientists. Here I wish only to draw attention to the phenomenon of interest and
pressure groups. 'Pressure groups,' it has been said, somewhat misleadingly,
'give us today a genuinely pluralist society in all spheres and levels of government. And without pluralism we should indeed be helpless before the
Great Leviathan.'[21] These pressure groups, however, often operate in a way
that would not be favoured by the British pluralists, pressuring governments
to adopt substantive policies which would benefit them.

I have alluded in a previous chapter to the notion of subsidiarity in
catholic social teaching. By 1891 the pope was stating that there should be
a right to form worker associations, while a later pope proclaimed that
small groups should be allowed a maximum of self-government, and that
large groups like the state should not arrogate to themselves functions
which can be performed efficiently by smaller societies. Johannes Messner
claims that subsidiarity is a natural law principle, which 'protects the particular rights of the natural and the free associations against the state's
claim to omnicompetence'. It is, he continued, 'a *fundamental principle of
the pluralistic society*'.[22] This principle of subsidiarity, has been widely
adopted within the European Community as one of its guiding axioms.
There should according to Jacques Delors, be 'a decentralised organisation
of responsibilities, with the aim of never entrusting to a larger unit what
can better be realised by a smaller one'.[23]

The term 'subsidiarity' is taken from the Latin *subsidium* meaning 'aid';
the idea is that each social organisation should assist smaller and weaker
organisations to fulfil their respective functions. Therefore the state should
adopt not a purely passive *laissez-faire* approach to social and economic
affairs, but an active role encouraging and facilitating the formation and
growth of different levels of association. Unfortunately it seems that subsidiarity is honoured more in the letter than in the spirit. The European
Commission pours out a continuous stream of regulations determining the
most minute issues throughout the Community, including, notoriously the
composition of the sausage and the temperature at which beer may be
stored.

Sharing much in common with the (basically catholic) notion of subsidiary function is the Dutch protestant idea of 'sphere sovereignty' (*souvereiniteit in eigen kring*), associated with a school of Calvinist political theology founded by Groen Van Prinsterer (1801–76) and Abraham Kuyper (1837–1920), culminating in the massive work of Herman Dooyeweerd (1894–1975), *De Wijsbegeerte der Wetsidee.*[24] These writers were critical of individualism and also of claims by the state to have command over all social activities of its citizens. The state was said to be sovereign but only in its sphere. Human institutions like family, school and economic enterprise (unlike province or municipality, which are historical phenomena, enjoying a degree of autonomy in the body politic) are part of God's gift in creation, and enjoy thereby an inherent right to autonomy and are not strictly speaking a part of the state at all.[25]

I I

In this section I shall examine the relationship between the political pluralism of Figgis and his contemporaries, and the concept of pluralism that developed among American political scientists in the last few decades to characterise the system of government which is said to operate in the United States. American pluralism can have both a descriptive and a normative content. Some theorists argue that: (a) pluralism, as they understand it, is the best form of government, and that (b) it is more or less realised in the USA. Others accept pluralism as an ideal, but deny that it is realised in contemporary America. Others again believe that some kind of pluralism does operate in the United States, but deny that it is good. Presumably, to complete the analysis, there are those who neither believe that pluralism is practised nor believe that it ought to be, but we would not call them pluralists!.

Political writers like David Truman write with a certain smugness about the American political system. The most satisfactory system of government is assumed to be a pluralist one, where representative democracy is supplemented by a large number of interest groups, each organised to achieve some specific end, and each endeavouring to influence 'the decision-making process' in accordance with this end. Thus minorities who feel strongly on a particular issue are able to make their voices heard and to influence the course of events. Pluralism is also believed to ensure that power is dispersed throughout the community; there is no single group of people able to determine governmental policy. In the tension which is created by conflicting group interests, individual freedom is thought to be preserved and the cross-cutting nature of group membership ensures a degree of stability to the political system. There is no over-all, total 'common good' or 'public interest', which the government attempts to impose upon the population; it tries simply to reach some temporary compromise between conflicting interests. Government is seen by certain of these writers as an *arena* in which contending groups meet and where compromise is reached; it is seen by others as the *referee* who searches for some kind of acceptable settlement of the conflicting claims made by groups. Clearly, the latter view is, in some respects, similar to that which Figgis advocated.

Many American pluralist writers believe that pluralism is the best form of government, and also that it is the form of government which operates in the United States. It is the pattern which 'modernising' nations must ever keep before their eyes. There is no system of government in all of history, declared Nelson D. Rockefeller after his celebrated tour of Latin America, 'better than our own flexible structure of political democracy, individual initiative, and responsible citizenship in elevating the quality of man's life'.[26]

In *The Torment of Secrecy*, Edward Shils puts forward a pluralist theory (as he conceives of it). He clearly believes that a pluralist state is not only the best kind of state, but is also the basic form of state existing in the United States. The McCarthyism of the early fifties is seen by him to be an aberration, a deviation from the American way of life, a disease temporarily afflicting an otherwise healthy body politic. This pluralism involves tolerating a large number of groups, so long as their demands are 'moderate'; that is, so long as their members do not go to 'an extreme in zealous attachment to a particular value'.[27] He follows here the ideas of Walter Lippmann, who asserted that 'It is inherent in the complex pluralism of the modern world that men should behave moderately'.[28] If a group is content to demand a little more of what it thinks good, rather than the complete fulfilment of its dreams, it can 'fall within the circle of pluralism'.

He sees this pluralist society as one composed of 'leaders and led', in which there must be 'a sense of affinity among the elites'.[29] This sense of affinity involves not an agreement to live and let live, but a determination to seek some kind of common good which will be imposed by the state, and which will reflect as far as possible the common interests of these acceptable in-groups. It also clearly implies the suppression of those groups which are thought to be 'extreme', whose leaders (presuming they also are composed of leaders and led) do not feel a sense of affinity with the leaders of other groups, or who reject the idea that a state should be concerned with imposing upon the population a substantive common good. Shils sees in the United States a situation where there is a general agreement among right-thinking people, those whom President Nixon referred to as the 'silent majority', those who feel strongly about nothing except the preservation of a state in which no one is permitted to feel strongly about anything else.

In the United States, businessmen may be called upon by the administration for certain tasks, but 'when they serve, they do not do so as businessmen but as government officials'.[30] In fact, one such businessman has gone further, and asserted that there is no distinction between the two roles. This double claim that pluralism is American and that it is good has led unfriendly critics to declare that pluralism is little more than an ideology (in the pejorative sense); that it is being used simply as the intellectual justification for perpetuating a *status quo* which is really preserved on quite other grounds.

Perhaps the most celebrated attack upon these American pluralist theories came from C. Wright Mills in his book on *The Power Elite*, where he argued forcefully that the USA was controlled by a coherent and sinister élite group, which determined all the important decisions of government according to their own narrow interests. This view gained a certain kind of popularity when President Eisenhower referred to a 'military-industrial complex' in the course of his farewell address.[31]

Pluralist writers have replied to the Mills theory of a power élite by making the general criticism that his theory is much too impressionistic, vague and lacking in empirical support. Also they have conducted empirical studies of power distribution in the United States, centring particularly on the local and regional levels of government. Robert Dahl's study of power in the city of New Haven, *Who Governs?*, is a classic in this field. His aim was to show that there are a number of quite distinct groups which have an effective voice in key decisions made in the city. Dahl's critics point out, however, that in over-emphasising the actual process of decision-making, he ignored all those forces which are able to prevent an issue from coming to the fore at all. Also it is observed that there is no clear criterion suggested for determining which issues are the 'key issues'. Nevertheless, these faults in Dahl's method do nothing to rehabilitate the assertions of Mills with respect to the existence of a power élite.

Even radical critics of American life, like Robert Paul Wolff, are dissatisfied with the 'power elite' theory. But the more valid point made by Mills was that the interest group system, as it operates in the United State, militates against large sections of the American public – the poor, the blacks and, in general, the unorganised. This fact has recently been reiterated by Wolff, who insists that the contemporary American state is organised in such a way that the well-established groups have their interests taken into account, but emerging groups find it difficult to make their voices heard. There is in the USA a great deal of intolerance of marginal, unrespectable groups who refuse to subscribe to the generally accepted norms of the average citizen. Herbert Marcuse has argued in a similar vein. Most of these criticisms are directed against pluralism as a descriptive theory, rather than against its normative aspect. What these writers are saying up to this point is that the contemporary USA is not, in fact, a genuine pluralist state. Some critics go further and attack the pluralist ideal; or, at least, they attack certain supposed corollaries of pluralism. H. S. Kariel has argued that the organisations which in the past were, with some justification, thought of as protecting the individual against unjust claims by the government, have themselves become oligarchic and oppressive. 'Our problem today,' he writes, 'is not how to strengthen the hierarchies of organized private power, but rather how to control them by some means short of establishing an illiberal political order.'[32]

In recent years there has been a revival of Rousseau's idea of a general will. Wolff attempts to show that the notion of a common good is meaningful and is a possible object of state policy. 'There must be some way,' he maintains, 'of constituting the whole society a genuine group with a group purpose and a conception of the common good'.[33] He correctly perceives that a pluralist would rule out such a project as impossible and undesirable. Furthermore, most pluralists would insist that any attempt to constitute a state of the kind envisaged by Wolff, having some single, coherent, all-embracing substantive purpose, would necessarily end in totalitarianism.

The difference between the British and the American conceptions of a pluralist state is not so much that the former is characterised by 'order', while in the latter we find 'a kaleidoscopic array of special interests'[34], or that one is static and the other is dynamic, the difference is rather that American pluralist theories see the group as exerting an influence in order to persuade the government to perform some substantive good which will be in the interest of that group. Most American theories envisage the groups as 'feverishly seeking to penetrate the policy-making arena',[35] or competing 'for control over the actions of the government'.[36] These theories assume that the government will, and ought to, play an active role in determining the end which should be pursued. They see the various groups bringing pressure to bear on the government, pulling it hither and yon, inducing it to bestow its patronage in a way calculated to benefit their own particular interests. So far from abandoning the pork-barrel state, they see politics as a contest for its appropriation.

From what has been said in previous chapters, it will be clear that, between these contemporary American theories and the notion of pluralism advocated by Figgis, there is a great gulf fixed. The British pluralists believed that the associations which comprise the state should not endeavour to force the government actively to intervene in the life of the people in order to realise some substantive purpose. These associations should be concerned simply with obtaining freedom to live life in a manner which they prefer, while recognising the rights of other groups to a similar freedom. If groups and parties in the state spent as much energy and money pursuing concrete ends of their choice, as they now spend on trying to persuade governments to pursue these ends on their behalf, the world would be a better place. The history of the labour movement in Britain provides a gruesome example of pressure group politics. Every five years or so, extraordinary efforts are made to put into political office a party which is believed to be in sympathy with the movement, and a number of other stratagems are employed in order to get Parliament to do what the movement might very well have done on its own. The industrial scene might have been very much brighter than it is today if workers had concentrated upon direct action along the lines recommended by the guild socialists, and tried to ensure that the state played as small a role as possible in the industrial affairs of the nation.

III

The idea that a state can exist only when the people share a common set of values is mistaken. Even in a relatively homogeneous state like the United Kingdom, values differ quite radically from one section of the population to another. Certainly, a majority of the people must share a belief in the importance of civil peace, combined with a willingness to allow their fellow citizens to live life as they choose to live it. They must also recognise some machinery which is the normal channel for resolving disputes, though this recognition will never be absolute. Individuals and groups will retain the ultimate right to use force in defending those rights which they believe to be vital. But the idea that governments must play an active and dynamic role in imposing or inculcating a single culture or set of values will lead either to totalitarianism or to civil war. 'The more conscience comes to the front,' wrote Acton, 'the more we consider, not what the state accomplishes, but what it allows to be accomplished'.[37] Indeed a pluralist must go further and see the role of the state not merely as allowing freedom to individuals and to groups, but as positively facilitating such freedom and encouraging citizens, by its structural arrangements, to join together in co-operative ventures to pursue some chosen substantive purpose which they share.

Legal Cases Cited

A. G. *v.* Great Northern Railway Co., 1 Drewry and Smales Rep. 154.

Barwick *v.* English Joint Stock Bank, L. R. 2 Exch. 259.

Cornford *v.* Carlton Bank [1899] 1 Q.B. 392.

D.P.P. *v.* Kent and Sussex Contractors Ltd [1944] K.B. 146.

Edwards *v.* Midland Railway Co. [1881] 50 L.J. Q.B. 281.

General Assembly of the Free Church of Scotland *v.* Overtoun (Lord) [1904] A.C. 515.

Henderson *v.* Midland Railway Co. [1871] 24 L.T.N.S. 881.

Kedroff *v.* St Nicholas Cathedral, 344 U.S. Sup. Ct. 1952 94.

Kent v. Courage & Co. Ltd [1890] 55 J.P, 264.

Osborne *v.* Amalgamated Society of Railway Servants [1901] A.C. 87.

R. *v.* Cory Bros. & Co. Ltd [1927] 1 K.B. 810.

R. *v.* I. C. R. Haulage Ltd [1944] K. B. 551.

Salomon *v.* Salomon & Co. [1897] A.C. 22.

Stevens *v.* Midland Counties Railway Co., 10 Exch. 352.

Sutton's Hospital Case [1613] 10 Co. Rep.

Taff Vale Railway Co. *v.* Amalgamated Society of Railway Servants [1901] A.C. 426.

Abbreviations

The following abbreviations are frequently used in the notes:

Authority: H. J. Laski, *Authority in the Modern State.*
Chaos: G. D. H. Cole, *Chaos and Order in Industry.*
Churches: J. N. Figgis, *Churches in the Modern State.*
Divine Right: J. N. Figgis, *The Divine Right of Kings.*
Essays: Lord Acton, *Essays on Freedom and Power.*
Fellowship: J. N. Figgis, *The Fellowship of the Mystery.*
Genossenschaftstheorie: O. von Gierke, *Die Genossenschaftstheorie und die deutsche Rechtsprechung.*
Gerson: J. N. Figgis, *Studies of Political Thought from Gerson to Grotius 1414–1625.*
Grammar: H. J. Laski, *A Grammar of Politics.*
'Grundbegriffe': O. von Gierke, 'Die Grundbegriffe des Staatsrechts' in *30 Zeitschrift für die gesammte Staatswissenschaft* (1874).
Hopes: J. N. Figgis, *Hopes for English Religion.*
Labour: G. D. H. Cole, *Labour in the Commonwealth.*
Political Theories: O. von Gierke, *Political Theories of the Middle Age* (edited with an introduction by F. W. Maitland).
Problem: H. J. Laski, *Studies in the Problem of Sovereignty.*
Self-Government: G. D. H. Cole, *Self-Government in Industry.*
Wesen: O. von Gierke, *Das Wesen der menschlichen Verbände.*

Note: The Mirfield MSS refer to Figgis Papers belonging to the Community of the Resurrection; they are now housed at the Borthwick Institute, in York.

Notes and References

Introduction

1. Jeffrey Weeks, in *Bulletin of the Society for the Study of Labour History*, 32, Spring 1976, p. 61.
2. Kedourie, *Perestroika in the Universities*, p. 26. Quoted by Shirley Robin Letwin, in *The Anatomy of Thatcherism*, p. 272.
3. See Letwin, *The Anatomy*, p. 261.
4. Recent examples in Britain would include such thinkers as Raymond Plant and David Miller on market socialism, and Paul Q. Hirst, 'Associational Socialism in a Pluralist State', *Journal of Law and Society*, 15, 1988, pp. 139f.; Hirst, ed., *The Pluralist Theory of the State: Selected Writings of G. D. H. Cole, J. N. Figgis, and H. J. Laski*, and Hirst, *Associative Democracy: New Forms of Economic and Social Governance*.
5. See, for example, the Introduction to Paul Q. Hirst, ed., *The Pluralist Theory of the State*.
6. See particularly Branko Horvat *et al.*, eds, *Self-governing Socialism: a Reader*; and Aloysius Balawyder, ed., *Cooperative Movements in Eastern Europe*.
7. Andras Bozokoi *et al.*, eds, *Post-Communist Transition: Emerging Pluralism in Hungary;* Uri Ra'anan *et al.*, *Russian Pluralism: Now Irreversible;* Tadensz Jarski, *A Troubled Transition: Poland's Struggle for Pluralism*.
8. C. J. Friedrich and Z. K. Brzezinski, *Totalitarian Dictatorship and Autocracy.*
9. See, for example, the work of H. Gordon Skilling, 'Interest Groups and Communist Politics', *World Politics*, 18, 1966, pp. 435f. and Skilling, (ed., with F. Griffiths), *Interest Groups in Soviet Politics.*
10. Jerry Hough, 'The Soviet System: Petrification or Pluralism?', *Problems of Communism*, March– April 1972, pp. 25f.
11. See Archie Brown, 'Pluralistic Trends in Czechoslovakia', *Soviet Studies.* 17, 1966, pp. 453f.
12. Hough, 'Pluralism, Corporatism and the Soviet Union', in Susan Solomon, ed., *Pluralism in the Soviet Union*, p. 57.
13. Archie Brown, 'Pluralism, Power and the Soviet Political System: a Comparative Perspective', in Solomon, ed., *Pluralism*, pp. 63f.
14. Brown, in Solomon, ed., *Pluralism*, p. 68.
15. Nicholls, *The Pluralist State* (1st edn), p. 81; see below p. 81.
16. Solomon, in Solomon, ed., *Pluralism*, pp. 11–12.
17. Nicholls, *The Pluralist State* (1st edn), pp. 80f. See below pp. 79f. Solomon made other ill-considered criticisms of pluralist writers for 'blending of normative and descriptive'; 'one reads in the pluralist writings that no organization (such as the state) can be absorptive of all the interests of citizens and that no organization ought to be all-absorptive' (p. 11). Misunderstanding G. E. Moore's argument she accuses them of committing the naturalistic fallacy. In fact their argument was that no organisation can succeed in being

all-absorptive, and that attempts to become so result in unfortunate and indeed evil consequences.

18. Archie Brown, 'New Thinking in the Political System', in Archie Brown, ed., *New Thinking in Soviet Politics,* pp. 19 and 24.
19. *Quadragesimo Anno,* section 79; in *Five Great Encyclicals,* p. 147
20. Hirst, *Associative Democracy,* p. 12.
21. In Michael Oakeshott, *On Human Conduct,* pp. 185ff.
22. Oakeshott was also one of my PhD examiners, subjecting me to a harrowing *viva* on the subject of political pluralism.
23. I also discuss this matter in Nicholls, *Three Varieties of Pluralism,* ch. 3.
24. A criticism powerfully argued by P. Bachrach and M. S. Baratz, *Power and Poverty: Theory and Practice.*
25. Dahl, *Dilemmas of Pluralist Democracy,* p. 45.
26. Dahl, *Dilemmas,* pp. 40f.
27. Dahl, *Dilemmas,* pp. 43f. A Rousseauesque point!
28. Dahl, *Dilemmas,* pp. 83f. See also the quotation from Stein Rokkan on pp. 66–7.
29. The phrase is used by Harold Laski; see P. Hirst, ed., *The Pluralistic Theory of the State,* p. 214.

1 Parentalism and Pluralism

1. For earlier discussions of English political pluralism see K. C. Hsiao, *Poitical Pluralism; H. M. Magid, English Political Pluralism; W. Y. Elliott, The Pragmatic Revolt in Politics;* Ernest Barker, *Political Thought in England: from Herbert Spencer to the Present Day;* F. W. Coker, 'The Technique of the Pluralist State', *American Political Science Review,* 15, 1921, pp. 186f, E. D. Ellis, 'Guild Socialism and Pluralism', *American Political Science Review,* 17, 1923, pp. 584f, E. D. Ellis, 'The Pluralist State', *American Political Science Review,* 14, 1920 pp. 393f, G. Sabine, 'Pluralism: a Point of View', *American Political Science Review,* 17, 1923, pp. 34f, N. Wilde, 'The Attack on the State', *International Journal of Ethics,* 30, 1920, pp. 349f, L. Rockow, *Contemporary Political Thought in England,* chs 6 and 7. Works published since the first edition of this book include, Andrew Vincent, *Theories of the State,* ch. 6; Paul Q. Hirst, *The Pluralist Theory of the State: Selected Writings of G. D. H. Cole, J. N. Figgis and H. J. Laski;* S. Ehrlich, *Pluralism, On and Off Course;* and P. P. Craig, *Public Law and Democracy in the United Kingdom and the United States of America,* ch. 5.
2. Figgis, *The Gospel and Human Needs,* p. 52.
3. For a discussion of Creighton, Acton and Maitland see appendix 2, to Figgis, *Churches,* pp. 226.
4. Laski, *A Grammar of Politics,* Preface to the First Edition.
5. See Kingsley Martin, *Harold J. Laski;* Bernard Zylstra, *From Pluralism to Collectivism: the Development of Harold Laski's Political Thought.*
6. See A. W. Wright, *G. D. H. Cole and Socialist Democracy,* and Margaret Cole, *The Story of Fabian Socialism.*
7. Balfour, *Essays Speculative and Political,* p. 198.

8. See, for example, Schiller, *Riddles of the Sphynx,* and *Studies in Humanism.*
9. Bradley, *Essays on Truth and Reality,* p. 268.
10. James, *A Pluralistic Universe,* p. 79.
11. James, *A Pluralistic Universe,* p. 321.
12. See below pp. 74f. This would be true also of the American Mary Parker Follett.
13. Figgis, *Antichrist,* pp. 30–1.
14. I do not wish to suggest that ideologies are merely rationalisations of self-interested groups or classes (though the word is frequently used in this pejorative sense). This is a large subject. Here I would merely assert (a) that it is impossible to understand human actions adequately unless we see them as purposive, and often following from conscious decisions; (b) that the decisions which people make are closely related to the beliefs they hold; (c) that these beliefs cannot satisfactorily be accounted for simply as mechanical consequences of physiological or social conditions; (d) that people sometimes hold beliefs because they think them to be true, and that one way of changing these beliefs is to convince them that they are false; and (e) that it is often important to consider whether a belief is true or not, and that this inquiry is distinct from (though sometimes connected to) a discussion about the origin of the belief.
15. See ch. 3 in David Nicholls, *Deity and Domination.*
16. For other examples see Terence Ball *et al.,* eds, *Political Innovation and Conceptual Change.*
17. I shall use the words synonymously throughout the book.
18. I have considered this conceptual modification of liberty, in relation to political developments in David Nicholls, 'Positive Liberty: 1880–1914', *American Political Science Review,* 56, 1962, pp. 114–28. Michael Freeden discusses the same events in *The New Liberalism: an Ideology of Social Reform;* for my response to his position see David Nicholls, *Deity and Domination,* p. 69.
19. In W. E. Connolly, ed., *The Bias of Pluralism,* p. 95.
20. E. Bernstein, *Evolutionary Socialism,* p. 169.
21. In G. B. Shaw, ed., *Fabian Essays,* p. 182
22. In *Fabian Essays,* p. 60. In some of his later essays, however, Webb was less optimistic about the outcome of this glide. See, for example, *Towards Social Democracy.*
23. Margaret Cole, *The Story of Fabian Socialism,* p. 148.
24. R. Michels, *Political Parties,* p. 113.
25. Craig, *Public Law and Democracy in the United Kingdom and the United States,* pp. 146–7. This book includes a most interesting attempt to relate various pluralist theories to legal and institutional developments. For Ehrlich see *Pluralism On and Off Course,* p. 49.
26. Barker, 'The Discredited State: Thoughts on Politics before the War', *The Political Quarterly,* 5, February 1915, p. 121.
27. H. S. Holland, 'The State', in B. F. Westcott *et al., The Church and New Century Problems,* p. 51.
28. W. J. H. Campion, in Charles Gore, ed., Lux Mundi: *a Series of Studies in the Religion of the Incarnation,* p. 444. See my criticism of this chapter in Robert Morgan, ed., *The Religion of the Incarnation,* pp. 172–88.

29. Maurice, *The Kingdom of Christ*, III, p. 76.
30. David Nicholls, *Deity and Domination*, passim, and 'Two Tendencies in Anglo-Catholic Political Theology', in Geoffrey Rowell, ed., *Tradition Renewed*, pp. 140–53.
31. *Churches*, p. 57.
32. Figgis, *Antichrist*, pp. 189 and 191.
33. Figgis, *Church Times*, 9 April 1914, p. 529. 'The root fact is this: our taste, our knowledge, our morals and our religion are able to exist because we live on the fruits of a system that is really slavery, and until this be changed all the honesty and devotion in the world will never prevent our religion from being half-hearted, our literature rococo, our architecture exotic, our culture mean and sickly, our art a succession of bad jokes and even our virtues at their very best rather an accident than an achievement.' Ibid.
34. For a note on the distinction between a secular and a secularist state see p. 96
35. *The Independent Review*, 7, 1905, p. 19.
36. J.F. Stephen, *Liberty Equality Fraternity*, p. 256; see also Henry Maine, *Popular Government*, p. 32. On Balfour see David Nicholls, 'Few are Chosen', *The Review of Politics*, 30, 1968, pp. 33–50.
37. *Churches*, p. 150.
38. *Churches*, p. 135.
39. See below Ch. 7.
40. Eliot, *Notes Towards the Definition of Culture*, p. 60.
41. I discuss briefly the relationship between British political pluralism and more recent American theories, and with concepts of a pluralist or segmented society in the Conclusion to this volume,
42. Aristotle, *Politics*, 5:11.
43. Proudhon, *Idée générale de la révolution au 19e siècle*, p. 344.

2   Liberty and the Division of Power

1. Bernard Crick, *In Defence of Politics*, p. 21.
2. Lippmann, *A Preface to Morals*, pp. 112–13. Recent discussions of 'the self' may be found in Michael Sandel, *Liberalism and the Limits of Justice*, and Charles Taylor, *Sources of the Self*.
3. 'A Person is composed of an internalization of organized social roles', H. H. Gerth and C. W. Mills, *Character and Social Structure*, p. 83; see also J. H. Fichter, *Sociology*, p. 212, and T. M. Newcomb, 'Community Roles in Attitude Formation', in *American Sociological Review*, 1942, 7, pp. 621f.
4. Lamprecht, 'The Need for a Pluralistic Emphasis in Ethics', in *Journal of Philosophy, Psychology and Scientific Method*, 1920, 17, pp. 562 and 569.
5. Sidgwick, *Methods of Ethics*, pp. 106–7. The same elementary point in made in more recent writers on the subject. See R. M. Hare, *The Language of Morals*, pp. 151f and P. H. Nowell Smith, *Ethics*, pp. 185f.
6. Bagehot, 'The Metaphysical Basis of Toleration', *Works*, VI, p. 227.
7. Bentley, *The Process of Government*, p. 371; see also T. V. Smith, *The Legislative Way of Life*, and *The Compromise Principle in Politics*.

8. Figgis, *Churches*, p. 263. For a recent writer who lays great emphasis on character, see Stanley Hauerwas, *Character and the Christian Life* and *A Community of Character.*
9. Laski, *Authority*, p. 121.
10. King, *Fear of Power*, p. 128. In his *Four Essays on Liberty*, Isaiah Berlin implies that Bentham saw that 'some laws increase the total amount of liberty in a society' (p. xlix). I am not convinced that he did. Bentham certainly 'favoured laws', but he justified them in terms of increasing happiness or decreasing pain, rather than in terms of increasing the total amount of liberty. This is what distinguishes him from a writer like Hobhouse, who insisted against most of his fellow empiricists that laws can increase the total freedom (though, of course, they decrease the freedom of those being coerced). Hobhouse thus put forward an explicitly *liberal* defence of legislation, which Bentham did not do. See David Nicholls, 'Positive Liberty, 1880–1914', *American Political Science Review*, 56, 1962, pp. 114f.
11. Hobhouse, *The Metaphysical Theory of the State*, p. 36.
12. King, *Fear*, p. 128.
13. Mill, *Principles of Political Economy*, book 5 ch. 11.
14. Lindsay, 'The State in Recent Political Theory', *Political Quarterly*, February 1914, p. 128.
15. Figgis, *Churches*, p. 116; Laski, *Authority*, pp. 54–5.
16. Mill, *On Liberty*, ch. 1. Mill also wrote, 'I fully admit that the mischief which a person does to himself may seriously affect, both through their sympathies and their interests, those nearly concerned with him and, in a minor degree, society at large ...', ibid., ch. 4. Mill's defence of liberty must, of course be seen in the context of his utilitarian philosophy.
17. Acton, *The History of Freedom*, p. 203.
18. Cambridge University Library, Add. MSS, 4901: 20.
19. Louise Creighton, *Life and Letters of Mandell Creighton*, I, p. 263.
20. Laski, 'The Literature of Politics', *The New Republic*, 17 November 1917, p. 6.
21. *Letter to the Duke of Norfolk*, p. 53. But see S. A. Grave, *Conscience in Newman's Thought*, also David Nicholls, 'Gladstone, Newman and the Politics of Pluralism', in James Bastable, ed., *Newman and Gladstone*, pp. 32f.
22. Figgis, *Hopes*, p. 116.
23. Sermon 9, Mirfield MSS.
24. Zylstra, *From Pluralism to Collectivism*, p. 38.
25. Acton, *The Rambler*, January 1860, p. 146.
26. Acton, *The History of Freedom*, p. 3.
27. Figgis, *Hopes*, p. 114.
28. Laski, *Authority*, pp. 55 and 37. Green wrote of freedom as 'a positive power of doing or enjoying something worth doing or enjoying, and that, too, something that we do or enjoy in common with others'. *Works*, III, p. 371.
29. Laski, *Grammar*, p. 142; in later editions he changed this passage.
30. Cole, *Social Theory*, p. 184.
31. Cole, *Social Theory*, p. 182.
32. Cole, *Labour*, p. 194.

33. Cole, *Self-Government*, p. 227.
34. Russell, *Principles of Social Reconstruction*, p. 228.
35. Russell, *Political Ideals*, p. 10.
36. Tocqueville, *Journeys to England*, p. 24.
37. Quoted in J. Charles-Brun's introduction to Proudhon's *Principe fédératif*, p. 123n.
38. Acton in Mirfield MSS. It was, of course, the Tory Samuel Johnson who called the Devil the first Whig.
39. Figgis, Lecture on Aquinas, Mirfield MSS, Notebook 2.
40. Acton, Essays *on Freedom and Power*, p. 35. Richard Niebuhr has pointed out how the American puritans were similarly suspicious of power; see *The Kingdom of God in America*, pp. 77f.
41. Figgis, Lecture III on Marsilius, Mirfield MSS, Notebook 3.
42. Acton, *Essays*, p. 101.
43. Acton, *Essays*, p. 48.
44. Acton, *Essays*, pp. 48 and 63; and *Letters to Mary Gladstone*, p. 124.
45. Maitland, Introduction to Gierke, *Political Theories*, p. xliii.
46. G. P. Gooch, Foreword to G. Ritter, *The Corrupting Influence of Power*, p. x.
47. Laski, *Authority*, p. 387.
48. Laski, *Authority*, p. 90.
49. Sorel, *Réflexions sur la violence*, p. 151.
50. Russell, *Political Ideals*, pp. 11–12, and *Principles*, p. 73. Compare the views of critics of pluralism: 'it is not force that is dangerous but the will embodied in it. The problem, therefore, is not that of limiting sovereignty, but of educating the sovereign.' Norman Wilde, 'The Attack on the State', *International Journal of Ethics*, 1920, 30, p. 370.
51. Burke, 'Substance of the Speech on Army Estimates' (1790), in *Works*, III, pp. 9–10.
52. Georges Goyau, *Ketteler*, p. 41. this association idea was, he held, particularly strong with the German people, *Die Arbeiterfrage und das Christenthum*, pp. 49–50. Gierke continually made a similar point in *Das deutsche Genossenschaftsrecht, cf. II, p. 32*.
53. 'This pulverisation method, this chemical solution of humanity into individuals, into grains of dust of equal value, into particle which a puff of the wind may scatter in all directions – this method is as false as are the suppositions on which it rests', Ketteler, *Die Arbeiterfrage*, p. 57. See J. F. Stephen's remark, 'The existence of such a state of society reduces individuals to impotence, and to tell them to be powerful, original and independent is to mock them. It is like plucking a bird's feathers in order to put it on a level with beasts, and then telling it to fly'. *Liberty, Equality, Fraternity*, p. 46.
54. For a discussion of this principle see below pp. 130f.
55. Maitland, 'Moral Personality and Legal Personality', in *Collected Papers*, III, p. 311; reprinted below in appendix D.
56. Figgis, *Antichrist*, p. 266.
57. Figgis, *Churches*, p. 101.
58. S. Mogi, *The Problem of Federalism*, p. 312.
59. Figgis, *Churches*, p. 81; and Figgis in A. J. Mason *et al.*, *Our Place in Christendom*, p. 94.

60. Acton, *Essays*, p. 160.
61. Figgis, *Churches*, p. 101. See H. Butterfield, *The Historical Development of the Principle of Toleration in British Life*, p. 3.
62. W. K. Jordan, *The Development of Religious Toleration in England*, I, p. 19. For a discussion of the growth of toleration in the USA see A. P. Stokes, *Church and State in the United States*, especially, I, p. 244.
63. Figgis, 'A Puritan Utopia', *Church Quarterly Review*, 1903, p. 126.
64. For example A. A. Seaton *The Theory of Toleration under the Later Stuarts*, p. 18; Maitland seems to have held this view too: 'Scepticism or doubt is the legitimate parent of toleration', 'Liberty and Equality'(1875), in *Collected Papers*, I, p. 95.
65. Figgis, *Gerson*, p. 118.
66. Figgis, *Churches*, p. 101.
67. M. de W. Howe, ed., *Holmes–Laski Letters*, pp. 246–7.
68. Figgis, *Gerson*, p. 180.

3   The Attack on Sovereignty

1. A. J. Balfour, *The Foundations of Belief*, p. 217.
2. Bryce, *Studies in History and Jurisprudence*, II, p. 50.
3. Austin, *The Province of Jurisprudence Determined*, pp. 225 and 244.
4. Maine, *Lectures on the Early History of Institutions*, pp. 358–9
5. Dicey, *Introduction to the Study of the Law of the Constitution*, pp. 70–1. F. W. Coker, criticising the ideas of Laski on sovereignty, denied that 'any political philosopher of any school in any era' has maintained this notion of a practical (or political) sovereign having unlimited power. 'The Technique of the Pluralist State', *American Political Science Review*, 15, 1921, p. 194.
6. Ritchie, *Principles of State Interference*, p. 68; see also Ritchie, *Darwin and Hegel*, pp. 238f. Ritchie maintained that in the USA the constitution was the legal sovereign. This clearly contravenes the Austinian requirement that the sovereign must be a person or body of persons which issues commands.
7. Bryce, *Studies*, II, p. 63.
8. Bryce, *Studies*, II, p. 73.
9. See also W. Y. Elliott, who wrote of '... that intangible but sovereign thing called public opinion'. *The Pragmatic Revolt in Politics*, p. 272.
10. He might, for instance say that it *must* have been the will of the electorate or it wouldn't have prevailed.
11. Sidgwick, *The Elements of Politics*, p. 658.
12. Rees in *Mind*, 59, 1950, pp. 495f., reprinted in W. J. Stankiewicz, ed., *Defence of Sovereignty*, pp. 209f. The editor himself makes an abortive defence of the idea of sovereignty.
13. Some of these points were made by critics of American pluralism, including Steven Lukes, *Power: a Radical View* and more perceptively P. Bachrach and M. S. Baratz, *Power and Poverty: Theory and Practice*.
14. Hobbes, *Leviathan*, 2: 21.
15. Kant, *Groundwork of the Metaphysic of Morals*, ch. 2.
16. Tussman, *Obligation and the Body Politic*, p. 8.

17. Tussman, *Obligation,* p. 26. For a later attempt to defend ideas of 'tacit consent', see Albert Weale, 'Consent', *Political Studies,* 26, 1978, pp. 65f. and David Nicholls, 'A Comment on "Consent"', *Political Studies,* 27, 1979, pp. 120f.

18. Gierke, *Genossenschaftstheorie,* pp. 641–2. Gierke's pupil Hugo Preuss criticised him on this question of sovereignty, maintaining that the theory of group personality asserted by Gierke logically calls into question even this notion of state sovereignty. *Gemeinde, Staat, Reich,* p. 112.

19. Expounding the ideas of Althusius, Gierke wrote, 'Moreover it (the state) is not absolute but bound by legal limitations, even though it may seem exempt from positive law so far as compulsion and punishment are concerned.' Gierke, *The Development of Political Theory,* p. 40. See also his discussion of the ideas of Althusius in *Natural Law and the Theory of Society,* pp. 70f.

20. Barker, Introduction to Gierke, *Natural Law,* p. lxxxii.

21. 'I must emphasise the fact', wrote S. Mogi, 'that the aims and methods of Gierke's *Genossenschaftstheorie* are pluralistic in essence ... and not unitarist.' *Otto von Gierke,* p. 230. Earlier Mogi had placed Gierke's theory 'mid-way between the pluralistic and unitaristic tendencies'. *The Problem of Federalism,* p. 1084n.

22. Figgis, *Gerson,* p. 171.

23. Quoted in Figgis, *Churches,* p. 5n.

24. Figgis, Lecture III on Marsilius, Mirfield MSS, Notebook 3. Compare Lord Acton: 'According to the old conservative legitimist principles the right of authority ought always to be sustained in the case of revolution – and the new democratic doctrine is that the will of the people ought ever to prevail. ... Both personify right. They talk of the rights of government or of the people. But the supreme right is the divine right; and that is to be found sometimes on the one side and sometimes on the other. There is no general presumption either way.' MSS in possession of Mr Douglas Woodruff (in 1974), who kindly let me see the Acton MSS in his possession.

25. That is, of sovereignty.

26. Lecture on Aquinas, Mirfield MSS, Notebook 2.

27. Cole, 'Conflicting Social Obligations', in *Proceedings of the Aristotelian Society,* XV, 1914–15, p. 152. See also Cole, *Self-Government,* p. 82.

28. Bosanquet, 'Note on Mr Cole's Paper', *Proceedings of the Aristotelian Society,* XV, 1914–15, p. 161.

29. Cole, 'Conflicting Social Obligations', p. 157. It has been alleged that in an unfinished book on Rousseau, Cole rejected these ideas of sovereignty. (N. Carpenter, *Guild Socialism,* p. 89n.)

30. Barker, *Political Thought in England,* p. 223. Yet Barker later denied ever having held a pluralist doctrine which 'dissolves and divides the sovereignty of the State among a plurality of different groups or communities'. Barker, *Age and Youth,* p. 76.

31. Benoist, *La politique,* p. 56.

32. Duguit, *Law in the Modern State,* p. 40.

33. Sub-heading in T. H. Green, *Lectures on the Principles of Political Obligation,* section G.

34. Laski, 'The Pluralistic State', in *The Philosophical Review,* 28, 1919, p. 571. See appendix C. below.

35. Laski, *Problem,* p. 23.
36. Cohen, *Reason and Nature,* p. 398. My italics.
37. Hobhouse, 'Compulsion', in J. A. Hobson, and M. Ginsberg, L. T. *Hobhouse,* pp. 318–9.
38. Laski, *Grammar,* p. 44.
39. Lindsay, 'The State in Recent Political Theory', *The Political Quarterly,* 1914, pp. 134–5.
40. Introduction to Rousseau, *The Social Contract,* p. xxvi.
41. Cole, 'Conflicting Social Obligations', p. 158; and Cole, *Self-Government,* p. 84.
42. Figgis, *Divine Right,* pp. 232 and 246.
43. Figgis, 'On Some Political Theories of the Early Jesuits', in *Transactions of the Royal Historical Society,* 1897, p. 107.
44. Figgis, *Churches,* p. x.
45. E.C.S. Wade and G.C. Phillips, *Constitutional Law,* pp. 309–10.
46. Laski, 'The Pluralistic State', p. 565; see below, Appendix C, p. 165.
47. Howe, ed., *Holmes–Laski Letters,* p. 9n.
48. Howe, ed. *Pollock–Holmes Letters,* II, p. 25.
49. Hart, 'Positivism and the Separation of Law and Morals', *Harvard Law Review,* 71, 1958, p. 604.
50. Bradley, 'The Sovereignty of Parliament: in Perpetuity?', in J. Jowell and D. Oliver, eds, *The Changing Constitution,* p. 36.
51. Dicey, *The Law of the Constitution,* p. 38
52. For a discussion of this case see N. P. Gravells, 'Disapplying an Act of Parliament Pending a Preliminary Ruling: Constitutional Enormity of Community Law Right?', *Public Law,* 1989, p. 568; also H. W. R. Wade, 'What has Happened to the Sovereignty of Parliament?', *Law Quarterly Review,* 107, 1991, p. 1.
53. Duguit, 'The Law and the State', Harvard Law Review, 1917, 31, p. 158. See also Duguit, *L'Etat, le droit objectif et la loi positive,* pp. 131 f.
54. W. Jethroe Brown, 'The Personality of the Corporation and the State', *Law Quarterly Review,* 21, 1905, p. 377.
55. Lecture on Aquinas, Mirfield MSS, Notebook 2.
56. Of the writers we have been considering only Cole retains the concept of sovereignty, in a Rousseauite sense. Gierke used the term but by no means subscribed to a positivist interpretation of sovereignty. In denying that Figgis rejected the idea of sovereignty, and asserting that Cole (as well as Laski) did reject it, Stanislas Ehrlich is very much off course, as he is in other things he says about the British political pluralists. Ehrlich, *Pluralism, On and Off Course,* p. 82.

4   Group Personality

1. Maitland, *Collected Papers,* III, pp. 308–9.
2. Spencer, *Principles of Sociology,* para. 219 (I, p. 474) and para. 511 (II, p. 548). See also 'The Social Organism', in *Essays Scientific, Political and Speculative,* I, p. 358.

3. Maine, *Lectures on the Early History of Institutions,* p. 396.
4. I have discussed the political ideas of these men briefly in David Nicholls, 'Positive Liberty, 1880–1914', *American Political Science Review,* 56, 1962, pp. 117f.
5. Durkheim, *The Division of Labour,* p. 28; see also H. E. Barnes, 'Durkheim's Contribution to the Reconstruction of Political Theory', *Political Science Quarterly,* 35, 1920, pp. 236f.; also Steven Lukes, *Emile Durkheim: his Life and Work,* pp. 542f.
6. See H. E. Barnes, in C. E. Merriam and Barnes, eds, *Political Theories: Recent Times,* pp. 384f.
7. Bradley, *Ethical Studies,* p. 157.
8. Green, *Principles of Political Obligation,* para. 141.
9. Hobhouse, *The Metaphysical Theory of the State,* p. 29. See also Hobhouse, *Development and Purpose,* p. 187 and *Social Development,* pp. 277f.
10. Introduction to Gierke, *Political Theories,* p. xli.
11. Figgis, *Churches,* pp. 87–8.
12. Figgis, *Churches,* p. 48. George Homans writes, 'Each of the sociologists – Durkheim, LeBon, Figgis, Brooks Adams, who began, just before World War I, to point out the signs of decay in our society, used the same metaphor. They said that society was becoming a dust heap of individuals without links to one another.' *The Human Group,* p. 457. See also W. J. H. Sprott, *Human Groups,* p. 184; R. M. MacIver and C. H. Page, Society, p. 213; K. Lewin, *Resolving Social Conflicts,* p. 146
13. Figgis, *The Will,* p. 129; also Figgis, *Gerson,* p. 80.
14. Creighton, *The Mind of St Peter,* p. 19.
15. Figgis, 'The Church and the Secular Theory of the State', *Church Congress Report,* 1905, pp. 190–1. See Appendix B, below.
16. Figgis, Lectures on Marsilius, Mirfield MSS, Notebook 3. See also Figgis, *Gerson,* p. 180, and Figgis, *Churches,* pp. 76–7.
17. Forsyth, *Theology in Church and State,* pp. 160 and 206.
18. Laski, *Grammar,* p. 256.
19. Laski, *Problem,* pp. 208–9.
20. Laski, *Problem,* p. 4; see also Laski, 'The Apotheosis of the State', *The New Republic,* July 1916, p. 303.
21. *The University of Chicago Law Review,* 15, 1948, p. 580.
22. Laski, *Authority,* p. 68; see the discussion of this issue in B. Zylstra, *From Pluralism to Collectivism,* pp. 53f.
23. Cole, *Labour,* p. 38.
24. Barker, *Political Thought in England,* p. 153.
25. Barker, 'The Discredited State', *The Political Quarterly,* February 1915, p. 113.
26. Wisdom, *Philosophy and Psychoanalysis,* p. 9. There are, however, some British empiricists who are critical of this individualism; see J. O. Urmson, *Philosophical Analysis,* p. 152 and P. F. Strawson, *Individuals,* pp. 110f.
27. Stebbing, *Ideals and Illusions,* pp. 162f.
28. Selznick, *TVA and the Grass Roots,* pp. 162f.
29. Dicey, 'The Combination Laws', *Harvard Law Review,* 17, 1904, p. 532.
30. Savigny, *Systems of Modern Roman Law,* section 60 (the English translation of the second volume is called *Jural Relations,* II, 1–2). Corporate persons

are thus 'artificial subjects admitted by means of a pure fiction', section 85 (II, p. 176).

31. Gierke, *Das deutsche Genossenschaftsrecht*, III, p. 279. Figgis accepted this view (*Churches*, p. 249). This position is attacked by H. A. Smith (*The Law of Associations*, p. 156), who argues that Innocent was not concerned with 'the working out of purely speculative theories'. Neither Gierke nor Figgis asserted that Innocent had explicitly enunciated the theory but rather that his statements on practical questions of the day assumed something very like the fiction theory (Figgis, *English Historical Review*, 1916, 31, p. 177.)

32. Detailed references to cases discussed can be found in the table on p. 136.

33. Pollock, *Essays in the Law*, p. 153

34. For a more detailed discussion of Gierke's ideas see J. D. Lewis, *The Genossenschaft Theory of Otto von Gierke*.

35. Gierke, 'Grundbegriffe', p. 302.

36. Gierke, *Wesen*, p. 10; see also 'Den Kern der Genossenschaftstheorie bildet die von ihr dem Phantom der persons ficta entgegengestellte Auffassung der Körperschaft als *realer Gesammtperson*', Gierke, *Genossenschaftstheorie*, p. 5. On Gierke's conceptions of group life and community see Anthony Black, ed., *Community in Historical Perspective*, and J. D. Lewis, *The Genossenschaft Theory of Otto von Gierke*.

37. *Suttons Hospital Case*.

38. *Osborne Case*. J. D. Mabbott has summarised the changing status of trade unions in English law in *The State and the Citizen*, p. 117

39. Vinogradoff, 'Jural Persons', *Columbia Law Review*, 24, 1924, p. 604.

40. *Kent and Sussex Contractors*.

41. Hallis, *Corporate Personality*, p. lviii n.

42. *Great Northern Railway case*.

43. Report of the Committee on Company Law Amendment (1945) Cmd 6659.

44. L. C. B. Gower, *Modern Company Law*, p. 93.

45. Maitland, *Collected Papers*, III, p. 319.

46. Figgis, *Fellowship*, p. 74.

47. M. de Wolfe Howe, 'Political Theory and the Nature of Liberty', *Harvard Law Review*, 67, 1953, p. 93.

48. Kingsley Martin, *Harold Laski*, p. 29.

49. Figgis, 'National Churches', in A. J. Mason, *et al., Our Place in Christendom*, p. 131.

50. Webb, *Legal Personality and Political Pluralism*, p. 55.

51. Figgis, *Churches*, p. 179 (my italics). It is also clear, from p. 250, that Figgis was fully aware that the effects of the decision were mitigated by legislation.

52. Pollock, *Essays in the Law*, p. 167.

53. Laski, *Grammar*, p. 256 (my itals).

54. Williams, in *Salmond on Jurisprudence* (11th edn), pp. 362–3.

55. Farrer, *The Freedom of the Will*, p. 79.

56. Hart, 'Definition and Theory in Jurisprudence', *Law Quarterly Review*, 70, 1954, p. 56.

57. Latham, *The Group Basis of Politics*, p. 8.

58. Webb, *Legal Personality*, p. vi.

59. At times, however, Gierke did seem to suggest that his belief in the social reality of groups was derived from the fact that they were treated as persons in law (*Wesen*, p. 15), but this does not reflect his settled opinion.

60. Webb, *Legal Personality*, p. 52.

61. Lloyd, *The Law Relating to Unincorporated Associations*, pp. 4–5.

62. Maitland, Introduction to Gierke, *Political Theories*, p. xxxviii.

5 The State, the Group and the Individual

1. See Figgis's essay on Maitland, Acton and Creighton in 'Three Cambridge Historians', *Churches*, pp. 227–65.

2. D. Runciman, of Trinity College, Cambridge, examines this theme at length in an unpublished fellowship dissertation of 1992.

3. Sidgwick, *Elements of Politics*, pp. 574f.

4. The term 'coerce' is widely defined and includes such things as joining together to boycott certain goods (p. 578). Attempts to ban this would result in depriving many oppressed groups from taking effective action to protect themselves.

5. Sidgwick, *Elements*, p. 588.

6. Hegel, *Philosophy of Right*, paragraphs 302f.

7. Hegel, 'The German Constitution', in T. M. Knox and Z. A. Pelczynski, eds, *Hegel's Political Writings*, p. 158.

8. Hegel, *Philosophy of Right*, paragraph 288.

9. Latham, 'The Group Basis of Politics', *American Political Science Review*, 46, 1952, p. 379.

10. Cole, 'Conflicting Social Obligations', *Proceedings of the Aristotelian Society*, 15, 1914–15, p. 142.

11. R. M. MacIver, *The Modern State*, p. 170n.

12. *Rerum Novarum*, section 38; in *Five Great Encyclicals*, p. 24. A. D. Lindsay adopted similar terminology.

13. Magid, *English Political Pluralism*, pp. 26–7.

14. B. Zylstra, *From Pluralism to Collectivism*, p. 192. According to P. P. Craig, this distinction was 'a characteristic trait of the pluralists', *Public Law and Democracy*, p. 142.

15. This is the assumption, for example, in T. J. Gorringe, *Discerning Spirit*, pp. 49f., and in most 'communitarians'.

16. Figgis, *Churches*, p. 103.

17. Oakeshott, *On Human Conduct*, p. 263.

18. Oakeshott, *On Human Conduct*, p. 253.

19. Figgis, 'Erastianism', in Ollard, Cross and Bond, eds, *Dictionary of English Church History*, p. 211.

20. Figgis, *Churches*, p. 251.

21. Figgis, *Divine Right*, p. 292.

22. Figgis, *Churches*, p. 90, and *Antichrist*, p. 259.

23. Dewey, *Reconstruction in Philosophy*, p. 203.

24. Hegel, 'The German Constitution', in T. M. Knox and Z. A. Pelczynski, eds, *Hegel's Political Writings*, p. 155.

25. Figgis, *Churches*, pp. 252–3.

26. Lecture on Aquinas, Mirfield MSS, Notebook 2.

27. Figgis, *Churches*, p. 252.
28. Dicey, 'The Combination Laws', *Harvard Law Review*, 17, 1904, p. 514.
29. Figgis, *Churches*, p. 46.
30. Figgis, 'The Church and the Secular Theory of the State', *Church Congress Report*, 1905, p. 190. Reprinted below as Appendix A.
31. Creighton, *The Church and the Nation*, p. 72.
32. Figgis, *Churches*, p. 45.
33. Laski, *Authority*, pp. 27 and 122.
34. Laski, in *Holmes-Laski Letters*, p. 622.
35. Laski, 'The Pluralistic State', p. 566. See below Appendix C.
36. H.A. Deane, *The Political Ideas of Harold J. Laski*, p. 19.
37. Laski, *Problem*, p. 23.
38. Laski, *Grammar*, p. 84.
39. Cole, *Chaos*, p. 55.
40. In *Self Government* and in *Labour*, Cole wrote of the state as nothing more than an association of consumers; in *Social Theory* he regarded this as *one* of the features of the state, while later in the same year he claimed, in *Guild Socialism Restated*, to have 'destroyed the idea that the State represents the consumer' (p. 120).
41. Cole, 'Conflicting Social Obligations', p. 158.
42. Russell, *Principles of Social Reconstruction*, p. 58.
43. Russell, *Principles*, p. 72.
44. Russell, *Democracy and Direct Action*, p. 6.
45. Barker, 'The Discredited State', *The Political Quarterly*, February 1915, p. 101. In a note added to the article Barker claimed that the World War was demonstrating that loyalty to the state was still a powerful force.
46. Ulam, *The Philosophical Foundations of English Socialism*, p. 86.
47. Laski, *Introduction to Contemporary Politics*, p. 69.
48. Figgis, *Churches*, p. 92.
49. Follett, *The New State*, pp. 291 and 312.
50. Follett, 'Community is a Process', *Philosophical Review*, 28, 1919, p. 580.
51. Follett, *The New State*, p. 312.
52. Ulam, *The Philosophical Foundations*, p. 86.
53. David Nicholls, 'Politics and Religion in Haiti', *Canadian Journal of Political Science*, 3, 1970, pp. 400f.; also *From Dessalines to Duvalier*, pp. 221f.
54. Furnivall, *Colonial Policy and Practice*, pp. 297f; and 'Some Problems of Tropical Economy', in Rita Hinden, ed., *Fabian Colonial Essays*, pp. 167f. I have considered social and cultural pluralism in more detail in Nicholls, *Three Varieties of Pluralism*, ch. 4.
55. See Vera Rubin, ed., *Social and Cultural Pluralism in the Caribbean*, and L. Kuper and M.G. Smith, eds, *Pluralism in Africa*. There is a useful bibliography in the latter book on pp. 491f.
56. Dahrendorf, *Class and Class Conflict in Industrial Society*, p. 316.
57. R. Bendix, in his English translation of G. Simmel, *The Web of Group Affiliations*.
58. David Nicholls, 'East Indians and Black Power in Trinidad', *Race*, 12, 1971, pp. 443f.; reprinted in Nicholls, *Haiti in Caribbean Context: Ethnicity, Economy and Revolt*.

6 The Ideological Foundations of a Secular State

1. Much has been written by sociologists and theologians on secularisation. See for example, Bryan Wilson, *Religion in Sociological Perspective*, Ch. 6; David Martin, *A General Theory of Secularization;* S. S. Acquaviva, *L'eclissi del sacro nella civiltà industriale;* H. Cox, *The Secular City*; J. B. Metz, *Zur Theologie der Welt.*
2. Chesterton, 'Epilogue', in Charles Gore *et al., The Return of Christendom,* p. 246. This idea of a world come of age, requiring a demythologised gospel, was hinted at by Dietrich Bonhoeffer, *Letters from Prison,* and popularised by John Robinson, *Honest to God;* relics of this view can be found in the many writings of Don Cupitt.
3. For example, Andrew Greeley, *Unsecular Man.*
4. Figgis, 'Respublica Christiana', in *Churches*, pp. 175f., and Figgis, 'Erastus and Erastianism', in *Divine Right*, pp. 293f.
5. Figgis, *Divine Right*, p. 199.
6. See Figgis, 'Some Political Theories of the Early Jesuits', *Transactions of the Royal Historical Society*, 1897, NS 11, pp 89f.
7. Laski, *Problem*, pp. 108 and 69n.
8. Figgis, *Civilisation at the Crossroads*, p. 32.
9. Figgis, *Churches*, p. 114.
10. Figgis, *Churches*, p. 112.
11. Figgis, *Fellowship,* pp. 100f.
12. Figgis, *Churches*, p. 130 and *Fellowship,* p. 101.
13. Hauerwas, *The Peaceable Kingdom*, p. 99.
14. See Yoder, *The Politics of Jesus;* Yoder, *The Original Revolution;* also Yoder, 'What would you do if?' *Journal of Religious Ethics,* 2, 1974, pp. 82f. Hauerwas, *The Peaceable Kingdom.*
15. Figgis, *Civilisation*, p. 171.
16. See Isaac Williams, 'On Reserve in Communicating Religious Knowledge', *Tracts for the Times,* no. 80; see also Robin C. Selby, *The Principle of Reserve in the Writings of John Henry Cardinal Newman.*
17. Lindbeck, *The Nature of Doctrine: Religion and Theology in a Postliberal Age,* p. 132.
18. Rawls, *A Theory of Justice.* See also Brian Barry, *The Liberal Theory of Justice,* and R. P. Wolff, *Understanding Rawls.* The debate between communitarians and liberals is explored in Will Kymlicka, *Liberalism, Community and Culture;* also in S. Mulhall and A. Swift, *Liberals and Communitarians.*
19. Taylor, *Philosophical Papers, II: Philosophy and the Human Sciences*; and *Hegel and Modern Society.* Michael J. Sandel, *Liberalism and the Limits of Justice.*
20. Introduction to David Nicholls, ed., *Church and State in Britain since 1820,* pp. 13f. and above, pp. 18f.
21. Figgis, *The Will to Freedom*, p. 301.
22. Figgis, *The Gospel and Human Needs,* p. 11. 'It is to betray the grossest ignorance of the world in which we live,' declared Figgis, 'to talk of our present controversies as though they were all being conducted in a rectory garden with everyone friendly and the most unbelieving ready, and indeed

anxious, to walk across the garden to the evening service if only you could make the path a little clearer. It is not a garden, it is a gulf which divides these people from the church', Figgis, *Antichrist*, pp. 12–13.

23.   Figgis, *Fellowship*, p. 146.

24.   Creighton, *The Church and the Nation*, p. 277.

25.   Figgis, *Religion and English Society*, p. 29.

26.   Figgis, *The Cambridge Review*, 3 February 1915, p. 179. G. le Bras made a similar point with respect to the church in France. 'Déchristianisation: mot fallacieux', *Social Compass*, 10, 1963, pp. 445f.

27.   Lippmann, *The Good Society*, ch. 15; and *The Public Philosophy*, ch. 8; both reprinted in Clinton Rossiter and James Lare, eds, *The Essential Lippmann*, pp. 172–3 and 176–8.

28.   Lippmann, *The Public Philosophy* ch. 8, in *The Essential Lippmann*, p. 179

29.   Neuhaus, 'From Civil Religion to Public Philosophy', in L. S. Rouner, ed., *Civil Religion and Political Theology*, p. 106.

30.   John Courtney Murray, 'The Problem of Pluralism in America', *Thought*, 29, 1954, p. 165.

31.   A recent attempt to rehabilitate the notion of a public philosophy may be found in William M. Sullivan, *Reconstructing Public Philosophy*.

32.   L. S. Rouner, 'To be at Home: Civil Religion as a Common Bond', in Rounder, ed., *Civil Religion*, p. 133. Civil religion may indeed be a bond, though not in the sense intended!

33.   Davidson, 'American Democracy as a Religion', *International Journal of Ethics*, 10, 1899, p. 26.

34.   Coleridge, *On the Constitution of Church and State, According to the Idea of Each.*

35.   Eliot, quoted in E. R. Norman, *Church and Society in England, 1770–1970*, p. 398; see also Eliot, *The Idea of a Christian Society.*

36.   Though Eliot did recognise an institutional pluralism, of a 'cross-cutting' kind. See his *Notes Towards the Definition of Culture*, p. 50.

37.   Rawls, *Political Liberalism*, pp. 133ff.

38.   Rescher, *Pluralism: Against the Demand for Consensus*, p. 134.

39.   *Pluralism*, p. 124. After what he says about different rational conclusions being dependent on differing circumstances, it is not clear in what way one person's position is thought to be *rationally superior* to those of others with different experiences. He maintains that a number of different and even conflicting evaluative, cognitive and practical positions can each be 'perfectly appropriate to one or another perspective basis' (p. 102). If the others who disagree with my position have rationally based their own position on their experience and circumstances, the only way my position can be superior is that my experience or circumstances are in some way 'superior' to theirs.

40.   *Pluralism*, p. 194.

41.   H. M. Relton, *Church and State*, p. 18.

42.   G. L. Prestige, *The Life of Charles Gore*, p. 352.

43.   Church Information Office, *Church and State*, paras 117f.

7 Authority in the Church

1. Clark Kerr, *Industrial Relations and the Liberal Pluralist*, p. 14.
2. Selznick, *Law Society and Industrial Justice*, p. 38. See also Grant McConnell, in J.R. Pennock and J.W. Chapman, eds, *Voluntary Associations*, p. 153.
3. Selznick, *Law*, p. 40.
4. De Maistre, *Du pape*, pp. 15–16.
5. Figgis, *Churches*, p. 135. Hobbes actually wrote 'the Papacy is no other than the *ghost* of the deceased *Roman empire*, sitting crowned upon the grave thereof.' *Leviathan*, 4:47, p. 457.
6. Figgis, *Fellowship*, p. 201; see also *Antichrist*, p. 263.
7. Figgis, *Hopes*, p. 71 and *Churches*, p. 136.
8. Figgis, *Churches*, pp. 151 and 237; also see Figgis in G. K. A. Bell, ed., *The Meaning of the Creed*, p. 193.
9. Tyrrell, *The Church and the Future*, p. 120n; see also Figgis, *The Gospel and Human Needs*, p. 137.
10. Figgis, *Fellowship*, p. 197.
11. Figgis, *Fellowship*, p. 60.
12. Newman, *The Via Media of the Anglican Church*, I, pp. xl, lxxx and 202n. See David Nicholls, 'Individualism and the Appeal to Authority', in Nicholls and F. Kerr, eds, *John Henry Newman: Reason, Rhetoric and Romanticism*, pp. 194f.
13. Figgis, *Churches*, p. 141. In *Deity and Domination* I argue this connection between ideas of God and the state, though suggest that the relationship is a dialectical one.
14. Figgis, *Fellowship*, p. 188.
15. Figgis, *Hopes*, p. 74.
16. Figgis, *Fellowship*, p. 189. 'Each nation, patriarchate, diocese, parish, finally the individual Christian, all bear their part', *Fellowship*, pp. 202–3.
17. Figgis, *Hopes*, p. 120
18. Figgis, 'Councils and Unity', in A. J. Mason *et al., Our Place in Christendom*, p. 119.
19. The conciliar movement, he wrote, 'stands for an incoate federalism and the rights of national groups, as against a centralising bureaucracy'. Figgis, 'Councils and Unity', p. 94.
20. Figgis, *Churches*, p. 146.
21. F. Dvornik, *National Churches and the Church Universal*, p. 6.
22. Figgis was preparing a MSS on Bossuet before he died in 1919. See also Figgis, 'National Churches', p. 122, and 'Some Recent Bossuet Literature', *Journal of Theological Studies*, 18, 1916–17, pp. 313f.
23. Figgis, 'National Churches', pp. 122f.
24. Figgis, *Hopes*, p. 80; see also *The Gospel and Human Needs*, p. 137.
25. Figgis, *Hopes*, pp. 59 and 63f.
26. Figgis, 'Councils and Unity', p. 91.
27. Figgis, *'National Churches'*, p. 140.
28. J. H. Newman, *A Letter Addressed to his Grace the Duke of Norfolk*, p. 66. For some of the ambiguities in Newman's position in this matter, see David Nicholls, 'Gladstone, Newman and the Politics of Pluralism', in J. D.

Bastable, ed., *Newman and Gladstone: Centennial Essays*, pp. 32f.; and S. A Grave, *Conscience in Newman's Thought.*

29. Figgis, *Fellowship*, p. 55; see also P. T. Forsyth, *The Principle of Authority*, p. 400.
30. Figgis, *Churches*, p. 154.
31. Sidgwick, *The Ethics of Conformity and Subscription;* also 'The Ethics of Religious Conformity' and 'Clerical Veracity', in *Practical Ethics.*
32. L. Creighton, *Life and Letters of Mandell Creighton*, II, p. 347; Charles Gore, *The Basis of Anglican Fellowship*, p. 26; J. F. Bethune-Baker, *The Miracle of Christianity;* H. Rashdall, 'Professor Sidgwick on the Ethics of Religious Conformity: a Reply', *The International Journal of Ethics*, 7, 1897, pp. 137f.; H. M. Gwatkin, *The Bishop of Oxford's Open Letter;* W. Sanday, *Bishop Gore's Challenge to Criticism.*
33. Tyrrell, *The Church and the Future*; Acton, *The History of Freedom*, pp. xviif.
34. Tyrrell, *The Church and the Future*, p. 145.
35. Figgis in Bell, ed., *The Meaning of the Creed*, p. 205.
36. Figgis, *Fellowship*, p. 270.
37. Figgis, *Hopes*, p. 120 and *Fellowship*, pp. 168 and 155.
38. Figgis, *Hopes*, p. 32.
39. Troeltsch, *The Social Teaching of the Christian Churches*, I, pp. 329f. and II, pp. 461f.
40. D. Warwick, 'The Centralisation of Ecclesiastical Authority: an Organisational Perspective', *Concilium*, January 1974, pp. 109–10.
41. K. Rahner, *Bishops: their Status and Function*, pp. 63f.
42. Rahner, 'Pluralism in Theology and the Unity of the Church's Profession of Faith', *Concilium*, June 1969, p. 49.
43. Rahner, 'Pluralism', p. 50.
44. Rahner, 'Pluralism', pp. 55–6.
45. Wiles, 'Theology and Unity', *Theology*, no. 77, 1974, pp. 4f. This 'inductive' approach is present in the thinking of Schleiermacher, as in that of Tyrrell and the Modernists. Does Wiles not mean provisional yet *adequate*?
46. Rahner, 'Pluralism', pp. 57 and 53. See W. M. Thompson, 'Rahner's Theology of Pluralism', *The Ecumenist*, January–February 1973, p. 20.
47. McConnell, 'The Spirit of Private Government', *American Political Science Review*, 52, 1958, p. 754.
48. See for example Nicholas Lash, *Change in Focus.*
49. Though some would maintain that the teaching is infallibly defined see John C. Ford and Germain Grisez, 'Contraception and the Infallibility of the Ordinary Magisterium', *Theological Studies*, 39, 1978.
50. Hill, *Ministry and Authority in the Catholic Church*, p. 4.
51. Hill, *Ministry*, p. 109.
52. Hill, *Ministry*, pp. 125–6.
53. Anglican-Roman Catholic International Commission, *The Final Report*, pp. 52 and 56.
54. *Final Report*, p. 72. A distinction prodigious deep, it might be thought.
55. *Final Report*, p. 63.

8   Conclusion

1.   David Miller *et al.*, eds, *Blackwell's Dictionary of Political Thought.*
2.   Figgis, *Divine Right*, p. 292.
3.   H. E. Barnes, 'Durkheim's Contribution to the Reconstruction of Political Theory', *Political Science Quarterly*, 35, 1920, pp. 236f.
4.   Newman, *Discussions and Arguments on Various Subjects*, p. 295. Sorel several times quoted Newman with approval, in his *Réflexions sur la violence.* See J. W. Scott, *Syndicalism and Philosophical Realism.*
5.   J. W. Scott, *Syndicalism and Philosophical Realism*, p. 161.
6.   *Syndicalist Railwayman*, September 1911.
7.   See S.T. Glass, *The Responsible Society.*
8.   See particularly K. Coates and T. Topham, *Workers' Control.*
9.   J. E. Gleeson, *What Distributism Means*, p. 1.
10. 'In the development of modern life we have been obsessed with the idea that size is of over-riding importance', Gleeson, *What Distributism Means*, p. 6. See E. F. Schumacher, *Small is Beautiful.*
11. See A. J. Penty, *The Restoration of the Gild System*; Penty, *Distributism: a Manifesto.*
12. J. E. F. Mann *et al., The Real Democracy.* See also H. Belloc and C. Chesterton, *The Party System*; H. Belloc, *The Servile State*; P. Derrick, *Lost Property*; H. E. Humphries, *Liberty and Property: an Introduction to Distributism.*
13. V. J. McNabb, *Communism or Distributism?*
14. For this aspect of Gierke's thought see Antony Black, *Guilds and Civil Society in European Thought from the Twelfth Century to the Present*; and a selection of Gierke's texts, mostly from vol. 1 of *Das deutsche Genossenschaftsrecht* edited by Black, *Community in Historical Perspective.*
15. On Durkheim's corporatism see Antony Black, *Guilds and Civil Society*, ch. 19.
16. Ernest Barker, *Reflections on Government*, pp. 347.
17. R. H. Bowen, *German Theories of the Corporative State*, p. 12.
18. See N. Harris, *Competition and the Corporate Society;* R. E. Pahl and J. T. Winkler, 'The Coming Corporatism', *New Society*, 10 October 1974; P. Schmitter, 'Still the Century of Corporatism', *Review of Politics*, 36, 1974, pp. 85f. As one writer remarked 'corporatism' was a growth industry among academics through the 1980s; see for example Alan Cawson, *Corporatism and Political Theory.*
19. Ross M. Martin, 'Pluralism and the New Corporatism', *Political Studies*, 31, 1983, p. 89. Government policy, it might be observed, which has emerged as a result of consultation with the corporations.
20. Alan Cawson, 'Pluralism, Corporatism and the Role of the State', *Government and Opposition*, 13, 1978, p. 190; Leo Panitch, 'The Development of Corporatism in Liberal Democracies', *Comparative Political Studies*, 10, 1977, p. 74.
21. 'Notes and Comments', in *The Political Quarterly*, 29, 1968, p. 4.
22. Messner, *Social Ethics: Natural Law in the Western World*, p. 213.
23. Delors, *Séance d'ouverture de la quarantième année academique du Collège de Europe*, Bruges, 1989; quoted in Paul Spicker, 'The Principles of Sub-

sidiarity and the Social Policy of the European Community', *Journal of European Social Policy*, 1, 1991, pp. 3–4. See also Gavin McCrone, 'Subsidiarity: its Implications for Economic Policy', *National Westminster Bank Review*, November 1992, pp. 46f.

24. Translated into English under the title *A New Critique of Theoretical Thought*.

25. The most convenient discussion of the idea of sphere sovereignty is to be found in H. Dooyeweerd, *Roots of Western Culture: Pagan, Secular, and Christian Options*, ch. 2. For a comparison between subsidiarity and sphere sovereignty see Jonathan Chaplin in F. McHugh and S. M. Natale, *Unfinished Agenda: Catholic Social Teaching Revisited*. See also unpublished PhD thesis by Chaplin: 'Pluralism, Society and the State' (London University, 1993).

26. Rockefeller, *The Quality of Life in the Americas*, p. 27.

27. Shils, *The Torment of Secrecy*, p 231.

28. Lippmann, *A Preface to Morals*, p. 270.

29. Shils, *Torment*, pp. 225 and 227.

30. Shils, *Torment*, p. 155n.

31. Eisenhower, however, saw this complex as a challenge to the authority of government, while Mills saw the government as a part of the power élite.

32. Kariel, *The Decline of American Pluralism*, p. 2. See also W. E. Connolly, ed., *The Bias of Pluralism*.

33. Wolff, *The Poverty of Liberalism*, p. 159.

34. D. Baskin, 'American Pluralism', *Journal of Politics*, 32, 1970, p. 85.

35. Baskin, 'American Pluralism', p. 85.

36. Wolff, *Poverty*, p. 151.

37. Cambridge University Library, Add. MSS, 5011: 235.

Appendix A
The Church and the Secular Theory of the State[1]
J. N. Figgis

There are two great tasks before the Church. Both are predominantly intellectual. Yet without them practical work must first become hollow and then disappear. Of these task the former has been treated – apologetics proper. We need to convince the individual that the Christian faith is not an excusable survival among the vulgar, not an emotional eccentricity of the cultivated, but is at once the condition and the consequence of personal and intellectual development, where it is complete. Education in its full sense, the making of a man, does not tolerate the faith of the Cross; it postulates it. The culture of the whole being is a 'schoolmaster to bring men to Christ'. To show this is our first and greatest task. It is the supreme achievement of Mandell Creighton, that he witnessed to the truth by what he was.

It is, however, with the second and the smaller of these tasks that this paper deals – the semi-political one of investigating the place of the self-conscious Church in the modern State. We have to show that the Church may claim a due independence, because it is a life not a contrivance; an organism not an organisation. Its claim to recognition is disinterested and serves the whole community – Christian and non-Christian. In a word, when the Church asks the State to acknowledge that it has real powers for developing itself, it is asking not for a privilege to be conceded, but for the facts to be realized. The Church is to fight not for its own hand, but for what is *true* about human life in society.

What is the enemy which we have to face?

'There are no rights but the rights of the State, there can be no authority but the authority of the republic.' These are the words of M. Combes anent the dissolution of the *Concordat* in France. In a couple of phrases they concentrate the notions of our adversaries. That there may be a juristic sense in which these words are true, I do not deny. Nothing is gained by ignoring facts. Legally, the State could establish Mohammedanism to-morrow – or rather in the next session of Parliament. But if we regard as a practical maxim a description of facts or an ideal for the future, the statement of M. Combes has no other merit but that of being indisputably false. Firstly, we may say that in England nobody now – unless a few absolute Socialists – believes it to be practically true of individuals. There are certain rights such as those for discussion, contract, and fair trial which have become *real* for all. Legally, indeed, they can be treated as the grant of the State. Actually, they are the result of age-long struggles and the expression of the English character. What we have now to secure is the liberty and power of self-development of *Societies* other than the State. It is in regard to such societies – to the Church, in fact – that for the next two generations or more the issue is going to be joined. The battle will be inevitable and terrific between those who believe and those who do not believe, that 'there are no rights but the rights of the State, there can be no authority but the authority of the republic'.

Let us try and see a little more clearly what it means. In his campaign against the religious orders, M. Combes declared that to take vows of obedience was to encroach upon the civil power, and to surrender what no one has a right to surrender. This dots the 'i's' a little. Take it in conjunction with the proposal – of another anti-clerical – to prohibit to religious uses those cathedrals which are the glory of France, and the symbol of the illustrious lineage of its people; and we shall see what the maxim expanded in practice may come to mean. They want, as they said, to create a *unité morale* through the State, the atmosphere of all education, the main source of the idea of duty. You can read more in the volume *Une Campagne Laique* of M. Combes. Dr Clifford's Letters are also illuminating. I mention these because issues are clear in France, without desiring to prejudge the question whether this attack be not the just nemesis of ultramontanism. The point is not what the French Church may or may not deserve; but that M. Combes stands for a certain notion of human society, and that notion is *false*. Here things are more confused, and Englishmen always more really tolerant even when they delude themselves into the belief that they are bigots. Yet the same idea is dominant in this country to-day, and it has to be met. And the only way possible to conquer a false idea is to put the true one into people's minds. 'Ideas rule the world, in the long run.'

What is the real objection to undenominationalism? It is not un-Christian. There is no theoretic reason why an undenominational system should not teach that love to Jesus of which all dogma is the inadequate intellectual expression and every Christian institution the imperfect realization. It might, indeed, be merely a matter of expediency whether or not undenominational solution of the education problem be not possible. But undenominationalism (and secularism too) as a universal principle means more than this. It means the denial of religion except as an individual luxury or a State-boon. The religious society is to be nothing – except to the fortunate classes – any more than the family is to pauper children in a workhouse. That the Church should be the home of the soul from its baptism is denied. The only home is the State. The State is to consider individuals only – and in no way to recognise churches for the educational period of the great majority of its citizens. To assert against this doctrine the rights of the parent, i.e., of the family as the unit instead of the individual, may be expedient, but it is not enough. What we must assert, are bound to assert, cannot help asserting if we have thought out our principles is this. The Church *has* real rights and true authority over all its members the moment they become such. The parent must bring the child, it is true. But the moment anyone has joined a church (or a club for that matter), he is not only John Smith, but an integral part of a society with a life of its own. We are fighting no selfish battle, advocating no private cause. It is public freedom that we want. We say that the world is *not*, as a fact, composed of a new vast unities known as States, set over against crowds of isolated individuals; but is a society of societies, each and all with rights, liberty and life of their own.

We do not need to deny the due rights of the civil power, as the guardian of property and interpreter of contract. We shall do no good by claiming for the Church powers which it is either inexpedient or unfair for it to exercise. We need enquiry. We must know the limits as well as the province of the Church within the modern State. I merely suggest the problem. What does the self-conscious life of the religious society mean in relation to affairs to-day? What is its essence? Only as knowing this shall we know what we must claim and where we are bound to stop. It is a new problem. In the mediaeval world, and for a long while after the Reformation, Church and State appeared as merely different departments of the same institution. Of course they quarrelled, as Government departments do. Even soldiers and civilians have been known to quarrel in the year of grace 1905. Now, however, this has ceased even in appearance. What we have to secure is our corporate existence, our real life functioning inside a State, itself made up of complex elements and tolerating all religions. The tolerant State is the true State. The uniform State of the past was founded on a lie. Religious persecution is fundamentally un-Christian. We are suffering for the sins of our fathers. But the State has yet to learn that she must tolerate not merely individual liberty but the religious society, must know that its life is real and must develop, and cannot (not *must* not) be stopped. This is our task; it is hard, but it is high. We have to do with the real facts of human society, not with prescriptive claims or traditional rights. We have the future with us, not merely the past.

Establishment cannot save us. Only this year our most eminent philosophic jurist expressed something like horror that in such a matter as divorce the clergy of the State Church should be permitted to have a different view of morals from that of the State.[2]

Disestablishment will not deliver us. France shows that. Only the truth can make us free.

The question, be it observed, is not the theological one. 'What is the Divine authority or nature of the Church?' but the political, 'What rights has the religious society which the State is bound to acknowledge on pain of being false to itself?'

Scotland has given us an example. In the case of the United Free Church, the most august Court of Judicature in the world found itself unable to allow that a religious community had any real life of its own, in fact was more than a company formed upon certain articles under the aegis of the State. No reasoning of Mr Haldane could convince those luminaries that the Church, so far as the law was concerned, could be anything more than a body of trustees. The idea of inherent corporate life they rejected. Such was the law; not so the facts. Even through a moribund and paralytic Parliament was driven a statute of far-reaching import to prevent *summum jus* being *summa injuria*. The fact is, that to deny to smaller societies a real life and meaning, a personality, in fact, is not anti-clerical, or illiberal, or unwise, or oppressive – it is untrue. And 'all the king's horses and all the king's men' cannot make that true which is untrue. The House of Lords cannot do it. Even the Roman Empire, with the mediaeval Papacy thrown in, the *fons et origo mali* cannot do it; because it is impossible. And we shall win.

But we shall not win yet. It may be a thousand years before we do or only a generation. It does not matter. We shall not win without a struggle – a struggle in which hard thought and patience must be ours; and that charity that comes of being sure. We need a clear intellectual knowledge of principles, and the will to fight for essentials – but for nothing else. This work – that of securing the liberty and real life of societies within the huge and complex modern State – will not be done by irresponsible chatter or by mere sentimentalism, in all ages the danger of religion. It will not be done by treating the Church of England as a *pis aller*, just good enough not to desert – so long as you can disobey the bishop. It cannot be done by individualist caprice masquerading as Catholic custom. Least of all will it be done by uncritical appeals to the *Corpus Juris Canonici*, a code relative to the conditions of mediaeval Europe, saturated with Papalism, and its earlier portions steeped in forgery.

Done, however, the work must and shall be, if the Church is not to vanish into a royal benevolent fund or dissolve into an academic debating society. We must have no want of charity or calumnies against Dissent, even though it should appear bigoted or refuse to understand us; if we do not know better, why are we Churchmen? We must not mistake rapid for wise action, or violent language for firmness. Ours must be perfect tolerance, but also entire conviction; unwearied thought and courage immovable; above all, the faith – the real faith that is strong and 'endures as seeing Him Who is invisible'. And then we are bound to win – we cannot help it – for it is we and not our adversaries, who are for truth and freedom in human society.

Notes

1. From *Church Congress Report* (1905) pp. 189f.
2. See A. V. Dicey, *Law and Public Opinion in England.*

Appendix B
Church and State[1]
J. N. Figgis

'Marvel not, my brethren, if the world hate you.' – 1 JOHN 3: 13.

The Festival of St Alban leads us to consider the quality and cause of martyrdom. Modern inquiry has dispelled the illusion that the persecution in the early Church was due merely to caprice or to personal unpopularity, or some abstract legal pedantry about *religio illicita*. The true case of the conflict between the Imperial administration and the Church has been definitely established by Sir William Ramsay in *The Church and the Roman Empire*. There he shows that the difference was one of vital principle. Christians were persecuted because they set up a 'new non-Roman unity,' repudiating the dogma of the omni-competence of the State. In other words, they were persecuted because they were a Church. The perception of this antagonism was more or less unconscious on both sides, from the day when Tacitus spoke of the Christians as *hostes humani generis* – i.e. at war with the current presuppositions of society – down to the final struggle under Diocletian. It was because the State demanded and the Church could not yield an unlimited allegiance (symbolised by the Emperor-worship) that the Christians made so many Roman holidays. Apart from this there might have been local riots or mere conservative cruelty. But what redeems even Galerius or Decius from sheer wickedness and lifts the struggle into the universal sphere is this claim of the new society to a life underived from the State, with the consequent right to impose limits on civil allegiance. it was because he saw this that St John wrote the words, 'Marvel not if the world hate you.' Why should they be surprised? It was the most natural thing in the world.

The dogma of State absolutism had come to the Roman Empire, the hard-won guerdon of millennial contests. The city-State recked nothing of the individual, save in and through itself – still less of any competing society. The whole world, *humanum genus*, took it as an axiom; political philosophers made it their starting-point; and the Imperial lawyers wove it into the complex system which still holds very largely the allegiance of the civilised world. Was it likely that men would surrender without a struggle those principles which seemed involved in the very notion of civil unity – or that the world-spirit in Rome would admit that its god was an idol? No. It was not likely, and it did not happen – the Church did not conquer without a war.

That war is still proceeding. With the peace of the Church under Constantine it might seem that the Christian idea of the State as the controlling power, guiding but not creating other societies, had come to its own. It was not so.

So deeply were men imbued with the notion of a single all-absorbing authority, that from persecution of the Church we pass to persecution by the Church, and witness for many centuries the dominance of the ideal of a great Church-State, with no freedom for other societies. More than this, the doctrine of the centrality of political power won its way into the inmost arcana of Church government; and found in the spectacle of an omnipotent world-priest a symbol more august, more enthralling, and more profoundly

161

dangerous to human society than any secular *Imperium*. It is the positive facts of the ancient compact city- State, developed into a universal system, made the corner-stone of law and politics governing alike the Church and the world, which are, as Bishop Stubbs said of the *Corpus Juris Civilis*, fatal alike to civil and religious liberty.

It is that *damnosa hereditas* we need to get rid of in the interests alike of a truly free State and a rightly functioning Church. *Libera Chiesa in libero Stato* is and must be our ideal. It is that battle – the battle of freedom in human society – that we of this Union are fighting. And we need to know what we are about. Some years ago I heard a remark of an eminent mathematician: 'The English people have not realised the idea of a Church.' It is true. That any corporate society, whether Church, or trade-union, or family, should assert its inherent life and by its claims on its members set limits to the moral omnipotence of the law is to most Englishmen, and especially English lawyers, unthinkable or repulsive. Our most eminent writer on Constitutional Law, Professor Dicey, writes with dislike, even in regard to the Act of 1857, that 'a clergyman, though an official of the State, is virtually allowed to pronounce immoral a marriage permitted by the morality of the State.'

That is a very mild expression of the attitude commonly taken to-day. Mr. Justice Darling's words in the case of Canon Thompson were stronger. It is that sentiment of the absolute supremacy of the civil law which our Union exists to combat; though it must be admitted that in the past it has been effectually contested by non-Catholic bodies like the Presbyterians and the Baptists.

Matthew Arnold was wont, in his inimitable way, to make fine sport of Mr. Miall, the Nonconformist M.P. of the seventies, and his words about maintaining 'the dissidence of Dissent and Protestantism of the Protestant religion.' We might adapt his words and declare that we exist to maintain 'the churchliness of Churchmanship and the Catholicity of the Catholic religion.'

It is for Christianity as a distinct entity for which we stand – no mere philosophic or ethical system – and for English Churchmanship with its peculiar note. Neither as against the State, of which we are citizens, nor as against that whole of which we are but a part, though a living part, do we lay claim to unlimited freedom. As citizens we bow to the just claims of that great England which bore us; as Catholics we would not if we could be severed from that stream of universal life which flows through the Church of the ages. While maintaining our distinction, we would not unduly press mere insularity. We claim to be not worse but better citizens, because we are loyal Churchmen. So we claim to be not worse but better Catholics because we are English Churchmen. Of the illimitable authority arrogated by the civil power, we say that it is false to the facts of human life in society; that we are doing a service to politics by asserting on the highest plane the doctrine of the inherent, underived, though not uncontrolled, life of societies within the State. In regard to the Church we say that we are laying down the lines upon which alone the reunion of Christendom is thinkable, in so far as we protest against the ultramontane theory of authority, which would centralise all Church life at one point, which is entangled with a narrow view of development, the outcome of conditions in the West for ever passed away, and which rests on certain notions of Roman jurisprudence, false no less to the fundamental facts of human life – the family, the town, the union – than to ecclesiastical development and national honour. Before I close, let me briefly review some ways in which at this moment we need to fight for this distinctness of our organic religion.

First, in the realm of thought. In her latest work, that lady, who attempted in *Robert Elsmere* to solve the religious problem for one generation, has returned to the Arnoldian ideal of Erastianism. In her earlier book she made her hero resign his preferments on adopting Unitarian views. Not so with Richard Meynell. The purpose of the book is to maintain the thesis that since the national Church is national no limits can be set to the opinions of its ministers. It is no question of altering the limits, but of denying them altogether. Other controversies have very striking claims of a similar nature. It is alleged that historical criticism must always be open to a priest; that a priest while still officiating as a priest is free to deny not merely the miraculous but every single historical element in the Christian creed, so that a Drews or a Jensen might occupy the thrones of Canterbury and York, with moralists like Nietzsche in London – at least that is where these principles logically lead. Such principles would seem ludicrous and impossible, even to their holders, were they not all based on an initial, though unstated, assumption, that the Church as a distinct society does not exist. If she does not exist, the place of any individual priest is a matter of convenience and law, and no opinion can matter. If she does exist, she must have some bond of cohesion beside the State.

More virulent still is the same tendency in regard to law. Baptism and Confirmation are repeatedly treated as of no value; not because they are bad conditions of membership, but because they are conditions at all. Men scorn the notion that the Church can lay any specific obligations upon her members. They do this rightly on their principle – for on their principles they do not believe in the reality of the Church at all. It is a name of certain delegated functions of the State. On many burning topics – education, the marriage law, even the status of a Disestablished body in Wales – we see widespread the same notion, that the Church has no right to any distinctive life of her own, and that those who claim it are obsolescent mediaevalists.

Even in the sphere of morals the same is true, though it is harder to prove it, for the whole topic is more vague. Still, there are easily discernible tendencies which claim for every one all the rights of Churchmen while repudiating every kind of obligation.

The notion that the Church has authority is simply repulsive to many who still continue to demand every privilege of membership. Yet this is to deny that the Church exists. No society of men but by the very nature of things has authority over its members; it cannot be a society with a permanent end and meaning without it. Nobody is quite the same person as a member of a society as he was apart from it. Thus it is no distant, farfetched idea for which we fight.

In claiming the rights of the Church we are claiming to lay down the true nature of the State; we are fighting for the just recognition of all those societies, from the family to the province, which in any great State arise in such uncounted variety. The battle of freedom in this century is the battle of small societies to maintain their inherent life as against the all-devouring Leviathan of the whole – a Leviathan not less but more dangerous if its form be democratic. It is for this freedom that we are fighting, and if it be true, as Acton said, that 'Liberty is not a means to a political end, but is itself the highest of all political ends,' we can claim that we are doing service no less valuable to the State than needful to the Church. So true is it that the Christian law is a perfect law of liberty, and that in Christ, and only in Christ, can all the families of the earth be blessed.

Note

1. Preached in St Alban's, Holborn, on Tuesday, June 18, 1912, at the Annual Festival of the English Church Union. First published in Figgis, *Antichrist, and other Sermons*, pp. 257–266.

Appendix C
The Pluralistic State[1]
H. J. Laski

Every student of politics must begin his researches with humble obeisance to the work of Aristotle; and therein, I take it, he makes confession of the inspiration and assistance he has had from the effort of philosophers. Indeed, if one took only the last century of intellectual history, names like Hegel, Green, and Bosanquet must induce in him a certain sense of humility. For the direction of his analysis has been given its perspective by their thought. The end his effort must achieve has been by no other thinkers so clearly or so wisely defined.

Yet the philosophic interpretation of politics has suffered from one serious weakness. It is rather with *staatslehre* than with *politik* that it has concerned itself. Ideals and forms have provided the main substance of its debates. So that even if, as with Hegel and Green, it has had the battles of the market-place most clearly in mind, it has somehow, at least ultimately, withdrawn itself from the arena of hard facts to those remoter heights where what a good Platonist has called[2] the 'pure instance' of the state may be dissected. Nor has it seen political philosophy sufficiently outside the area of its own problems. Aristotle apart, its weakness has lain exactly in those minutiae of psychology which, collectively, are all-important to the student of administration. Philosophy seems, in politics at least, to take too little thought for the categories of space and time.

The legal attitude has been impaired by a somewhat similar limitation. The lawyer, perhaps of necessity, has concerned himself not with right but with rights, and his consequent preoccupation with the problem of origins, the place of ultimate reference, has made him, at least to the interested outsider, unduly eager to confound the legally ancient with the politically justifiable. One might even make out a case for the assertion that the lawyer is the head and centre of our modern trouble; for the monistic theory of the state goes back, in its scientific statement, to Jean Bodin. The latter became the spiritual parent of Hobbes, and thence, through Bentham, the ancestor of Austin. On Austin I will make no comment here; though a reference to an ingenious equation of Maitland's may perhaps be pardoned.[3]

It is with the lawyers that the problem of the modern state originates as an actual theory; for the lawyer's formulae have been rather amplified than denied by the philosophers. Upon the historic events which surround their effort I would say one word, since it is germane to the argument I have presently to make. We must ceaselessly remember that the monistic theory of the state was born in an age of crisis and that each period of its revivification has synchronised with some momentous event which has signalised a change in the distribution of political power. Bodin, as is well known, was of that party which, in an age of religious warfare, asserted, lest it perish in an alien battle, the supremacy of the state.[4] Hobbes sought the means of order in a period when King and Parliament battled for the balance of power. Bentham published his *Fragment* on the eve of the Declaration of Independence; and Adam Smith, in the same year, was outlining the programme of another and profounder revolution. Hegel's philosophy was the outcome of a vision of German multiplicity destroyed by the unity of France. Austin's book was conceived when the middle classes of France and England had, in their various ways, achieved the conquest of a state hitherto but partly open to their ambition.

It seems of peculiar significance that each assertion of the monistic theory should have this background. I cannot stay here to disentangle the motives through which men so different in character should have embraced a theory as similar in substance. The result, with all of them, is to assert the supremacy of the state over all other institutions. Its primary organs have the first claim upon the allegiance of men; and Hobbes's insistence[5] that corporations other than the state are but the manifestations of disease is perhaps the best example of its ruthless logic. Hobbes and Hegel apart, the men I have noted were lawyers; and they were seeking a means whereby the source of power may have some adequate justification. Bentham, of course, at no point beatified the state; though zeal for it is not wanting in the earlier thinkers or in Hegel. What, I would urge, the lawyers did was to provide a foundation for the moral superstructure of the philosophers. It was by the latter that the monistic state was elevated from the plane of logic to the plane of ethics. Its rights then became matter of right. Its sovereignty became spiritualised into moral preeminence.

The transition is simple enough. The state is today the one compulsory form of association;[6] and for more than two thousand years we have been taught that its purpose is the perfect life. It thus seems to acquire a flavour of generality which is absent from all other institutions. It becomes instinct with an universal interest to which, as it appears, no other association may without inaccuracy lay claim. Its sovereignty thus seems to represent the protection of the universal aspect of men – what Rousseau called the common good – against the intrusion of more private aspects at the hands of which it might otherwise suffer humiliation. The state is an absorptive animal; and there are few more amazing tracts of history than that which records its triumphs over the challenge of competing groups. There seems, at least today, no certain method of escape from its demands. Its conscience is supreme over any private conception of good the individual may hold. It sets the terms upon which the lives of trade-unions may be lived. It dictates their doctrine to churches; and, in England at least, it was a state tribunal which, as Lord Westbury said, dismissed hell with costs.[7] The area of its enterprise has consistently grown until today there is no field of human activity over which, in some degree, its pervading influence may not be detected.

But it is at this point pertinent to inquire what exact meaning is to be attached to an institution so vital as this. With one definition only I shall trouble you. 'A state,' writes Mr Zimmern,[8] 'can be defined, in legal language, as a territory over which there is a government claiming unlimited authority.' The definition, indeed, is not quite correct; for no government in the United States could claim, though it might usurp, unlimited power. But it is a foible of the lawyers to insist upon the absence of legal limit to the authority of the state; and it is, I think ultimately clear that the monistic theory is bound up with some such assumption. But it is exactly here that our main difficulty begins to emerge. The state, as Mr Zimmern here points out, must act through organs; and, in the analysis of its significance, it is upon government that we must concentrate our main attention.[9]

Legally, no one can deny that there exists in every state some organ whose authority is unlimited. But that legality is no more than a fiction of logic. No man has stated more clearly than Professor Dicey[10] the sovereign character of the King in Parliament; no man has been also so quick to point out the practical limits to this supremacy. And if logic is thus out of accord with the facts of life the obvious question to be asked is why unlimited authority may be claimed. The answer, I take it, is reducible to the belief that government expresses the largest aspect of man and is thus entitled to institutional expression of the area covered by its interests. A history, of course, lies back of that attitude, the main part of which would be concerned with the early struggle of the modern state to be born. Nor do I think the logical character of the doctrine has all the sanction claimed for it. It is only with the decline of theories of natural law that Parliament becomes the complete master of its destinies. And the internal limits which the jurist is driven to admit prove, on examination, to be the main problem for consideration.

There are many different angles from which this claim to unlimited authority may be proved inadequate. That government is the most important of institutions few, except theocrats, could be found to deny; but that its importance warrants the monistic assumption herein implied raises far wider questions. The test, I would urge, is not an *a priori* statement of claim. Nothing has led us farther on the wrong path than the simple teleological terms in which Aristotle stated his conclusions. For when we say that political institutions aim at the good life, we need to know not only the meaning of good, but also those who are to achieve it, and the methods by which it is to be attained. What, in fact, we have to do it to study the way in which this monistic theory has worked; for our judgment upon it must depend upon its consequences to the mass of men and women. I would not trouble you unduly with history. But it is worth while to bear in mind that this worship of state-unity is almost entirely the offspring of the Reformation and therein, most largely, an adaptation of the practice of the medieval church. The fear of variety was not, in its early days, an altogether unnatural thing. Challenged from within and from without, uniformity seemed the key to self-preservation.[11] But when the internal history of the state is examined, its supposed unity of purpose and of effort sinks, with acquaintance, into nothingness. What in fact confronts us is a complex of interests; and between not few of them ultimate reconciliation is impossible. We cannot, for example, harmonise the modern secular state with a Roman Church based upon the principles of the Encyclical of 1864; nor can we find the basis of enduring collaboration between trade-unions aiming at the control of industry through the destruction of capitalistic organization and the upholders of capitalism. Historically, we always find that any system of government is dominated by those who at the time wield economic power; and what they mean by 'good' is, for the most part, the preservation of their own interests. Perhaps I put it too crudely; refined analysis would, maybe, suggest that they are limited by the circle of the ideas to which their interests would at the first instance give rise. The history of England in the period of the Industrial Revolution is perhaps the most striking example of this truth. To suggest, for instance, that the government of the younger Pitt was, in its agricultural policy, actuated by some conception of public welfare which was equal as between squire and labourer, is, in the light of the evidence so superbly discussed by Mr and Mrs Hammond, utterly impossible.[12] There is nowhere and at no time assurance of that consistent generality of motive in the practice of government which theory would suppose it to possess.

We cannot, that is to say, at any point, take for granted the motives of governmental policy, with the natural implication that we must erect safeguards against their abuse. These, I venture to think, the monistic theory of the state at no point, in actual practice, supplies. For its insistence on unlimited authority in the governmental organ makes over to it the immense power that comes from the possession of legality. What, in the stress of conflict, this comes to mean is the attribution of inherent rightness to acts of government. These are somehow taken, and that with but feeble regard to their actual substance, to be acts of the community. Something that, for want of a better term, we call the communal conscience, is supposed to want certain things. We rarely inquire either how it comes to want them or to need them. We simply know that the government enforces the demand so made and that the individual or group is expected to give way before them. Yet it may well happen, as we have sufficiently seen in our experience, that the individual or the group may be right. And it is difficult to see how a policy which thus penalises all dissent, at least in active form, from government, can claim affinity with freedom. For freedom, as Mr Graham Wallas has finely said,[13] implies the chance of continuous initiative. But the ultimate implication of the monistic state in a society so complex as our own is the transference of that freedom from ordinary men to their rulers.

I cannot here dwell upon the more technical results of this doctrine, more particularly on the absence of liability for the faults of government that it has involved.[14] But it is in some such background as this that the pluralistic theory of the state takes its origin. It agrees with Mr. Zimmern that a state is a territorial society divided into government and subjects, but it differs, as you will observe, from his definition in that it makes no assumptions as to the authority a government should possess. And the reason for this fact is simply that it is consistently experimentalist in temper. It realized that the state has a history and it is unwilling to assume that we have today given to it any permanence of form. There is an admirable remark of Tocqueville's on this point which we too little bear in mind.[15] And if it be deemed necessary to dignify this outlook by antiquity we can, I think, produce great names as its sponsors. At least it could be shown that the germs of our protest are in men like Nicholas of Cusa, like Althusius, Locke, and Royer-Collard.

It thus seems that we have a twofold problem. The monistic state is an hierarchical structure in which power is, for ultimate purposes, collected at a single centre. The advocates of pluralism are convinced that this is both administratively incomplete and ethically inadequate. You will observe that I have made no reference here to the lawyer's problem. Nor do I deem it necessary; for when we are dealing, as the lawyer deals, with sources of ultimate reference, the questions are no more difficult, perhaps I should also add, no easier, than those arising under the conflict of jurisdictions in a federal state.

It is with other questions that we are concerned. Let us note, in the first place, the tendency in the modern state for men to become the mere subjects of administration. It is perhaps as yet too early to insist, reversing a famous generalisation of Sir Henry Maine, that the movement of our society is from contract to status; but there is at least one sense in which that remark is significant. Amid such vague enthusiasm for the thing itself, every observer must note a decline in freedom. What we most greatly need is to beware lest we lose that sense of spontaneity which enabled Aristotle to define citizenship as the capacity to rule not less than to be ruled in turn.[16] We believe that this can best be achieved in a state of which the structure is not hierarchical but coordinate, in which, that is to say, sovereignty is partitioned upon some basis of function. For the division of power makes men more apt to responsibility than its accumulation. A man, or even a legislature that is overburdened with a multiplicity of business, will not merely neglect that which he ought to do; he will, in actual experience, surrender his powers into the hands of forceful interests which know the way to compel his attention. He will treat the unseen as non-existent and the inarticulate as contented. The result may, indeed, be revolution; but experience suggests that it is more likely to be the parent of a despotism.

Nor is this all. Such a system must needs result in a futile attempt to apply equal and uniform methods to varied and unequal things. Every administrator has told us of the effort to arrive at an intellectual routine; and where the problems of government are as manifold as at present that leads to an assumption of similarity which is rarely borne out by the facts. The person who wishes to govern America must know that he cannot assume identity of conditions in North and South, East and West. He must, that is to say, assume that his first duty is not to assert a greatest common measure of equality but to prove it. That will, I suggest, lead most critical observers to perceive that the unit with which we are trying to deal is too large for effective administration. The curiosities, say of the experiment in North Dakota, are largely due to this attempt on the part of predominating interests to neglect vital differences of outlook. Such differences, moreover, require a sovereignty of their own to express the needs they imply. Nor must we neglect the important fact that in an area like the United States the individual will too often get lost in its very vastness. He gets a sense of impotence as a political factor of which the result is a failure properly to estimate the worth of citizenship. I cannot stay to analyze the result of that mistaken estimate. I can only say here that I am convinced that it is the nurse of social corruption.

Administratively, therefore, we need decentralisation; or, if you like, we need to revivify the conception of federalism which is the great contribution of America to political science. But we must not think of federalism today merely in the old spatial terms. It applies not less to functions than to territories. It applies not less to the government of the cotton industry, or of the civil service, than it does to the government of Kansas and Rhode Island. Indeed, the greatest lesson the student of government has to learn is the need for him to understand the significance for politics of industrial structure and, above all, the structure of the trade-union movement.[17] The main factor in political organization that we have to recover is the factor of consent, and here trade-union federalism has much to teach us. It has found, whether the unit be a territorial one like the average local, or an industrial like that envisaged by the shop-steward movement in England, units sufficiently small to make the individual feel significant in them. What, moreover, this development of industrial organization has done is to separate the processes of production and consumption in such fashion as to destroy, for practical purposes, the unique sovereignty of a territorial parliament. It is a nice question for the upholders of the monistic theory to debate as to where the effective sovereignty of America lay in the controversy over the Adamson law; or to consider what is meant by the vision of that consultative industrial body which recent English experience seems likely, in the not distant future, to bring into being.[18]

The facts, I suggest, are driving us towards an effort at the partition of power. The evidence for that conclusion you can find on all sides. The civil services of England and France are pressing for such a reorganization.[19] It is towards such a conclusion that what we call too vaguely the labour movement has directed its main energies.[20] We are in the midst of a new movement for the conquest of self-government. It finds its main impulse in the attempt to disperse the sovereign power because it is realised that where administrative organization is made responsive to the actual associations of men, there is a greater chance not merely of efficiency but of freedom also. That is why, in France, there has been for some time a vigorous renewal of that earlier effort of the sixties in which the great Odillon-Barrot did his noblest work;[21] and it does not seem unlikely that some reconstruction of the ancient provinces will at last compensate for the dangerous absorptiveness of Paris. The British House of Commons has debated federalism as the remedy for its manifold ills;[22] and the unused potentialities of German decentralisation may lead to the results so long expected now that the deadening pressure of Prussian domination has been withdrawn. We are learning, as John Stuart Mill pointed out in an admirable passage,[23] that 'all the facilities which a government enjoys of access to information, all the means which it possesses of remunerating, and therefore of commanding, the best available talent in the market, are not an equivalent for the one great disadvantage of an inferior interest in the result'. For we now know that the consequent of that inferior interest is the consistent degradation of freedom.[24]

I have spoken of the desire for genuine responsibility and the direction in which it may be found for administrative purposes. To this aspect the ethical side of political pluralism stands in the closest relation. Fundamentally, it is a denial that a law can be explained merely as a command of the sovereign for the simple reason that it denies, the sovereignty of anything save right conduct. The philosophers since, particularly, the time of T. H. Green, have told us insistently that the state is based upon will; though they have too little examined the problem of what will is most likely to receive obedience. With history behind us, we are compelled to conclude that no such will can by definition be a good will; and the individual must therefore, whether by himself or in concert with others, pass judgment upon its validity by examining its substance. That, it is clear enough, makes an end of the sovereignty of the state in its classical conception. It puts the state's acts – practically, as I have pointed out, the acts of its primary organ, government – on a moral parity with the acts of any other association. It gives to the judgments of the state exactly the power they inherently possess by virtue of their moral content, and no other. If the English state should wish, as in 1776, to refuse colonial freedom; if Prussia should choose to embark upon a *Kulturkampf*; if any state, to take the decisive instance, should choose to embark upon war; in each case there is no *a priori* rightness about its policy. You and I are part of the leverage by which that policy is ultimately enacted. It therefore becomes a moral duty on our part to examine the foundations of state-action. The last sin in politics is unthinking acquiescence in important decisions.

I have elsewhere dealt with the criticism that this view results in anarchy.[25] What is more profitable here to examine is its results in our scheme of political organization. It is, in the first place, clear that there are no demands upon our allegiance except the demands of what we deem right conduct. Clearly, in such an aspect, we need the means of ensuring that we shall know right when we see it. Here, I would urge, the problem of rights becomes significant. For the duties of citizenship cannot be fulfilled, save under certain conditions; and it is necessary to ensure the attainment of those conditions against the encroachments of authority. I cannot here attempt any sort of detail; but it is obvious enough that freedom of speech,[26] a living wage, an adequate education, a proper amount of leisure, the power to combine for social effort, are all of them integral to citizenship. They are natural rights in the sense that without them the purpose of the state cannot be fulfilled. They are natural also in the sense that they do not depend upon the state for their validity. They are inherent in the eminent worth of human personality. Where they are denied, the state clearly destroys whatever claims it has upon the loyalty of men.

Rights such as these are necessary to freedom because without them man is lost in a world almost beyond the reach of his understanding. We have put them outside the power of the state to traverse; and this again must mean a limit upon its sovereignty. If you ask what guarantee exists against their destruction in a state where power is distributed, the answer, I think, is that only in such a state have the masses of men the opportunity to understand what is meant by their denial. It is surely, for example, significant that the movement for the revival of what we broadly term natural law should derive its main strength from organized trade-unionism. It is hardly less important that among those who have perceived the real significant of the attitude of labour in the Taff Vale and Osborne cases should have been a high churchman most deeply concerned with the restoration of the church.[27] That is what coordinate organization will above all imply, and its main value is the fact that what, otherwise, must strike us most in the modern state is the inert receptiveness of the multitude. Every student of politics knows well enough what this means. Most would, on analysis, admit that its dissipation is mainly dependent upon an understanding of social mechanisms now largely hidden from the multitude. The only hopeful way of breaking down this inertia is by the multiplication of centres of authority. When a man is trained to service in a trade-union, he cannot avoid seeing how that activity is related to the world outside. When he gets on a school-committee, the general problems of education begin to unfold themselves before him. Paradoxically, indeed, we may say that a consistent decentralisation is the only effective cure for an undue localism. That is because institutions with genuine power become ethical ideas and thus organs of genuine citizenship. But if the Local Government Board, or the Prefect, sit outside, the result is a balked disposition of which the results are psychologically well known. A man may obtain some compensation for his practical exclusion from the inwardness of politics by devotion to golf. But I doubt whether the compensation is what is technically termed sublimation, and it almost always results in social loss.

Here, indeed, is where the main superiority of the pluralistic state is manifest. For the more profoundly we analyze the psychological characteristic of its opposite, the less adequate does it seem relative to the basic impulses of men. And this, after all, is the primary need to satisfy. It was easy enough for Aristotle to make a fundamental division between masters and men and adapt his technique to the demands of the former; but it was a state less ample than a moderate sized city that he had in mind. It was simple for Hobbes to assume the inherent badness of men and the consequent need of making government strong, lest their evil nature bring it to ruin; yet even he must have seen, what our own generation has emphasized, that the strength of governments consists only in the ideas of which they dispose. It was even simple for Bentham to insist on the ruling motive of self-interest; but he wrote before it had become clear that altruism was an instinct implied in the existence of the herd. We know at least that the data are more complex. Our main business has become the adaptation of our institutions to a variety of impulses with the knowledge that we must at all costs prevent their inversion. In the absence of such transmutation what must mainly impress us is the wastage upon which our present system is builded. The executioner, as Maistre said, is the corner-stone of our society. But it is because we refuse to release the creative energies of men.

After all, our political systems must be judged not merely by the ends they serve, but also by the way in which they serve those ends. The modern state provides a path whereby a younger Pitt may control the destinies of a people; it even gives men of leisure a field of passionate interest to cultivate. But the humbler man is less fortunate in the avenues we afford; and if we have record of notable achievement after difficult struggle, we are too impressed by the achievement to take due note of the anguish upon which it is too often founded. This, it may be remarked, is the touchstone by which the major portion of our institutions will be tested in the future; and

I do not think we can be unduly certain that they will stand the test. The modern state, at bottom, is too much an historic category not to change its nature with the advent of new needs.

Those new needs, it may be added, are upon us, and the future of our civilization most largely depends upon the temper in which we confront them. Those who take refuge in the irrefutable logic of the sovereign state may sometimes take thought that for many centuries of medieval history the very notion of sovereignty was unknown. I would not seek unduly to magnify those far-off times; but it is worth while to remember that no thought were dearer to the heart of medieval thinkers than ideals of right and justice. Shrunken and narrow, it may be, their fulfilment often was; but that was not because they did not know how to dream. Our finely articulated structure is being tested by men who do not know what labour and thought have gone into its building. It is a cruder test they will apply. Yet it is only by seeking to understand their desires that we shall be able worthily to meet it.

Notes

1. From 28 *Philosophical Review* (1919) 562ff.
2. Barker, *Political Thought in England from Herbert Spencer to Today*, pp. 68f.
3. *Cf. The Life of F. W. Maitland*, by H. A. L. Fisher, p. 117.
4. The background of his book has recently been exhaustively outlined by Roger Chauviré in his *Jean Bodin* (Paris, 1916), esp. pp. 312f.
5. *Leviathan*, chap. xliv.
6. I say today; for it is important to remember that, for the Western World, this was true of the Church until the Reformation.
7. A. W. Benn, *History of English Rationalism in the Nineteenth Century*, vol. ii, p. 133.
8. *Nationality and Government*, p. 56.
9. Cf. my *Authority in the Modern State*, pp. 26ff.
10. Cf. *The Law of the Constitution* (8th ed.), pp. 37ff.
11. Cf. Professor McIlwain's introduction to his edition of the *Political Works of James I*, and my comment thereon, *Pol. Sci. Quarterly*, vol. 34, p. 290.
12. See their brilliant volume, *The Village Labourer* (1911).
13. Cf. his article in the *New Statesman*, Sept. 25, 1915. I own my knowledge of this winning definition to Mr A. E. Zimmern's *Nationality and Government*, p. 57.
14. Cf. my paper on the Responsibility of the State in England, 32 *Harv. L. Rev.*, p. 447.
15. *Souvenirs*, p. 102.
16. *Politics*, bk. iii, c.1, 1275a.
17. A book that would do for the English-speaking world that M. Paul-Boncour did twenty years ago for France in his *Fédéralisme. Economique* would be of great service.
18. See the Report of the *Provisional Joint Committee of the Industrial Conference*, London, 1919.
19. See my *Authority in the Modern State*, chap. v.
20. Cf. Cole, *Self-Government in Industry*, passim, esp. chap. iii.

21. Odillon-Barrot, *De la centralization.* [sic]
22. *Parliamentary Debates,* June 4th and 5th, 1919.
23. *Principles of Political Economy* (2nd ed.), vol. ii, p. 181.
24. On all this, cf. my *Problem of Administrative Areas* (Smith College Studies, vol. iv, no. 1).
25. *Authority in the Modern State*, pp. 93 - 4.
26. Cf. the brilliant article of my colleague, Professor Z. Chafee, Jr., in 32 *Harv. L. Rev.,* 932f.
27. J. Neville Figgis, *Churches in the Modern State.* The recent death of Dr Figgis is an irreparable blow to English scholarship.

Appendix D
Moral Personality and Legal Personality[1]
F. W. Maitland

The memory of Henry Sidgwick is not yet in need of revival. It lives a natural life among us, and will live so long as those who saw and heard him draw breath. Still the generations, as generations must be reckoned in this place, succeed each other rapidly, and already I may be informing, rather than reminding, some of you when I say that among his many generous acts was the endowment of a readership in English Law, of which one of his pupils was fortunate enough to be the first holder. If that pupil ventures to speak here this afternoon, it will not be unnatural that he should choose his theme from the borderland where ethical speculation marches with jurisprudence.

Ethics and Jurisprudence. – That such a borderland exists all would allow, and, as usually happens in such cases, each of the neighbouring powers is wont to assert, in practice, if not in theory, its right to define the scientific frontier. We, being English, are, so I fancy, best acquainted with the claims of ethical speculation, and in some sort prejudiced in their favour. We are proud of a long line of moralists, which has not ended in Sidgwick and Martineau and Green, in Herbert Spencer and Leslie Stephen, and we conceive that the 'jurist', if indeed such an animal exists, plays, and of right ought to play, a subordinate, if not subservient, part in the delimitation of whatever moral sciences there may happen to be. I am not sure, however, that the poor lawyer with antiquarian tastes might not take his revenge by endeavouring to explain the moral philosopher as a legal phenomenon, and by classing our specifically English addiction to ethics as a by-product of the specifically English history of English law. That statement, if it be more than the mere turning of the downtrodden worm, is obviously too large, as it is too insolent, a text for an hour's lecture. What I shall attempt will be to indicate one problem of a speculative sort, which (so it seems to me) does not get the attention that it deserves from speculative Englishmen, and does not get that attention because it is shrouded from their view by certain peculiarities of the legal system in which they live.

The Natural Person and the Corporation – Texts, however, I will have. My first is taken from Mr Balfour. Lately in the House of Commons the Prime Minister spoke of trade unions as corporations. perhaps, for he is an accomplished debater, he anticipated an interruption. At any rate, a distinguished lawyer on the Opposition benches interrupted him with 'The trade unions are not corporations.' 'I know that,' retorted Mr Balfour, 'I am talking English, not law.' A long story was packed into that admirable reply.[2]

And my second text is taken from Mr Dicey, who delivered the Sidgwick lecture last year. 'When,' he said, 'a body of twenty, or two thousand, or two hundred thousand men bind themselves together to act in a particular way for some common purpose, they create a body, which by no fiction of law, but by the very nature of things, differs from the individuals of whom it is constituted'.[3] I have been waiting a long while for an English lawyer of Professor Dicey's eminence to say what he said – to talk so much 'English'. Let me repeat a few of his words with the stress where I should like it to lie: 'they create a body, which by *no fiction of law, but by the very nature of things,* differs from the individuals of whom it is constituted'. So says Blackstone's successor. Blackstone himself would, I think, have inverted that phrase, and would have ascribed to a fiction of law that phenomenon – or whatever we are to call it – which Mr Dicey ascribes to the very nature of things.

Now for a long time past the existence of this phenomenon has been recognised by lawyers, and the orthodox manner of describing it has been somewhat of this kind. Besides men or 'natural persons', law knows persons of another kind. In particular it knows the corporation, and for a multitude of purposes it treats the corporation very much as it treats the man. Like the man, the corporation is (forgive this compound adjective) a right-and-duty-bearing unit. Not all the legal propositions that are true of a man will be true of a corporation. For example, it can neither marry nor be given in marriage; but in a vast number of cases you can make a legal statement about x and y which will hold good whether these symbols stand for two men or for two corporations, or for a corporation and a man. The University can buy land from Downing, or hire the guildhall from the Town, or borrow money from the London Assurance; and we may say that *exceptis excipiendis* a court of law can treat these transactions, these acts in the law, as if they took place between two men, between Styles and Nokes. But further, we have to allow that the corporation is in some sense composed of men, and yet between the corporation and one of its members there may exist many, perhaps most, of those legal relationships which can exist between two human beings. I can contract with the University: the University can contract with me. You can contract with the Great Northern Company as you can with the Great Eastern, though you happen to be a shareholder in the one and not in the other. In either case there stands opposite to you another right-and-duty-bearing unit – might I not say another individual? – a single 'not-yourself' that can pay damages or exact them. You expect results of this character, and, if you did not get them, you would think ill of law and lawyers. Indeed, I should say that, the less we know of law, the more confidently we Englishmen expect that the organised group, whether called a corporation or not, will be treated as person: that is, as right-and-duty-bearing unit.

Legal Orthodoxy and the Fictitious Person. – Perhaps I can make the point clearer by referring to an old case. We are told that in Edward IV's day the mayor and commonalty – or, as we might be tempted to say, the municipal corporation – of Newcastle gave a bond to the man who happened to be mayor, he being named by his personal name, and that the bond was held to be void because a man cannot be bound to himself.[4] The argument that is implicit in those few words seems to us quaint, if not sophistical. But the case does not stand alone; far from it. If our business is with medieval history and our aim is to re-think it before we re-present it, here lies one of our most serious difficulties. Can we allow the group – gild, town, village, nation – to stand over against each and all of its members as a distinct person? To be concrete, look at Midsummer Common. It belongs, and, so far as we know, has always in some sense belonged, to the burgesses of Cambridge. But in what sense? Were they co-proprietors? Were they corporators? Neither – both?

I would not trouble you with medievalism. Only this by the way: If once you become interested in the sort of history that tries to unravel these and similar problems, you will think some other sorts of history rather superficial. Perhaps you will go the length of saying that much the most interesting person that you ever knew was *persona ficta*. But my hour flies.

To steer a clear or any course is hard, for controversial rocks abound. Still, with some security we may say that at the end of the Middle Age a great change in men's thoughts about groups of men was taking place, and that the main agent in the transmutation was Roman Law. Now just how the classical jurists of Rome conceived their *corpora* and *universitates* became in the nineteenth century a much debated question. The profane outsider says of the Digest what some one said of another book:

> Hic liber est in quo quaerit sua dogmata quisque
> Invenit et pariter dogmata quisque sua.

Where people have tried to make antique texts do modern work, the natural result is what Mr Buckland has happily called 'Wardour Street Roman Law'.[5] Still, of this I suppose there can be no doubt, that there could, without undue pressure, be obtained from the Corpus Juris a doctrine of corporations, which, so far as some main outlines are concerned, is the doctrine which has ruled the modern world. Nor would it be disputed that this work was done by the legists and canonists of the Middle Age, the canonists leading the way. The group can be a person: co-ordinated, equiparated, with the man, with the natural person.

With the 'natural' person – for the personality of the *universitas*, of the corporation, is not natural – it is fictitious. This is a very important part of the canonical doctrine, first clearly proclaimed, so we are told, by the greatest lawyer that ever sat upon the chair of St Peter, Pope Innocent IV. You will recall Mr Dicey's words: 'not by fiction of law, but by the very nature of things'. Invert those words, and you will have a dogma that works like leaven in the transformation of medieval society.

If the personality of the corporation is a legal fiction, it is the gift of the prince. It is not for you and me to feign and to force our fictions upon our neighbours. 'Solus princeps fingit quod in rei veritate non est.'[6] An argument drawn from the very nature of fictions thus came to the aid of less questionably Roman doctrines about the illicitness of all associations, the existence of which the prince has not authorised. I would not exaggerate the importance of a dogma, theological or legal. A dogma is of no importance unless and until there is some great desire within it. But what was understood to be the Roman doctrine of corporations was an apt lever for those forces which were transforming the medieval nation into the modern State. The federalistic structure of medieval society is threatened. No longer can we see the body politic as *communitas communitatum*, a system of groups, each of which in its turn is a system of groups. All that stands between the State and the individual has but a derivative and precarious existence.

Do not let us at once think of England. English history can never be an elementary subject: we are not logical enough to be elementary. If we must think of England, then let us remember that we are in the presence of a doctrine which in Charles II's day condemns all – yes, all – of the citizens of London to prison for 'presuming to act as a corporation'. We may remember also how corporations appear to our absolutist Hobbes as troublesome entozoa. But it is always best to begin with France, and there, I take it, we may see the pulverising, macadamising tendency in all its glory, working from century to century, reducing to impotence, and then to nullity, all that intervenes between Man and State.

The State and the Corporation. – In this, as in some other instances, the work of the monarchy issues in the work of the revolutionary assemblies. It issues in the famous declaration of August 18, 1792: 'A State that is truly free ought not to suffer within its bosom any corporation, not even such as, being dedicated to public instruction, have merited well of the country.'[7] That was one of the mottoes of modern absolutism: the absolute State faced the absolute individual. An appreciable part of the interest of the French Revolution seems to me to be open only to those who will be at pains to give a little thought to the theory of corporations. Take, for example, those memorable debates touching ecclesiastical property. To whom belong these broad lands when you have pushed fictions aside, when you have become a truly philosophical jurist with a craving for the natural? To the nation, which has stepped into the shoes of the prince. That is at least a plausible answer, though an uncomfortable suspicion that the State itself is but a questionably real person may not be easily dispelled. And as with the churches, the universities, the trade-guilds, and the like, so also with the communes, the towns and villages. Village property – there was a great deal of village property in France – was exposed to the dilemma: it belongs to the State, or else it belongs to the now existing villagers. I doubt we Englishmen, who never clean our slates, generally know how clean the French slate was to be.

Associations in France. – Was to be, I say. Looking back now, French lawyers can regard the nineteenth century as the century of association, and, if there is to be association, if there is to be group- formation, the problem of personality cannot be evaded, at any rate if we are a logical people. Not to mislead, I must in one sentence say, that even the revolutionary legislators spared what we call partnership, and that for a long time past French law has afforded comfortable quarters for various kinds of groups, provided (but notice this) that the group's one and only object was the making of pecuniary gain. Recent writers have noticed it as a paradox that the State saw no harm in the selfish people who wanted dividends, while it had an intense dread of the comparatively unselfish people who would combine with some religious, charitable, literary, scientific, artistic purpose in view. I cannot within my few minutes be precise, but at the beginning of this twentieth century it was still a misdemeanour to belong to any unauthorized *association* having more than twenty members. A licence from the prefect, which might be obtained with some ease, made the *association* non-criminal, made it licit; but personality – 'civil personality', as they say in France – was only to be acquired with difficulty as the gift of the central government.

Now I suppose it to be notorious that during the last years of the nineteenth century law so unfavourable to liberty of association was still being maintained, chiefly, if not solely, because prominent, typically prominent, among the *associations* known to Frenchmen stood the *congrégations* – religious houses, religious orders. The question how these were to be treated divided the nation, and at last, in 1901, when a new and very important law was made about 'the contract of association', a firm line was drawn between the non-religious sheep and the religious goats. With the step then taken and the subsequent woes of the congregations I have here no concern; but the manner in which religious and other groups had previously been treated by French jurisprudence seems to me exceedingly instructive. It seems to me to prove so clearly that in a country where people take their legal theories seriously, a country where a Prime Minister will often talk law without ceasing to talk agreeable French, the question whether the group is to be, as we say, 'a person in the eye of the Law' is the question whether the group as group can enjoy more than an uncomfortable and precarious existence. I am not thinking of attacks directed against it by the State. I am thinking of collisions between it and private persons. It lives at the mercy of its neighbours, for a law- suit will dissolve it into its constituent atoms. Nor is that all. Sometimes its neighbours will have cause to complain of its legal impersonality. They will have been thinking of it as a responsible right-and-duty-bearing unit, while at the touch of law it becomes a mere many, and a practically, if not theoretically, irresponsible many.

Group-Personality. – During the nineteenth century (so I understand the case) a vast mass of experience, French, German, Belgian, Italian, and Spanish (and I might add, though the atmosphere is hazier, English and American), has been making for a result which might be stated in more than one way. (1) If the law allows men to form permanently organised groups, those groups will be for common opinion right-and-duty-bearing units; and if the law-giver will not openly treat them as such, he will misrepresent, or, as the French say, he will 'denature' the facts: in other words, he will make a mess and call it law. (2) Group-personality is no purely legal phenomenon. The law-giver may say that it does not exist, where, as a matter of moral sentiment, it does exist. When that happens, he incurs the penalty ordained for those who ignorantly or wilfully say the thing that is not. If he wishes to smash a group, let him smash it, send the policeman, raid the rooms, impound the minute-book, fine, and imprison; but if he is going to tolerate the group, he must recognize its personality, for otherwise he will be dealing wild blows which may fall on those who stand outside the group as well as those who stand within it. (3) For the morality of common sense the group is person, is right-and-duty-bearing unit. Let the moral philosopher explain this, let him explain it as illusion, let him explain it away; but he ought not to leave it unexplained, nor, I think, will he be able to say that it is an illusion which is losing power, for, on the contrary, it seems to me to be persistently and progressively triumphing over certain philosophical and theological prejudices.

You know that classical distribution of Private Law under three grand rubrics – Persons, Things, Actions. Half a century ago the first of these three titles seemed to be almost vanishing from civilised jurisprudence. No longer was there much, if anything, to be said of exceptional classes, of nobles, clerics, monks, serfs, slaves, excommunicates or outlaws. Children there might always be, and lunatics; but women had been freed from tutelage. The march of the progressive societies was, as we all know, from status to contract. And now? And now that forlorn old title is wont to introduce us to ever new species and new genera of persons, to vivacious controversy, to teeming life; and there are many to tell us that the line of advance is no longer from status to contract, but through contract to something that contract cannot explain, and for which our best, if an inadequate, name is the personality of the organised group.

Fact or Fiction? – Theorising, of course, there has been. I need not say so, nor that until lately it was almost exclusively German. Our neighbours' conception of the province of jurisprudence has its advantages as well as its disadvantages. On the one hand, ethical speculation (as we might call it) of a very interesting kind was until these last days too often presented in the unattractive guise of Wardour Street Roman Law, or else, raising the Germanistic cry of 'Loose from Rome!' it plunged into an exposition of medieval charters. On the other hand, the theorising is often done by men who have that close grasp of concrete modern fact which comes of a minutes and practical study of legal systems. Happily it is no longer necessary to go straight to Germany. That struggle over 'the contract of association' to which I have alluded, those woes of the 'congregations' of which all have heard, invoked foreign learning across the border, and now we may read in lucid French of the various German theories. Good reading I think it; and what interests me especially is that the French lawyer, with all his orthodoxy (legal orthodoxy) and conservatism, with all his love of clarity and abhorrence of mysticism, is often compelled to admit that the traditional dogmas of the law-school have broken down. Much disinclined though he may be to allow the group a real will of its own, just as really real as the will of a man, still he has to admit that if n men unite themselves in an organised body, jurisprudence, unless it wishes to pulverize the group, must see $n + 1$ persons. And that for the mere lawyer should I think be enough. 'Of heaven and hell he has no power to sing.' and he might content himself with a phenomenal reality – such reality, for example, as the lamp- post has for the idealistic ontologist. Still, we do not like to be told that we are dealing in fiction, even if it be added that we needs must reign, and the thought will occur to us that a fiction that we needs must feign is somehow or another very like the simple truth.

Why we English people are not interested in a problem that is being seriously discussed in many other lands, that is a question to which I have tried to provide some sort of answer elsewhere.[8] It is a long, and you would think it a very dreary, story about the most specifically English of all our legal institutes; I mean the trust. All that I can say here is that the device of building a wall of trustees enabled us to construct bodies which were not technically corporations and which yet would be sufficiently protected from the assaults of individualistic theory. The personality of such bodies – so I should put it – though explicitly denied by lawyers, was on the whole pretty well recognised in practice. That something of this sort happened you might learn from one simple fact. For some time past we have had upon our statute book the term 'Unincorporate body'. Suppose that a Frenchman saw it, what would he say? 'Unincorporate body: inanimate soul! No wonder your Prime Minister, who is a philosopher, finds it hard to talk English and talk law at the same time.'

One result of this was, so I fancy, that the speculative Englishman could not readily believe that in this quarter there was anything to be explored except some legal trickery unworthy of exploration. The lawyer assured him that it was so, and he saw around him great and ancient, flourishing and wealthy groups – the Inns of Court at their head – which, so the lawyer said, were not persons. To have crossexamined the lawyer over the bodiliness of his 'unincorporate body' might have brought out some curious results; but such a course was hardly open to those who shared our wholesome English contempt for legal technique.

The Ultimate Moral Unit. – Well, I must finish; and yet perhaps I have not succeeded in raising just the question that I wanted to ask. Can I do that in two or three last sentences? It is a moral question, and therefore I will choose my hypothetical case from a region in which our moral sentiments are not likely to be perplexed by legal technique. My organised group shall be a sovereign state. Let us call it Nusquamia. Like many other sovereign states, it owes money, and I will suppose that you are one of its creditors. You are not receiving the expected interest and there is talk of repudiation. That being so, I believe that you will be, and indeed I think that you ought to be, indignant, morally, righteously indignant. Now the question that I want to raise is this: Who is it that really owes you money? Nusquamia. Granted, but can you convert the proposition that Nusquamia owes you money into a series of propositions imposing duties on certain human beings that are now in existence? The task will not be easy. Clearly you do not think that every Nusquamian owes you some aliquot share of the debt. No one thinks in that way. The debt of Venezuela is not owed by Fulano y Zutano and the rest of them. Nor, I think, shall we get much good out of the word 'collectively', which is the smudgiest word in the English language, for the largest 'collection' of zeros is only zero. I do not wish to say that I have suggested an impossible task, and that the right-and-duty-bearing group must be for the philosopher an ultimate and unanalysable moral unit: as ultimate and unanalysable, I mean, as is the man. Only if that task can be performed, I think that in the interests of jurisprudence and of moral philosophy it is eminently worthy of circumspect performance. As to our national law, it has sound instincts, and muddles along with semi-personality and demi-semi-personality towards convenient conclusions. Still, I cannot think that Parliament's timid treatment of the trade unions has been other than a warning, or that it was a brilliant day in our legal annals when the affairs of the Free Church of Scotland were brought before the House of Lords, and the dead hand fell with a resounding slap upon the living body. As to philosophy, that is no affair of mine. I speak with conscious ignorance and unfeigned humility; only of this I feel moderately sure, that those who are to tell us of the very nature of things and the very nature of persons will not be discharging their duties to the full unless they come to close terms with that triumphant fiction, if fiction it be, of which I have said in your view more than too much, and in my own view less than too little.

Notes

1. The Sidgwick Lecture, 1903, delivered at Newnham College, Cambridge, and printed in H. A. L. Fisher (ed.), *The Collected papers of Frederic William Maitland* (Cambridge University Press, 1911) vol. iii, pp. 304–19.
2. *The Standard*, 23 April 1904. *Mr Balfour:* 'The mere fact that funds can be used, or are principally used, for benefit purposes, is surely not of itself a sufficient reason for saying that trade unions, and trade unions alone, out of all the corporations in the country, commercial –' *Sir R. Reid:* 'The trade unions are not corporations.' *Mr Balfour:* 'I know; I am talking English, not law' (*cheers and laughter*).
3. Professor Dicey's lecture on the Combination Laws is printed in *Harvard Law Review*, xvii 511.
4. Year Book, 21 Edw. IV, f. 68: 'Come fuit ajudgé en le cas del Maior de Newcastle ou le Maior et le Cominalty fist un obligation a mesme le person que fuit Maior par son propre nosme, et pur ceo que il mesme fuit Maior, et ne puit faire obligation a luy mesme, il [=l'obligation] fuit tenus voide.'
5. Buckland, 'Wardour Street Roman Law', *Law Quarterly Review*, xvii 179.
6. Lucas de Penna, cited in Gierke, *Das deutsche Genossenschaftsrecht*, iii 371.
7. 'Considérant qu'un État vraiment libre ne doit souffrir dans son sein aucune corporation, pas même celles qui, vouées à l'enseignement public, ont bien mérité de la patrie.'
8. Maitland, 'Trust und Korporation', Wien, 1904 (from *Grünhut's Zeitschrift fur das Privat- und Öffentliche-Recht*, vol. xxxii).

Bibliography

J. E. E. D. Acton, *Essays on Freedom and Power,* ed. G. Himmelfarb (Boston: 1956).
—— *The History of Freedom* (London: 1907).
—— *The Letters of Lord Acton to Mary Gladstone* (London: 1904).
Anglican-Roman Catholic International Commission, *The Final Report* (London: 1982).
Aristotle, *Politics*, ed. E. Barker (London: 1948).
J. Austin, *The Province of Jurisprudence Determined* (London: 1861).
W. Bagehot, *Works* (London: 1915).
Aloysius Balawyder, (ed.), *Cooperative Movements in Eastern Europe* (London: 1980).
Terence Ball, *et al.,* (eds), *Political Innovation and Conceptual Change* (Cambridge: 1989).
E. Barker, *Age and Youth* (London: 1953).
—— *Reflections on Government* (Oxford: 1942).
—— *Political Thought in England from Herbert Spencer to the Present Day* (London: 1915).
—— *Political Thought in England 1848–1914* (London: 1928).
Brian Barry, *The Liberal Theory of Justice* (Oxford: 1973).
James Bastable, (ed.), *Newman and Gladstone* (Dublin: 1978)
G. K. A. Bell (ed.), *The Meaning of the Creed* (London: 1921).
H. Belloc, *The Servile State* (London: 1927).
—— and C. Chesterton, *The Party System* (London: 1911).
C. Benoist, *La politique* (Paris: 1894).
A. F. Bentley, *The Process of Government* (Chicago, 1908).
I. Berlin, *Four Essays on Liberty* (London: 1969).
Eduard Bernstein, *Evolutionary Socialism* (New York: 1961).
J. F. Bethune-Baker, *The Miracle of Christianity* (London: 1914).
Antony Black, (ed.), *Community in Historical Perspective* (Cambridge: 1990).
—— *Guilds and Civil Society in European Thought from the Twelfth Century to the Present* (London: 1984).
Dietrich Bonhoeffer, *Letters and Papers from Prison* (London: 1959).
R. H. Bowen, *German Theories of the Corporative State* (New York: 1947).
Andras Bozokoi, *et al.,* (eds), *Post-Communist Transition: Emerging Pluralism in Hungary* (London: 1992).
F. H. Bradley, *Ethical Studies* (London: 1876).
J. Bryce, *Studies in History and Jurisprudence* (Oxford: 1901).
H. Butterfield, *The Historical Development of the Principle of Toleration in British Life* (London: 1957).
N. Carpenter, *Guild Socialism* (New York: 1922).
Alan Cawson, *Corporatism and Political Theory* (Oxford: 1986).
Church Information Office, *Church and State* (London: 1970).
K. Coates and T. Topham (eds.), *Workers' Control* (London: 1970).
M. Cohen, *Reason and Nature* (London: 1931).

G. D. H. Cole, *Chaos and Order in Industry* (London: 1920).
—— *Guild Socialism Restated* (London: 1920).
—— *Labour in the Commonwealth* (London: 1918).
—— *Self-Government in Industry* (London: 1917).
—— *Social Theory* (London: 1920).
Margaret Cole, *The Story of Fabian Socialism* (Stanford, Calif: 1961).
S. T. Coleridge, *On the Constitution of Church and State, According to the Idea of Each* (London: 1972).
W. E. Connolly (ed.), *The Bias of Pluralism* (New York: 1969).
P. P. Craig, *Public Law and Democracy in the United Kingdom and the United States* (Oxford: 1990).
L. Creighton, *The Life and Letters of Mandell Creighton* (London: 1904).
Mandell Creighton, *The Mind of St Peter* (London: 1904).
B. Crick, *In Defence of Politics* (Harmondsworth: 1964).
R. Dahrendorf, *Class and Class Conflict in Industrial Society* (London: 1959).
Joseph de Maistre, *Du pape* (Paris: 1845).
P. Derrick, *Lost Property* (London: 1947).
P. Devlin, *The Enforcement of Morals* (London: 1965).
J. Dewey, *Reconstruction in Philosophy* (London: 1921).
A. V. Dicey, *An Introduction to the Study of the Law of the Constitution* (London: 1908).
H. Dooyeweerd, *Roots of Western Culture: Pagan, Secular, and Christian Options* (Toronto: 1979).
—— *A New Critique of Theoretical Thought* (Philadelphia: 1969).
L. Duguit, *Law in the Modern State* (London: 1921).
——, *L'état, le droit objectif et la loi positive* (Paris: 1901).
E. Durkheim, *The Division of Labor* (New York: 1933).
F. Dvornik, *National Churches and the Church Universal* (London: 1944).
Stanislas Ehrlich, *Pluralism, On and Off Course* (Oxford: 1982).
T. S. Eliot, *The Idea of a Christian Society* (London: 1939).
—— *Notes towards the Definition of Culture* (London: 1967).
W. Y. Elliott, *The Pragmatic Revolt in Politics* (New York: 1928).
A. Farrer, *The Freedom of the Will* (London: 1958).
J. H. Fichter, *Sociology* (Chicago: 1957).
J. N. Figgis, *Antichrist and Other Sermons* (London: 1913).
—— *Christianity and History* (London: 1905).
—— *Churches in the Modern State* (London: 1913).
—— *The Divine Right of Kings* (Cambridge: 1914).
—— *The Fellowship of the Mystery* (London: 1915).
—— *The Gospel and Human Needs* (London: 1909).
—— *Hopes for English Religion* (London: 1919).
—— *Political Aspects of S. Augustine's 'City of God'* (London: 1921).
—— *Religion and English Society* (London: 1911).
—— *Studies of Political Thought from Gerson to Grotius 1414–1625* (Cambridge: 1916).
—— *The Will to Freedom* (London: 1917).
Five Great Encyclicals (New York: 1939).
M. P. Follett, *The New State* (New York: 1918).
P. T. Forsyth, *The Principle of Authority* (London: 1952).

182   *Bibliography*

—— *Theology in Church and State* (London: 1915).
Michael Freeden, *The New Liberalism: an Ideology of Social Reform* (Oxford: 1978).
J. S. Furnivall, *Colonial Policy and Practice* (Cambridge: 1948).
Otto von Gierke, *Das deutsch Genossenschaftsrecht* (Berlin: 1868–1913).
—— *The Development of Political Theory* (London: 1939).
—— *Die Genossenschaftstheorie und die deutsche Rechtsprechung* (Berlin: 1887).
—— *Natural Law and the Theory of Society* (Cambridge: 1934).
—— *Political Theories of the Middle Age* (Cambridge: 1900).
—— *Das Wesen der menschlichen Verbände* (Berlin: 1902).
S. T. Glass, *The Responsible Society* (London: 1966).
J. E. Gleeson, *What Distributism Means* (London: 1935).
Charles Gore, *The Basis of Anglican Fellowship in Faith and Organization* (London: 1914).
—— (ed.), *Lux Mundi: a Series of Studies in the Religion of the Incarnation* (London: 1890).
——, *et al.*, *The Return of Christendom* (London: 1922).
T. J. Gorringe, *Discerning Spirit* (London: 1990).
L. C. B. Gower, *The Principles of Modern Company Law* (London: 1957).
G. Goyau, *Ketteler* (Paris: 1907).
S. A. Grave, *Conscience in Newman's Thought* (Oxford: 1989).
Andrew Greeley, *Unsecular Man* (New York: 1972).
T. H. Green, *Lectures on the Principles of Political Obligation* (London: 1895).
H. M. Gwatkin, *The Bishop of Oxford's Open Letter* (London: 1914).
F. Hallis, *Corporate Personality* (London: 1930).
R. M. Hare, *The Language of Morals* (London: 1952).
N. Harris, *Competition and the Corporate Society* (London: 1972).
H. L. A. Hart, *Law, Liberty and Morality* (London: 1963).
—— *The Concept of Law* (Oxford: 1963).
Stanley Hauerwas, *Character and the Christian Life* (Notre Dame, Ind.: 1989).
—— *A Community of Character* (Notre Dame, Ind., 1981).
—— *The Peaceable Kingdom* (Notre Dame, Ind: 1983).
G. W. F. Hegel, *The Philosophy of Right* (London: 1942).
Hegel's Political Writings (Knox and Pelczynski, eds.) (Oxford: 1964).
Edmund Hill, *Ministry and Authority in the Catholic Church* (London: 1988).
R. Hinden (ed.), *Fabian Colonial Essays* (London: 1945).
Paul Q. Hirst, *Associative Democracy: New Forms of Economic and Social Governance* (Cambridge: 1993).
—— (ed.), *The Pluralist Theory of the State: Selected Writings of G. D. H. Cole, J. N. Figgis, and H. J. Laski* (London: 1989).
T. Hobbes, *Leviathan* (Oxford: 1946).
L. T. Hobhouse, *Development and Purpose* (London: 1913).
—— *Social Development: Its Nature and Conditions* (London: 1924).
—— *The Metaphysical Theory of the State* (London: 1918).
J. A. Hobson and M. Ginsberg, *L. T. Hobhouse* (London: 1931).
S. G. Hobson, *National Guilds and the State* (London: 1920).
George Homans, *The Human Group* (London: 1951).
Branko Horvat, *et al.*, (eds), *Self-governing Socialism: a Reader* (New York: 1975).
M. de W. Howe (ed.), *Holmes-Laski Letters* (London: 1953).

—— (ed.), *Pollock-Holmes Letters* (Cambridge: 1942).

K. C. Hsiao, *Political Pluralism* (London: 1927).

H. E. Humphries, *Liberty and Property: an Introduction to Distributism* (London: 1928).

W. James, *A Pluralistic Universe* (London: 1909).

Tadensz Jarski, *A Troubled Transition: Poland's Struggle for Pluralism* (London: 1989).

W. K. Jordan, *The Development of Religious Toleration in England* (London: 1932).

H. M. Kallen, *Cultural Pluralism and the American Ideal* (Philadelphia: 1956).

H. S. Kariel, *The Decline of American Pluralism* (Stanford: 1967).

Kedourie, E. *Perestroika in the Universities* (London: 1989).

Clark Kerr, *Industrial Relations and the Liberal Pluralist* (Berkeley: 1955).

W. E. von Ketteler, *Die Arbeiterfrage und das Christenthum* (Mainz: 1864).

P. King, *Fear of Power* (London: 1967).

T. M. Knox and Z. A. Pelczynski, (eds), *Hegel's Political Writings* (Oxford: 1964).

I. Kramnick and B., Sheerman, *Harold Laski: a Life on the Left* (London: 1993).

L. Kuper and M. G. Smith (eds.), *Pluralism in Africa* (Berkeley and Los Angeles: 1969).

Will Kymlicka, *Liberalism, Community and Culture* (Oxford: 1989).

Nicholas Lash, *Change in Focus* (London: 1973).

H. J. Laski, *Authority in the Modern State* (New Haven: 1919).

—— *A Grammar of Politics* (London: 1925).

—— *Introduction to Contemporary Politics* (Seattle: 1939).

—— *Studies in the Problem of Sovereignty* (New Haven: 1917).

E. Latham, *The Group Basis of Politics* (Ithaca: 1952).

Shirley Robin Letwin, *The Anatomy of Thatcherism* (London: 1992).

K. Lewin, *Resolving Social Conflicts* (London: 1973).

J. D. Lewis, *The Genossenschaft Theory of Otto von Gierke* (Madison: 1935).

George Lindbeck, *The Nature of Doctrine: Religion and Theology in a Postliberal Age* (Philadelphia: 1984).

W. Lippmann, *A Preface to Morals* (London: 1929).

D. Lloyd, *The Law Relating to Unincorporated Associations* (London: 1938).

J. D. Mabbott, *The State and the Citizen* (London: 1955).

F. McHugh and S. M., Natale, *Unfinished Agenda: Catholic Social Teaching Revisited* (Langham, Md: 1994).

R. M. MacIver and C. H., Page, *Society: an Introductory Analysis* (London: 1949).

V. J. McNabb, *Communism or Distributism?* (London: 1937).

H. M. Magid, *English Political Pluralism* (New York: 1941).

H. Maine, *Lectures on the Early History of Institutions* (London: 1893).

—— *Popular Government* (London: 1890).

F. W. Maitland, *Collected Papers* (Cambridge: 1911).

J. E. F. Mann *et al.*, *The Real Democracy* (London: 1913).

David Martin, *A General Theory of Secularization* (Oxford: 1978).

Kingsley Martin, *Harold Laski (1893–1950): a Biographical Memoire* (London: 1953).

A. J. Mason *et al.*, *Our Place in Christendom* (London: 1916).

F. D. Maurice, *The Kingdom of Christ* (London: 1838).

C. E. Merriam and H. E. Barnes, (eds), *Political Theories: Recent Times* (New York: 1924).

Johannes Messner, *Social Ethics: Natural Law in the Western World* (St Louis and London: 1964).
Robert Michels, *Political Parties* (New York: 1962).
J. S. Mill, *On Liberty* (London: 1903).
—— *The Principles of Political Economy* (London: 1883).
David Miller *et al.*, (eds), *Blackwell's Dictionary of Political Thought* (Oxford: 1987).
B. Mitchell, *Law, Morality and Religion in a Secular Society* (London: 1970).
S. Mogi, *Otto von Gierke* (London: King, 1932).
—— *The Problem of Federalism* (London: 1931).
Robert Morgan (ed.), *The Religion of the Incarnation* (Bristol: 1989).
S. Mulhall, and A. Swift, *Liberals and Communitarians* (Oxford: 1992).
M. Newman, *Harold Laski: a Political Biography* (London: 1993).
J. H. Newman, *A Letter addressed to his Grace the Duke of Norfolk on the Occasion of Mr Gladstone's Recent Expostulation* (London: 1875).
——, *Discussions and Arguments on Various Subjects* (London: 1872).
——, *The Via Media of the Anglican Church* (London: 1899).
David Nicholls (ed.), *Church and State in Britain since 1820* (London: 1967).
——, *Deity and Domination: Images of God and the State in the Nineteenth and Twentieth Centuries* (London: 1989).
——, *Haiti in Caribbean Context: Ethnicity, Economy and Revolt* (London: 1985).
——, and F., Kerr, (eds), *John Henry Newman: Reason, Rhetoric and Romanticism* (Bristol: 1991).
H. R. Niebuhr, *The Kingdom of God in America* (Chicago: 1937).
E. R. Norman, *Church and Society in England, 1770–1970* (Oxford: 1976).
P. H. Nowell-Smith, *Ethics* (Harmondsworth: 1954).
Michael Oakeshott, *On Human Conduct* (Oxford: 1975).
S. L. Ollard *et al.*, *Dictionary of English Church History* (London: 1912).
S. Orwell and I. Angus (eds.), *The Collected Essays, Journalism and Letters of George Orwell* (Harmondsworth: 1970).
J. R. Pennock and J. W. Chapman (eds.), *Voluntary Associations* (New York: 1969).
A. J. Penty, *Distributism: a Manifesto* (London: 1937).
—— *The Restoration of the Gild System* (London: 1906).
F. Pollock, *Essays in the Law* (London: 1922).
—— *A First Book of Jurisprudence* (London: 1923).
G. L. Prestige, *The Life of Charles Gore, A Great Englishman* (London: 1935).
H. Preuss, *Gemeinde, Staat, Reich* (Berlin: 1889).
P. J. Proudhon, *L'idée générale de la révolution du 19e siècle* (Paris, 1929).
—— *Du principe fédératif* (Paris, 1921).
Uri Ra'anan, *et al*, *Russian Pluralism: Now Irreversible* (New York: 1993).
K. Rahner, *Bishops: their Status and Function* (London: 1964).
—— *Theological Investigations* (London: 1962f).
John Rawls, *Political Liberalism* (New York: 1993).
—— *A Theory of Justice* (Oxford: 1972).
H. M. Relton, *Church and State* (London: 1936).
Nicholas Rescher, *Pluralism: Against the Demand for Consensus* (Oxford: 1993).
D. G. Ritchie, *Darwin and Hegel* (London: 1893).
—— *The Principles of State Interference* (London: 1891).
G. Ritter, *The Corrupting Influence of Power* (Hadleigh: 1952).

John Robinson, *Honest to God* (London: 1963).
L. Rockow, *Contemporary Political Thought in England* (London: 1925).
Clinton Rossiter, and James, Lare, (eds), *The Essential Lippmann* (New York: 1965).
L. S. Rouner, (ed.), *Civil Religion and Political Theology* (Notre Dame, Ind: 1986).
J. J. Rousseau, *Social Contract and Discourses* (London: 1913).
Geoffrey Rowell, (ed.), *Tradition Renewed* (London: 1986).
V. Rubin (ed.), *Social and Cultural Pluralism in the Caribbean* (New York: 1960).
B. Russell, *Democracy and Direct Action* (London: 1919).
—— *Political Ideals* (New York: 1917).
—— *Principles of Social Reconstruction* (London: 1916).
Salmond on Jurisprudence (ed. G. Williams) (London: 1957).
W. Sanday, *Bishop Gore's Challenge to Criticsm* (London: 1914).
Michael J. Sandel, *Liberalism and the Limits of Justice* (Cambridge: 1982).
F. C. von Savigny, *Jural Relations* (London: 1884).
—— *System of Modern Roman Law* (Madras: 1867).
E. F. Schumacher, *Small is Beautiful* (London: 1974).
J. W. Scott, *Syndicalism and Philosophical Realism* (London: 1919).
A. A. Seaton, *The Theory of Toleration under the Later Stuarts* (Cambridge: 1911).
Robin C. Selby, *The Principle of Reserve in the Writings of John Henry Cardinal Newman* (Oxford: 1975).
P. Selznick, *Law Society and Industrial Justice* (New York: 1969).
—— *TVA and The Grass Roots* (Berkeley: 1949).
G. B. Shaw (ed.), *Fabian Essays* (London: 1889).
E. Shils, *The Torment of Secrecy* (Glencoe: 1956).
H. Sidgwick, *The Elements of Politics* (London: 1908).
—— *The Ethics of Conformity and Subscription* (London: 1870).
—— *The Methods of Ethics* (London: 1890).
—— *Practical Ethics* (London: 1898).
G. Simmel, *Conflict and The Web of Group Affiliations* (Glencoe: 1955).
H. A. Smith, *The Law of Associations* (Oxford: 1914).
G. Sorel, *Réflexions sur la violence* (Paris: 1910).
Herbert Spencer, *Essays Scientific, Political and Speculative* (London: 1868).
——, *Principles of Sociology* (London: 1877).
W. J. H. Sprott, *Human Groups* (Harmondsworth: Penguin 1958).
W. J. Stankiewicz (ed.), *In Defence of Sovereignty* (London: 1969).
L. S. Stebbing, *Ideals and Illusions* (London: 1944).
J. F. Stephen, *Liberty Equality Fraternity* (London: 1874).
A. P. Stokes, *Church and State in the United States* (New York: 1950).
P. F. Strawson, *Individuals* (London: 1959).
William M., Sullivan, *Reconstructing Public Philosophy* (Berkeley Calif.: 1982).
Charles Taylor, *Hegel and Modern Society* (Cambridge: 1979).
—— *Sources of the Self* (Cambridge: 1989).
—— *Philosophical Papers, II: Philosophy and the Human Sciences* (Cambridge: 1985).
A. de Tocqueville, *Journeys to England and Ireland* (London: 1958).
Ernst Troeltsch, *The Social Teaching of the Christian Churches* (London: 1931).
J. Tussman, *Obligation and the Body Politic* (New York: 1960).

George Tyrrell, *The Church and the Future* (London: 1910).

A. B. Ulam, *The Philosophical Foundations of English Socialism* (Cambridge, Mass: 1951).

J. O. Urmson, *Philosophical Analysis* (Oxford: 1956).

Andrew Vincent, *Theories of the State* (Oxford: 1987).

L. C. Webb (ed.), *Legal Personality and Political Pluralism* (Carlton: 1958).

S. Webb, *Towards Social Democracy* (London: 1919).

B. F. Westcott, *et al.*, *The Church and New Century Problems* (London: n.d.).

M. Wiles, *The Remaking of Christian Doctrine* (London: 1974).

Isaac Williams, 'On Reserve in Communicating Religious Knowledge', *Tracts for the Times*, no. 80 (London: 1837).

Bryan Wilson, *Religion in Sociological Perspective* (Oxford, 1982).

J. Wisdom, *Philosophy and Psycho-analysis* (Oxford: 1953).

R. P. Wolff, *The Poverty of Liberalism* (Boston: 1968).

——, *Understanding Rawls* (Princeton, N. J.:1977).

A. W. Wright, *G. D. H. Cole and Socialist Democracy* (Oxford: 1979).

John Howard, Yoder, *The Politics of Jesus* (Grand Rapids, Mich.: 1972).

——, *The Original Revolution* (Scottsdale, Pa.: 1971).

B. Zylstra, *From Pluralism to Collectivism* (Assen: 1968).

Index

Delors, J., 130
democracy, 12, 86, 88, 131, 145
Dewey, J., 83, 106
Dicey, A. V., 38ff, 49, 51, 63, 83, 159, 162,
 165, 173f, 175
disestablishment, 159
distributism, 128
divine right of kings, 49
Dooyeweerd, H., 131
Duguit, L., 5, 46f, 50, 52f, 71, 85
Durkheim, E., 56ff, 126, 128
Duvalier, F., 18, 91

Eastern Europe, xif, 96
economy, 9, 86f, 166
education, x, 9, 84, 95, 103, 131, 157
Ehrlich, S., 8, 146
Eisenhower, D. D., 133, 156
Eliot, G., 103,
Eliot, T. S., 14, 107
Elliott, W. Y., 144
elites and elitism, xviii, 12, 132F
England, *see* Great Britain
equality, 28f,
Erastus, and erastianism, 97, 163
ethnicity, xvf, 93f
Eucken, R., 1, 4f
European Community, xiiif, xvi, 51f, 130
excommunication, 116

Fabian Society and fabianism, xi, 3, 8, 127
family, 131, 158, 162
Farrer, A. M., 71
fascism, 5, 127f
federalism, 33f, 115, 153, 168
Figgis, J. N., xiif, xv, xvii, 1ff, 10, 12, 13, 20,
 21, 22, 25f, 30, 33ff, 43ff, 48, 50f, 53f,
 56, 59f, 61, 67, 69, 75, 76, 79ff, 82ff,
 88, 89, 93, 96ff. 102f, 109f, 112ff, 126,
 128, 132, 134, 147f, 151
Follett, M. P., 89f
force, *see* power
Forsyth, P. T., 60
France, 9, 11, 12, 29, 44, 61, 75, 77, 86,
 126f, 158f, 165, 168, 175f
Franco, F., 91
Frankfurter, F., 69
Free Church of Scotland, 67ff, 72, 73, 86, 179
freedom, *see* liberty
Friedrich, C. J., xii
Froude, J. A. , 30
functionalism, 3, 8, 31, 46, 86, 128ff, 167f
fundamentalism, 113
Furnivall, J. S., 92f

general will, 42, 44ff, 86, 134
 see also common good
Germany, 6, 7, 8, 9, 12, 51, 61, 73, 75, 86,
 129, 169
Gierke, O. von, 2, 43f, 47, 52f, 56, 58f, 60,
 63, 64f, 71, 72, 128, 145, 148
Gladstone, W. E., 21, 25
Gleeson, J. E., 128
Goerdeler, C. F., 90
Gollwitzer, H., 90
Gorbachev, M., xiii
Gore, C., 2, 110, 117
Great Britain, xv, 9, 11, 34, 36, 44, 48, 49f,
 75, 94f, 108, 127, 135, 157f, 168, 175
Green, T. H., 6, 27, 41f, 58, 77f, 85, 164, 169
Groen van Prinsterer, G., 131
group personality, xiii, 3, 14, 44, 53, chapter
 4, appendix D
groups, xvf, 6, 13ff, 32, 34, 46f, 57f, chapter
 4, 75ff, 82, 108, 111, 114f, 118, 126,
 128, 130, 135, 158f, 163, 174ff
guild socialism, xi, 8, 13, 30, 87, 126ff, 135
Gwatkin, H. M., 117

Hart, H. L. A. , 51, 72
Hayek, F. von, 62
Hegel, G. W. F., 77f, 83, 128, 164
Hill, E., 122f
Hirst, P. Q., viii, xvi
Hoadley, B., 35
Hobbes, T. and hobbism, 22, 26, 31, 41, 44,
 54, 76, 83, 112, 153, 164f, 170, 175
Hobhouse, L.T., 6, 23, 47, 58, 142
Holland, H. S., 10
Holmes, O. W., 3, 51
Homans, G., 62
Hooker, R., 54
hospital trusts, x
Hough, J., xii
Hume, D., 22
Huxley, T. H. 107

idealism, 16, 47f, 53, 57f, 78, 89
ideology, 140
India, 51, 96
individualism, xx, 16, 32, 56ff, 76f, 83, 85,
 89, 113f, 131, 143, 158
Innocent IV, pope, 64, 148, 175
Institute of Economic Affairs, ix
interest groups, 130f, 133, 135
Italy, 9, 12, 129

James, W., 1f, 127
Jesuits, 97